THE DAY OF THE TYPHOON

Flying with the RAF tankbusters in Normandy

THE DAY OF THE TYPHOON

Flying with the RAF tankbusters in Normandy

JOHN GOLLEY

 PSL **Patrick Stephens, Wellingborough**

First published in 1986

British Library Cataloguing in Publication Data

Golley, John
The Day of the Typhoon.
1. Great Britain. Royal Air Force—History
2. World War, 1939-1945—Aerial operations,
British   3. Typhoon (Fighter plane)
I. Title
940.54'4941   D786

ISBN 0-85059-758-7

*Patrick Stephens Limited is part of the
Thorsons Publishing Group.*

Photoset in 11 on 12 pt Plantin
by MJL Typesetting Services Limited.
Printed in Great Britain on Onslow White Wove
Vol 18 80 gsm, and bound by Biddles Limited,
Guildford, Surrey, for the publishers,
Patrick Stephens Limited, Denington Estate,
Wellingborough, Northants, NN8 2QD, England.

Contents

"Boys, meet Mr. Jones. He flies a Rocket-Typhoon."

A cartoon which says everything. Reproduced by kind permission of Arthur Reed and Wing Commander Roland Beamont DSO DFC. 'Bee' Beamont was a legendary Wing leader and Typhoon test pilot who fathered the progress of the machine during its turbulent childhood.

Foreword

by Wing Commander Roland Beamont, CBE, DSO*,
DFC*, DL, FRAeS

Much has been written about the Hurricane and Spitfire in the battles of France and Britain in 1940, and of the courage and spirit of their pilots. The heroic deeds and almost unbelievable dedication in the face of fierce casualties of the crews of Bomber Command throughout the whole of World War 2 have been very fully recorded. But until recent years very little has been said about the important and at some points vital role played by the Typhoon squadrons in the last years of the war, and especially in the final crucial battles to liberate Europe.

After an inauspicious entry into service with the RAF in 1942, bedevilled by mechanical and structural failures, and being less than attractive to pilots due to its heavy and cumbersome appearance in contrast to the beauty of line of the Spitfire, the Typhoon's true qualities began to show through in early 1943 when some determined squadrons based on the South Coast for anti-'Tip and Run raider' patrols also set about exploring the aircraft's capabilities in a wide range of low-level offensive operations over France and the Low Countries.

Faster than the Me 109 and Fw 190 at low level, heavily armed and with excellent controllability and gun-aiming stability the Typhoon soon proved to be a first class ground-attack aircraft, and after coming close to total cancellation the production programme was firmly re-established in 1943 to introduce them as the standard fighter-ground-attack aircraft for the RAF.

In this book John Golley has set out to record events in one of the most successful Typhoon squadrons through the eyes of a young pilot joining his first squadron, gaining combat experience in a long and arduous operational tour, surviving when more than fifty per cent of his colleagues did not, gaining a commission and finally returning home 'Tour Expired'. The result is a fascinating and authentic account of the thoughts, experiences, stresses and excitements of a squadron pilot in continuous daily combat in the harsh conditions of front line field service.

The casualties sustained by the Typhoons from Normandy through to the Baltic were high indeed but the squadrons, led by the brilliant Wing and squadron commanders who have never been in short supply in the Royal Air Force, wavered not at all. Individual cases of extraordinary courage were countless, but perhaps the most outstanding mark of the Typhoon pilots was their almost casual acceptance of the intense dangers which faced them daily. Of course they had their fears, like all fighting men, but they dismissed them, as described so well by John Golley, and just carried on and hit the enemy wherever he could be found; and that is the true courage.

The book is uniquely successful in recreating the atmosphere of crew-room (or tent) life, and the split-second reactions of combat at a time when the Typhoon Wings were spearheading the assault by our combined forces against Hitler's Europe; and the author, who himself fought through the heaviest battles in his Typhoon, is eminently well qualified to write it.

In the great tradition of the Royal Air Force, the Typhoon fighter pilots of the 2nd Tactical Air Force played a major part in the battle for Europe, and this book is a fitting tribute to them, to the Hawker Typhoons and to the men who kept them flying.

RPB, July 1985

Introduction

The rocket Typhoon was the most lethal air-to-ground attack fighter to emerge from the Second World War. During the Invasion of Europe it played a major role in supporting Allied armies and proved that air power alone is capable of destroying attacking enemy armoured divisions. Any pilot who has flown high performance aircraft in close support battle conditions knows that this is a highly dangerous, brutal and bloody business. Rocket Typhoon pilots in Normandy during the weeks following the Invasion had a very rugged life. Casualties were heavy. They were living in tents on airstrips close to enemy lines and in the early days came under shellfire. Rarely a night went past without a bomber circling around hour after hour and finally dropping its load. Whenever weather permitted they flew off to attack heavily defended targets or made reconnaissances. For them, the war was a non-stop affair in which they were personally involved almost on a day-to-day basis—if they were lucky enough to survive.

Many of these men came from distant parts of the British Empire but together with their counterparts from the United Kingdom they provided a rare blend of competitive and explosive talent. This book characterizes some of the pilots on a particular Typhoon squadron during the traumatic period when the success of the Normandy landings hung in the balance.

I have often been asked why I became a Typhoon pilot and what made me do it. My answer is that I had no choice in the matter. I was determined to become a fighter pilot having been mesmerized by the Battle of Britain like many of my contemporaries throughout the world. By the time I was flying Hurricanes, the new Typhoon 1A—fastest aircraft in the world— had been handed over to squadrons and become operational. This happened in late 1942 and early '43 when there was an urgent need to train as many Typhoon pilots as possible to be ready for the Invasion of Europe. None of us had the slightest idea what we were letting ourselves in for when we converted on to this monster. There had been insufficient time to perfect its development and it had a terrible reputation in those early days. Sabre engines kept seizing up and tails falling off.

Sitting in the cockpit for the first time was a nightmare for the novice pilot when the Austin-7 type door was closed on either side and the lid clamped down over his head. The climax came when a member of the ground crew reached in a hand to bolt the thing shut. For the pilot it was rather like being locked in a sardine tin with no hope of escaping until he brought the bastard down. The Typhoon swung viciously on take-off and oxygen had to be used constantly, even on the ground, because of oil fumes infiltrating the cockpit. Surprisingly, I never saw anybody panic and try to get out before their first solo but some killed themselves during training flights.

Typhoon pilots—most of them in their late teens and early twenties—were of an age to readily accept discipline and did what they were told without question. The main fear for many of them was that they might make clots of themselves and prang the aircraft and possibly get chucked off the course. Even worse was to be labelled as 'lacking in moral fibre'. To be tagged, 'LMF' was like having a terrible disease and any sufferer was immediately cut out of the community by the RAF like a cancer. This was brutal but effective treatment because any man who had lost his nerve could infect a squadron and reduce its effectiveness.

There was never any rank consciousness among pilots, especially on squadrons, but it was customary to call the CO 'Sir'. Many Typhoon squadrons at this time had a high percentage of non-commissioned pilots. This proved to be an advantage for NCO pilots because they were given more time to acquire operational experience before being pitchforked, like many officers, into leadership.

Every Typhoon pilot in Normandy was continually updated on the military situation. He knew why particular targets were selected for rocket attacks. His daily life during those vital weeks when the success of the Invasion hung in the balance was determined by the battle line situation which provides the thread for this book.

What happened in the air depended on the progress of the battle and one cannot divorce the two. Whenever Typhoons were ordered to attack specific targets there was a very good reason and it is only by understanding that reason that the reader can partake in Typhoon operations. Most targets were sticky operations involving flying through intense flak which caused heavy casualties. There was no one particular reason why Typhoon pilots were prepared and even eager to take on such killing odds and stay with it. But some of the compulsions which drove them become clearer in the telling of this story and offer the reader some explanation why they cheerfully and aggressively carried out any operation allotted to them. Air-Chief-Marshal Sir Harry Broadhurst who commanded twenty squadrons of rocket-firing Typhoons in the 2nd Tactical Air Force, said, 'I suppose that flying one of these aircraft was the most dangerous task the Air Force has ever asked anybody to do'.

John Golley
October 1985

11

'Life is too short to be little'
Benjamin Disraeli

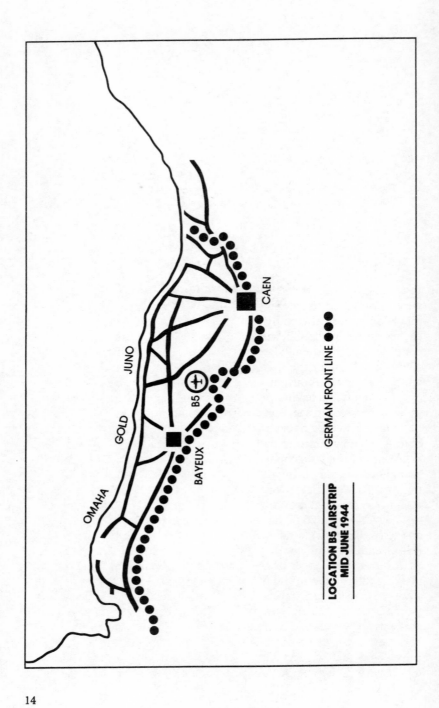

OMAHA

GOLD

JUNO

B5

BAYEUX

CAEN

LOCATION B5 AIRSTRIP
MID JUNE 1944

GERMAN FRONT LINE ●●●

Chapter 1

D-Day

In the evening of 5 June 1944, two Typhoon pilots of 245 Squadron were summoned to Intelligence and briefed to carry out a weather recce. Their task was to fly south of Brest, keeping well away from the coastline of the Cherbourg Peninsula, and to report on cloud conditions in that area. They had strict instructions to maintain RT silence throughout the flight and in no circumstances were they to engage enemy aircraft or shoot up anything at sea. Both were experienced pilots having previously carried out weather recces and, as far as they could see, the job was purely routine. The countryside had been lashed by heavy rain and gale force winds during the day before but now summer had suddenly reappeared. Everybody was keyed up for the Invasion to kick off but the only odd thing that the two pilots noticed during their briefing session was a couple of high ranking Army officers, or 'brown jobs' as the RAF called them, lurking in the background but saying nothing.

They took off at 20.00 hours from Holmsley South, a large airfield about twelve miles outside Bournemouth and climbed on course into a beautiful sunny evening. The flight proved uneventful. To the east, the stubby finger of the Cherbourg Peninsula was silent and glowing under the sun and in the west, way out in the Atlantic, there were wisps of high curved tail cirrus denoting the approach of frontal systems. There was no doubt that cloud was on its way and that was all they would be able to report when they got back. There had been no sign of the Luftwaffe or acknowledgement of their presence from trigger happy German gunners in the Port of Cherbourg. Down below, as they crossed back over the Channel, a few spritely white horses broke up the glossy surface of a calm sea making little white sparkling crinkles of froth and foam.

As the pattern of the South Coast began to unroll on the horizon they suddenly saw that from Poole right across to Portsmouth and beyond the coast was alive with shipping crawling slowly out of inlets and estuaries. Great bunches of ships were multiplying at assembly points offshore and they knew at once that they were witnessing the formation of a gigantic D-Day armada and that the show was on.

Coming from the quiet and seemingly peaceful coastline of Normandy basking in evening sunlight and then flying back over an empty Channel to find the English coast in a frenzy of activity and bursting at its seams with craft of all sizes, shapes and descriptions was a breathtaking experience. Both pilots were conscious that the well-kept secret of Operation Overlord was now out of the bag as far as they were concerned, and they would be able to report that they had seen no sign of activity or anything unusual going on in and around the enemy coast.

They were excited as they approached the airfield at Holmsley South wondering what would happen when they landed. It seemed unbelievable that all this was occurring and yet the Germans didn't seem to have got wind of it. It dawned on them as they came in to land that they had witnessed history in the making, but the enormity of the operation was beyond imagination. Armed guards surrounded them after they had climbed out of their aircraft and escorted them to Intelligence. They were told officially that the D-Day show was on and that after debriefing they would be confined under armed guard for obvious reasons. There really wasn't much to report except that frontal systems were probably on their way into Normandy from the Atlantic and everything appeared to be very quiet in that part of the world.

About midnight the guards took them back to Intelligence and they found the large room crammed full of Typhoon pilots and officers from other services. The place was full of tobacco smoke and a high level of excited conversation. When a red-tabbed Army officer accompanied by the Wing leader and other top brass strode onto the platform there was absolute silence. The officer held up his hand and calmly announced that Operation Overlord was now under way. 'Gentlemen', he said dramatically pointing to his watch, 'I have to inform you that at this moment, British, Canadian and American paratroopers are dropping into Normandy to capture vital targets.'

It took a few seconds before the full impact of this statement penetrated and then there were cheers and yells relieving the tension. Pilots got up from their wooden chairs waving their arms about and slapping each other on the back. For them it was a champagne moment and they erupted. Gradually the noise and frolic simmered down and finally subsided when the 'brown job' pulled strings which rolled up the cover of a huge map of the Normandy coast from the Ouistreham Estuary in the east across to the base of the Cherbourg Peninsula in the west. Slowly and methodically, pointing to arrows on the map, he outlined the pattern of the Allied assault plan.

This seemed a little tedious at the time because most pilots were anxious to know what was in store for them and wanted to get on with it. When finally the Wing leader got to his feet amidst a round of cheers, all ears were strained to catch the 'gen'. The particular job of rocket Typhoons, he explained, would be to patrol behind the area of the beaches and shoot up German reinforcements being brought up to neutralize the Allied landings. Selected gun positions, Panzer and SS headquarters and anything spotted on the roads would be fair game. Spitfire cover would dominate the upper echelons of the air, he said, allowing Typhoons to operate at low level without having to worry about the Luftwaffe.

The first D-Day op was to be an armed recce south of Caen and the Wing would take off at 04.45 hours formating with navigation lights on and cross the Channel at a height of about 3,000 feet. This was going to be a novelty because until now Typhoon Squadrons had flown out at wave-top level in order to get under German radar and then climbed furiously when in sight of the French coast. With the Invasion under way there was no further need for deceptive tactics. The Wing leader also pointed out, with a smile, that the D-Day planners had divided the air itself into various layers with specific air corridors for crossing out and coming back. Lower layers for ground attack fighters from 1,500 to 3,500 feet and other layers for medium and heavy bombers left the upper air free for top level fighter cover. These layers, or bands, had been set up to accommodate the variety of aircraft using them and the air corridors served as traffic routes. Transport and supply aircraft were to have their own air corridors once airstrips had been established in Normandy.

There was nothing new about carrying out an armed recce over the Caen-Bayeux area as far as most pilots were concerned because they were familiar with the territory and the type of operation involved. Hitherto, it had just been another job to fly over Normandy and comb the countryside for targets, or rocket heavily defended posi-

17

tions, but today was D-Day.

After the briefing pilots drifted back to billets or messes laughing and joking amongst themselves having been stimulated by the great news. To take part in the D-Day operation was the climax of their ambition and something which they had always looked forward to. Knowing that our chaps would soon be ashore on the ground over there was a comforting thought and nobody had the slightest doubt about the eventual outcome. During the past two years Typhoon air-to-ground attacks had made Northern France a very uncomfortable place for the enemy and the time had now come for full retribution in which each pilot could play his part.

Those going on the first show were due to be called in three hours time and sleep was out of the question. Nobody got much rest that night, except for an odd doze, because the atmosphere was too tense. Many wondered what it was going to be like flying over the beaches and whether the Luftwaffe would show up. Typhoon pilots rarely got an opportunity to have a crack at German fighters because there hadn't been many of them around and when they appeared on the odd occasions, high flying Spitfires were quick to dive down and get in first.

Having to take-off at night with navigation lights on was a novel experience for most of them. Few pilots had any night-flying expertise in Typhoons and only a handful had carried out night-intruder operations over Northern France. When they arrived at dispersals, jumping out of their trucks at about 04.15 hours, the night was alive with shaded torches and vehicle lights. Their introduction to D-Day was having to fumble around in cockpits in the dim light of faintly glowing instruments and with the aid of ground crews who shone a weak beam to help them get settled in. It wasn't easy in the dark, especially as they were excited, to plug in leads, adjust oxygen knobs, clip in parachute and harness straps and then do a cockpit check before starting up.

Once Sabre engines coughed and roared into life and they started to taxi out, guided by ground crews, all concentration was focused on the nav lights of the man in front. No pilot could relax for a second as the Wing lined up for take-off. Each man's eyes were glued to his partner's lights as, in pairs, they charged down the runway and began climbing into a night sky. Thirty-two Typhoons combining four squadrons, numbers 245, 181, 175 and 174, were airborne and on their way to Normandy. Each squadron, stacked one under another, formed in two Flights of finger-fours. The collective fire power of the Wing included 256 rockets, with semi armour piercing high explosive heads, and 17,920 20-mm cannon shells which made it an awesome strike force.

Gradually eyes became accustomed to formating at night and tension eased off. The soft air with little or no turbulence helped pilots to keep station without having to continually manipulate controls and most began to find the experience 'just a piece of cake' and were able to take notice of what was going on around them. With one hand resting on the spade grip of the stick and the other wrapped gently around the throttle bar and feet automatically moving for rudder control, pilots could relax, conscious of the vibrant power of the one-and-a-half-ton Napier Sabre engine in front of them. Stuffed inside Mae Wests, clamped down by harness straps and with an oxygen mask clipped across their faces they became very warm inside the 'office' especially as they were flying at a low altitude of only 3,000 feet. It seemed only minutes later that a faint finger of dawn wiped the skyline in the east giving them a horizon which made all the difference.

The RT crackled out the order to switch nav lights off as down below they caught their first glimpse of white horses in the blackness of the Channel. The air began to get a little bumpy and soon they could make out vague shapes of ships and lines of foam as the night evaporated quickly in the path of a rising sun whose rays began to probe the sky away to their left. A thousand feet below great chunks of cloud were drifting in from the Atlantic, silhouetted in purple and brown against the golden background of the sunrise.

Now they could see unending lines of shipping plugging their way through a roughening sea and approaching the Normandy coast, battleships, cruisers and destroyers were standing off in a giant semi-circle, their guns belching fire as the naval bombardment hotted up. Broadside to the coast, the great ships slid backwards and forwards in the sea from the recoil of their own big guns. From the air it presented an incredible picture of sheer stark naval power and strength with seemingly hundreds of ships pounding away at about eighty miles of Normandy coast stretching from Ouisterham in the east right across to the base of the Cherbourg Peninsula.

As the Wing crossed the coastline the sky was punctured by black powder puffs of bursting shells as German flak batteries opened up. Red and yellow tracer curved its way upwards from the ground, some of it whizzing out of cloud below, before falling away in a giant hoop. In seconds the Typhoons had left the coastal flak belt behind them as the Wing leader gave the order for 'Line astern, go!' and 32 Typhoons broke their finger-four formation and tucked in behind one another in a long descending line. Down below on their right was the city of Bayeux looking majestic and unscathed but Caen to the east was belching up great clouds of smoke and obviously burning. Quite heavy cloud had been building up and now covered some six-tenths of the landscape as one after another the Typhoons did a wing-over and dived down towards the south-east of the smoking city of Caen.

The aircraft shot through a hole in the clouds like a long snake, following the Wing leader and then pulling out of a steepish dive at about 1,000 feet, well under the cloud base. Tracer was coming up from several gun positions in the hinterland, exposing their locations, and aircraft were detailed over the RT to peel off to go and deal with them. The air was becoming very bumpy and pilots had to work hard to keep station, especially those at the end of the whiplash when the Wing leader banked this way and that searching for targets.

The RT was chattering away as pilots reported signs of movement and dived down to investigate, but the main roads from Flers, Falaise, Argentan and Alencon leading to Caen were empty. They had expected to find German units moving up into the Caen area or at least a few motorized columns rushing about but the enemy in those parts seemed to be asleep and unaware of what was happening.

As they flashed over the countryside, stabs of sunlight poked through the clouds, highlighting the pastoral scene. Instant pictures of water towers in mushroom shape, yellow fields of barley, rich brown soil, tree-lined roads, lush green woods, ancient churches in grey granite villages rotated beneath them as they banked, searching for anything that moved.

Chasing along a road south of Caen with woods on either side they caught a glimpse of something hidden under the trees. A reflection from the sun, almost like a come-hither wink, and immediately a pair of Typhoons dived down to take a closer look. The Germans promptly opened fire, sending up a carpet of light flak. The Wing, circling above under the cloud base, was extremely vulnerable to well directed flak at that height so the order was given to go right in and rocket the wooded area. Opening into echelon and fanning out in the dive to keep clear of each other, they attacked, spraying the foliage of the woods with cannon shells to keep the gunners' heads down. Some concentrated their fire directly at the source of the tracer while others fired salvos of rockets into that area of the woods. One Typhoon was seen to go straight in and explode with a great orange flash and others had been hit by flak. Pilots were confident that there must be something big down there but it was a frustrating business attacking a hidden enemy and not knowing what damage they had inflicted.

On the way home they could see an enormous pall of smoke and fire which enveloped Caen or what remained of it. The earth all along the coast behind the seaside towns was vomiting muck and dust from exploding naval shells. The whole panoramic scene was like a giant firework display, enlivened by never-ending hoops of coloured tracer with Caen as the bonfire. They climbed through a hole in bulbous lively cloud to find a sky filled with aeroplanes flying through a curtain of heavy flak draped along the coastline.

The Wing landed back at Holmsley South shortly after 06.00 hours having been airborne for an hour-and-a-quarter. Everybody at base was keen and anxious to know what it was like over on the other side but there was no time to say much before the trucks arrived to take them to Intelligence. A few thumbs-up signs and fatuous remarks about the op being a piece of cake and they were driven off for the post mortem. This proved to be longer than usual with pilots being questioned about every little detail of the flight and what they had seen on the ground. Anything, however trivial, was duly noted down and the Intelligence officers appeared to be well satisfied with the way things were going because it was obvious that the Germans behind the coastal belt weren't showing signs of moving up armour towards the beach-head. After discussion amongst the pilots, the exact location of the gun positions which they attacked, together with that of the suspected armour in the woods south of Caen, was meticulously pin-pointed on Intelligence maps.

Shortly after debriefing it was announced that the Wing would be taking off again at 07.15 hours. Pilots all wanted to take part in this one because it would be possible to see the first assault waves going up the beaches as the actual landings took place. Squadron and Flight commanders took preference so there was no chance for anybody else who had been on the first show to go in again as all Squadrons had been topped up with pilots during preceding weeks and there was no shortage of talent.

Despite the early hour the airfield was running in top gear with all kinds of vehicles rumbling around its perimeter and aircraft being re-armed and refuelled for the next show. The intermittent noise of Sabre engines being run up was supplemented by the steady drone of bombers on their way to France. There was an air of expectancy and enthusiasm as WAAFS and ERKS pedalled bicycles to and fro with waves and cheerful grins. In addition there was a family atmosphere about the place and nobody had to pull rank or enforce discipline.

Talk in the mess over eggs and bacon centred on why the Luftwaffe hadn't put in an appearance. Various theories were put forward but it was generally agreed that the Invasion had caught them on the hop because of yesterday's bad weather. Most expected that they would be up in force later on. An Australian said that if the bastards bounced him he was going to poop off a few rockets and put the fear of God into them. This seemed a fair idea because German pilots didn't have rockets and would probably crap themselves if they saw a few coming at them!

The dawn show had been disappointing especially the empty roads with nothing major to prang and those lucky bastards on the next one might have a party. But they had been 'first in' on D-Day so it was bully for them. Anyway, the attack on the woods had been a fair prang and they were convinced that there must have been some armour hidden under those trees.

The second show landed back shortly after 08.30 hours and had seen landing craft battering their way towards the beaches which had now become an inferno of tracer and shells. German arcs of fire, from concrete gun emplacements at regular intervals along the coast, opened out like fans but it looked from the air as if some small segments of beaches were escaping the major onslaught. The Navy was still pounding away and shoals of medium bombers were darting across the landscape. During the armed recce the Wing had seen no sign of any German aircraft or anything of major consequence on the roads leading towards Caen and the beach-head. Further recces were carried out during the day but apart from attacking gun positions, plastering woods suspected of containing armour and generally combing the countryside for targets there was little else to report.

There had been some casualties but nothing like those expected. 245 Squadron, for example, had two pilots picked out of the Channel and one who managed to get back to base with severe head wounds. In addition, several Squadron aircraft had been damaged by flak, but none seriously.

*　　　　　*　　　　　*

During the next few days the war began to sort itself out as the Allied bridgehead along the Normandy coast became firmly established. Pilots could see from maps in the Intelligence room that the British Second Army had penetrated a few miles inland and had reached the northern perimeters of Caen. The Americans had done likewise advancing out of their beachhead areas of Utah and Omaha at the base of the Cherbourg Peninsula.

Pilots were told that it wouldn't be long before the Wing would be operating from landing strips in Normandy and most took the opportunity of living it up while they had the chance. Many wondered how the advance party, who had gone over there to set up the strip, were getting on and thought that their chums must be having a fairly rugged time. Ops were now becoming fairly hairy experiences as the Germans were moving up armoured and infantry divisions and squadrons were steadily losing pilots. Flak was a Typhoon pilot's biggest problem and it was getting heavier all the time, but there were compensations. There was a thin slice of friendly territory over there now in which one could force land in an emergency. Also, the Channel was full of shipping and if a pilot was forced to bale out he had a splendid chance of being picked out of the water pronto and revived with a touch of Naval gin! Not that anybody worried about such matters, but they were comforting thoughts to have at the back of one's mind!

Very few Typhoon pilots had ever set foot in France and they hadn't the remotest idea what it would be like when they got there. Many were anticipating booze-ups in the mess and parties in shady cafés as they moved up the line. Illusions of wine, women and song from films and books about World War 1 pilots who staggered from one piss-up to another were tempting thoughts. A quick breakthrough to Paris by the brown jobs was considered to be on the cards and everything was going to be very French and exciting.

On 15 June, the Wing was briefed to attack a Panzer headquarters in the environs of a little town called Villers Bocage. This place was about 25 miles inland from the beaches of Arromanches and south of Bayeux and at the junction between the British Second Army and the First US Army. The Second Panzer Division had been attacking the Americans at Caumont, three or four miles to the west, and the British 7th Armoured Division in the Villers Bocage area. Our brown jobs were just about to mount a push when the First Panzer Division suddenly arrived and established its headquarters in a château outside the town. The disposition of Allied troops in the general locality was carefully pointed out and pilots were warned to keep clear of the high ground outside the town which was occupied by the 7th Armoured Division.

This was a typical close support operation for which Typhoons were especially suited and pilots were busy checking their maps when the Wing was told that it would land in Normandy, on its airstrip there, before flying back to Holmsley South. The strip, code named B5, was only a few minutes flying time from Villers Bocage and, on the map, looked only a finger tip into Normandy but everybody was pleased to know that things were moving at last and within an hour after take-off they would actually be landing in France.

There were great boiling cauldrons of cumulus cloud, with dirty grey bottoms and milky orange tops hanging over the countryside as they crossed the coast. Barrage balloons, moored to shipping offshore, looked like cocktail sausages swinging about in a gusty wind. The floating 'Mulberry' harbour was doing a busy trade and since the landings there hadn't been a puff of smoke from German gun batteries along the coast.

Diving down towards Villers Bocage through virile cumulus was uncomfortable and needed physical strength to keep the bucking bronco under control. As they broke cloud, cotton wool mist vanished from windscreens and the colourful tapestry of Normandy stared them in the face. The target pin-point, a fork in the main road leading from Caen to the south-west, showed up quite clearly as they circled to position themselves for the attack. Panzer gunners, with eyes trained on the long line of Typhoons, opened fire with medium flak which burst in boxes uncomfortably close to the formation so they wasted no time hanging about under the cloud base and dived down to prang the château and surrounding woods. It was all over in a few minutes as they fired rockets in salvos with a liberal dose of cannon shells for good measure and pulled up and away to re-form on their way to the strip.

Landing in France for the first time was going to be quite an event and most pilots wondered what it was going to be like as they flew north-east towards the landing beaches. They hadn't long to ponder before they were back in line astern formation and making a gentle dive to join the circuit prior to landing. The strip looked very short and rough after the runways of Holmsley South and was surrounded by woods and orchards with dark green tents blending into the natural landscape. Sandbagged ack-ack positions covered all approaches and they were surprised to see a solitary Typhoon standing disconsolately outside a canvas maintenance hangar which poked its roof through an orchard. Gun flashes were winking away all around the Caen area as, with undercarriages down, they crossed out over the coast before turning back to make a curved approach towards the mouth of the strip.

Coming in over the barrage balloons they dropped off the last few hundred feet with full flap down and gave engines a final burst before thumping onto the uneven wire mesh. Sturdy wide undercarriages took the strain as Squadron Typhoons rocked and rolled down the strip sending up clouds of dust. With brakes squealing they came to a standstill and were waved into dispersal points by their old chums who had gone over shortly after D-Day.

Greetings were short lived as shells came whining over and pilots dived smartly into adjacent slit trenches having got the message loud and clear. Despite the bravado and jokes it was a fairly terrifying experience being under shellfire especially for the first time. Those whose initial reaction was to disregard the funk holes soon changed their attitude and were glad to get their bums underground with the rest.

Ground crews handed out mugs of compo tea which didn't taste too bad and some pilots were about to take a look around the place when the Wing was ordered to fly back to base at Holmsley South. It had been nice seeing familiar faces but a bit galling having to fly off to home comforts leaving those poor bastards out there under shellfire. The most frustrating thing about the trip had been the shelling, when they had been forced to crouch down in slit trenches with their Typhoons only a few yards away. It was a humiliating experience and when they landed back at Holmsley the Wing leader sent off two Typhoons to pin-point the gun flashes in the woods on the southern outskirts of the strip and have a go at them.

Everybody had expected that they would be off to Normandy permanently but the plan was for them to operate over there from the strip on a daily basis flying home after ops. It wasn't until the third week in June that the Wing finally left Holmsley—on D-Day plus twenty.

Chapter 2

B5—Le Fresne Camilly

They had only been on the strip a short time before they got a rude awakening. It happened after lunch in early July when 245 Squadron was preparing for a show. Their Typhoons, armed with rockets and 20-mm cannon shells, were dispersed alongside a hedge on the eastern side of the wire mesh runway. Ground crews were helping pilots with last minute preparations and some pilots were climbing into their cockpits when the attack took place. Three German fighters roared in from the east under cover of low cloud, hedge-hopping over tree tops and setting their gunsights on the line of 245 Squadron Typhoons.

Nobody on the strip paid much attention to the sound of low-flying aircraft because they were too accustomed to it and carried on with what they were doing. The Luftwaffe hadn't put in an appearance to date, not even on D-Day, so a ground straffing attack was the last thing anybody expected. Frequently a German bomber droned round and round over the invasion beaches far into the night before dropping its load, but that was all. It had become a perpetual nuisance and people couldn't understand why our night fighters didn't shoot it down.

The first indication of an attack was when the strip's ack-ack gunners opened fire with resounding crashes. Yellow flashes spurted out from the gun ports of three Focke-Wulf 190's as shells scissored up the dusty top soil making everybody dive for cover. Some were lucky enough to fling themselves into adjacent slit trenches and others lay prone on the ground protecting their heads with their arms. Pilots in cockpits lowered their seats and ducked down behind the armour plating of their aircraft. Some, about to get in, jumped off the wing and rolled underneath apparently oblivious of the fact that they were taking refuge under 186 gallons of high octane fuel!

The lightning strike was over in seconds and followed by an uncanny silence. Momentarily, the action froze and all movement ceased as if somebody had stopped a film running through a projector. Slowly, men got to their feet looking around to take stock of the situation. On the far side of the strip a fire was pumping up clouds of black smoke. The urgent and penetrating sound of blood wagons rushing about made people conscious of casualties. Some of the ground crew had collected flak splinters and one Sergeant had his windpipe severed by a piece of flying metal. Blood was bubbling from his throat and he was making gurgling noises being unable to breathe air into his lungs. He would have died if Doc Saunders, the Squadron medical officer, hadn't passed by in his jeep at that particular moment. Somebody shouted for him and miraculously the MO had a piece of glass tubing in his battledress pocket which he inserted into the severed windpipe. A chum held everything in place while they drove the Sergeant over to the hospital tent for emergency repairs.

The strip was a shambles with vehicles darting about sending up clouds of fine Normandy dust. Those pilots who had been getting ready for the show were gathered in small groups walking about and inspecting the damage done to their machines. In the event 245 Squadron, which had been in the direct line of attack from the Focke-Wulfs, had escaped very lightly. A couple of Typhoons had to be written off and others had sustained minor damage but by the merest fluke, cannon shells from the FWs hadn't penetrated fuel tanks or exploded ammunition. Had this happened, most of the Squadron's aircraft might have been destroyed and very heavy casualties inflicted.

Minutes previously pilots had been desperately diving for cover to escape from cannon shells, but now this was conveniently forgotten. All they could talk about was the damage they would have inflicted with their rockets in similar circumstances. Most agreed that those German pilots had had the opportunity of a lifetime having an entire squadron of Typhoons in their gunsights strung out like a line of sitting ducks. The efficiency of the Focke-Wulf as a ground attack fighter was discussed at great length and they concluded that without rockets it wasn't in the same category as their Typhoons. The fact that the Germans had given them a dose of their own medicine and put the fear of God into most of them was never mentioned.

Squadron Leader Jack Collins, the CO, drove up in his jeep and told them that the show had been cancelled and that the Squadron had been stood down for the rest of the day. There was nothing else to do but to filter back to their tents through a gap in the hedge which separated their living quarters from their aircraft lined up on the other side. The cloud was lowering and had filled in previous gaps making the air warm and humid. On their right, a field of corn wavered gently in a light breeze, producing a rich smell of Normandy countryside. It was a scene disfigured only by the poles and canvas of the field latrine standing up on a hump in the middle.

They were still talking and arguing amongst themselves as they gathered round a large sawn-off tree trunk which acted as a table. This had soon become a focal point for chit-chat and was conveniently situated just inside a gap in the hedge serving as the entrance to the living quarters. The pilots' dark green tents were pitched in a line alongside the hedge which was about four feet high and interspersed with thin spindly looking trees. It ran right down the length of the cornfield where wooded land sloped sharply from a plateau into the environs of the ancient village of Le Fresne Camilly.

The strip, coded B5, was the fifth airfield to be established in the British and Canadian sector of the Normandy landings. Only about four miles inland from the Invasion beaches of Courseulles, St. Aubin, Luc and Lion-sur-Mer, it had only recently been freed from shell-fire which had come from German units dug into surrounding woods. These had now been 'flushed out' from their positions but the front line was still less than a mile away to the south, where the country road from Le Fresne Camilly bisected the major road from Bayeux to Caen.

The wire mesh strip which served as a runway was over 1,000 yards long and ran from north to south along the plateau. Surrounding orchards were used to give cover for maintenance hangars and as dispersal points for aircraft requiring servicing. The main HQ was situated at the southern end of the runway and the three squadrons were dispersed to the east and west of it. Anti-aircraft defences were dug in around the perimeters, and slit trenches were adjacent to all working areas.

The Focke-Wulf attack had literally come out of the blue and was a sharp reminder that the Luftwaffe was still around. Not that the Squadron had been feeling complacent because the war was too close to them. The guns in the Caen area, only a few miles away, barked

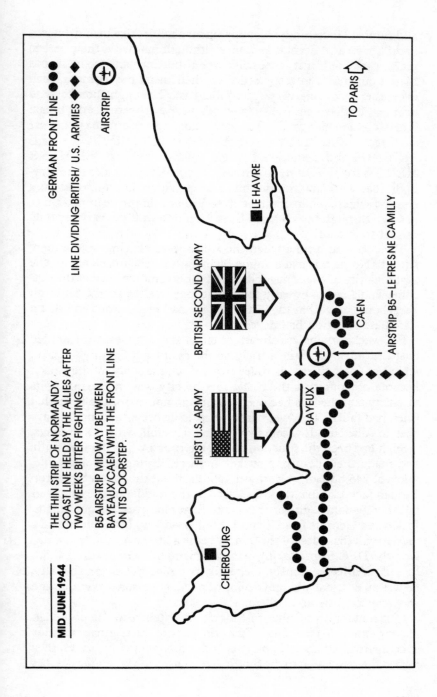

MID JUNE 1944

THE THIN STRIP OF NORMANDY
COAST LINE HELD BY THE ALLIES AFTER
TWO WEEKS BITTER FIGHTING.

B5 AIRSTRIP MIDWAY BETWEEN
BAYEAUX/CAEN WITH THE FRONT LINE
ON ITS DOORSTEP.

●●● GERMAN FRONT LINE
◆◆◆ LINE DIVIDING BRITISH/ U.S. ARMIES
⊕ AIRSTRIP

LE HAVRE

BRITISH SECOND ARMY

FIRST U.S. ARMY

CHERBOURG

BAYEUX

CAEN

AIRSTRIP B5—LE FRESNE CAMILLY

TO PARIS

and rumbled incessantly. Coming under shellfire day in and day out hadn't been a pleasant experience although many did their best to make a joke out of it, especially when the Germans in the woods blared out music interspersed with their usual obscenities. However, there was one very funny incident. The night bomber had dropped leaflets over the strip which were discovered at daybreak. There was a blonde on the front cover holding a telephone to her ear with the words, 'THINK OF YOUR DEAR WIFE OR GIRL FRIEND', and underneath it said, 'WILL YOU EVER HEAR HER SWEAT VOICE AGAIN?'. The 'SWEAT' bit made everybody roar with laughter but more was to come. On the back was a coupon which, when completed, would entitle the bearer to a free passage through the German lines where he would be given preferential treatment!

This came at a time when the Allies were clawing onto a mere sliver of Normandy and hanging on literally by their back teeth! The vast majority of chaps never doubted for one moment what the outcome would be but by early July, some four weeks after the landings, everybody knew that the initial assault had petered out and that a stalemate situation had developed.

For weeks an endless stream of tanks and vehicles had rumbled past the outskirts of the airfield on the road from Creully to Caen, which was only five or six miles away. From the sound of the guns it became obvious that the battle for the city was increasing in its intensity and the lads had been waiting anxiously for the news that Caen had fallen. This was hardly surprising because it should have been in Allied hands within two or three days following the landings.

Such had been the situation on the afternoon when the Luftwaffe had made their lightning strike. Gathered round their log table, pilots of 245 Squadron were still talking about the event. Squadron Leader Jack Collins, their CO, was in the middle of the group. A tallish, raw-boned, gingery man with light blue eyes and buck teeth, Jack was a Geordie from Tyneside who said very little but smiled a lot. He was the oldest of the bunch, being a little over thirty and had won the DFC before taking over command of 245 Squadron about fifteen months previously. Generally regarded as being rather shy, he was an efficient and brave pilot who led by personal example and was respected by all of them.

Jack nodded from time to time as he listened to the chit-chat. Having exhausted the topic of the efficiency of the German machine as compared with their Typhoons under similar circumstances, they turned their attention to the Spitfire cover over the beach-head. Ches

West, a Canadian, remarked in his nasal tone, 'Aw shit. How the hell did those Krauts get through? They should have had their asses clobbered long before they reached us, for sure.' Any mention of Spitfires usually got them going because Spitfire pilots were referred to 'as those lucky bastards who pedal around high up in the sky without having to take all the ground shit pumped up at the Typhoons'. It was generally agreed that the Spits should have shot down the FW's because that was what they were bloody well paid to do. Jack Collins laughed but pointed out that he thought those German pilots had put up a pretty good show. 'Anyway', he said, 'They're all probably dead by now. None of them had stood a cat in hell's chance of getting back'.

Tubby Sago, an Australian, turned to his friend Terry Gray, 'I wish to Christ I could have got my arse off the deck and had a go at the bastards', he said. Tubby had built up an intense hatred of the Kraut ever since his great chum McKillop had been drowned in the Channel seven or eight months before D-Day. This had all come out a week or so previously when some German prisoners were being marched across the perimeter of the airstrip. Tubby had suddenly leapt into his Typhoon and pressed the cannon button sending 20-mm shells over their heads. The German column had scattered and gone to ground and it was some days before that terrified lot were rounded up. Naturally, nobody had any idea how it could possibly have happened!

While pilots were drinking compo tea out of mugs Benny Bennet hobbled in through the gap in the hedge. This stocky little Canadian Flight Sergeant with dark curly hair, brown eyes, wide mouth and dimples had long since become a Squadron character. Everything happened to Benny. After the German attack he was seen to be lying on the ground writhing in agony. Thinking that he must, at least, have had his guts shot out, a couple of the lads raced over with a stretcher only to find that he had sprained his ankle jumping off his wing. He might equally well have been dead because the perspex hood of his cockpit was shot to pieces and his fuselage damaged by shrapnel. Somewhat sheepishly he had explained that no bones were broken and the medics had put a compress on his ankle. This was too much for Paddy Gray (not to be confused with Terry Gray) who asked Benny, admist general laughter, whether somebody in sick quarters had actually managed to remove his flying boot. Nobody had ever seen Benny without his flying boots. It was rumoured that he never took them off, not even for a bath! And he certainly hadn't had one of those since he landed in Normandy!

Paddy Gray told some of the new chaps round the log table about some of Benny's charmed life; the time when he was dive bombing in the area of the Cherbourg Peninsula long before D-Day and had a 500-lb bomb hang-up—which is usually fatal. Having one bomb left on the hook normally makes the Typhoon one wing heavy but for some reason it didn't on that occasion, not for Benny! He brought the bomb back to base at West Hampnett and as he landed it dropped off and bounced high over his wing but didn't explode. The rest of the Squadron had watched his approach and landing in horror from the safety of slit trenches. Another time, Paddy told them, Benny ran out of fuel and tried to stretch his glide in order to belly land on a soccer pitch. His Typhoon stalled and flicked over on to its back and Benny went in upside down, his Sabre engine burying itself several feet below ground.

Everybody was convinced that Benny had had it but when they arrived on the scene they heard him yelling, trapped in his cockpit down in the hole, 'Get me out. Get me out'. All he suffered was slight scratches on the backs of his hands and he was later seen in the Sergeants' mess with his hands bandaged while a sympathetic WAAF fed him a boiled egg with a spoon.

Benny appeared to take no notice of the laughter but he knew that Paddy had been talking about him. He sat on the edge of the log table to take the weight off his ankle, flipped a Sweet Caporal cigarette from the pack and stuck it in the corner of his mouth. Looking across at Paddy's group he gave them a victory sign and lit up, blowing smoke from his nostrils. A new arrival, by the name of Cartwright, had been trying hard to establish himself with the Squadron since he landed on the strip 48 hours earlier—he was anxious to find somebody who would give him the low-down on operational flying and he sat himself beside Benny hoping that Benny would give him some gen. Cartwright couldn't understand why he had been ignored and hadn't the faintest idea that he was fast becoming an irritant. After endless months of training and routine flying duties he had at last been posted to an operational squadron and was bubbling over with enthusiasm. The CO, Jack Collins, had welcomed him to the Squadron and made him feel at home but since then nobody had taken the slightest notice of him.

Tapping Benny on the shoulder Cartwright asked him brightly whether he would be down for the early morning show but Benny didn't respond, so he asked him again. After a silence, Benny deliberately took the cigarette out of his mouth and ground the butt into the dust with his sound heel. Slowly and seemingly painfully he got to his feet and hobbled towards his tent saying to Cartwright, 'I don't effing know. You'll having to go and ask your Flight commander, Jimmy Wilson.' Benny wasn't being deliberately short with Cartwright. Any 'sprog' pilot joining the Squadron was cold shouldered until he had proved himself on ops. A new man found this difficult to understand especially arriving on the Squadron full of bounce, expecting to be on ops as soon as he had signed in and dumped his kit.

It was really like being a new boy at school, the seasoned pilots acting in a lordly and arrogant manner towards new entrants. They formed an elite and jealously guarded group whatever their rank. Enthusiasm and a desire to win the war single handed were qualities frowned upon by the fraternity. Understatement was the name of the game. Non-conformity was essential. Cartwright would learn all about it if he was lucky enough to survive. Meanwhile he would have to do his own thing—get on with it.

As the Squadron was stood down for the rest of the day and there were no further ops, the crowd around the log table began to break up. Flying Officer George Wharry, a Canadian, had to air test his aircraft but the rest were 'off the hook'. The trouble with B5 for most of the chaps was that when they had time on their hands there was little to do except play cards or take a trip out somewhere. Pilot Officer Dud Nott and Flying Officer Maxie Maxwell thought it might be a good idea to borrow the CO's jeep and shove off to Fontaine Henri and do a recce around those parts but Jack Collins needed his transport. The Met officer wouldn't part up with a truck so it had to be cards.

Flight Lieutenants Bob Lee, known as the Colonel, and Bob Monk always had a bridge four going on in Lee's tent. They played endless rubbers and were very toffee-nosed about anybody daring to raise the flap and disturb them. Poker, whist and pontoon were popular pastimes as was 'rolling the bones'. Escape packets had long since been opened and the money used for gambling and Warrant Officer Terry Gray usually came out with wads of francs whenever a dice session got going.

Terry's namesake, Warrant Officer Paddy Gray, shared a tent with Flight Sergeant Bob Stanford and they were cribbage fanatics. That afternoon they decided to walk down to the village of Le Fresne Camilly to buy eggs and have a jar of cider. The food on the strip still consisted of a relentless diet of tinned mushy stew and hard biscuits. There was no fresh bread or other such refinements so they occasionally made up an egg-and-potato mixture which they cooked in a billy-can outside the tent. The penalty for pinching potatoes out of the fields was the firing squad but nobody bothered to read the notices.

Flight Lieutenant Jimmy Wilson, B Flight commander, had previously told Stanford that he was down for the early show and would be flying 'R' (Robert). Bob Stanford was brassed off because his own personal Typhoon 'U' (Uncle) had been a write-off after the Focke-Wulf attack and no pilot enjoyed flying another man's machine. 'R' (Robert) belonged to Ches West and he knew Ches wouldn't be happy either.

The water wagon drove up as Gray and Stanford were buckling on Smith and Wesson revolvers so they waited for the jerry-cans to be filled. Bob thought to himself what a bloody monotonous job it must be to have to drive around the airfield filling up cans. He felt at that moment how lucky he was to be a pilot with everything done for him and then he remembered that he might find it a trifle difficult to take over that water wagon because he had never driven anything in his life except an aeroplane.

Gray was wearing khaki battledress but Stanford always wore his blue. Most of the chaps wore khaki now, the idea being that a Typhoon pilot who either baled out or crash landed behind the lines could identify himself as a brown job. The Germans hated rocket Typhoon pilots and had threatened to string them up to the nearest lamp-post. Pilots could easily remove their wings and badges of ranks and pass themselves off as Privates. Stanford had been rummaging around trying to find a box of matches to light his pipe while his chum carefully laced up the tent flaps and tidied the gear outside. Paddy was like that, methodical and deliberate in everything he did; the way he opened his silver cigarette case, looking into it before carefully selecting a weed and then snapping it shut almost with a flourish. This calculated act was not completed until he had replaced the case in his breast pocket and buttoned it up. He also turned back the cuffs of his battledress blouse in a neat and orderly fashion and was fastidious about his dress and appearance. Gray was soft-spoken, serious, and rarely got himself worked up about anything. When he did, he would stalk off in a huff and his slightly bandy legs would become more apparent. There was an Irish look about him with his gingery hair and freckles. He was of average height, slim and slightly-built like his friend Stanford.

Stanford was six months younger than Gray and had recently celebrated his twenty-first birthday. He was fairish, round-faced and looked younger than his years. More outgoing than Paddy he liked to fool about and ignore the more serious aspects of life. Both men were experienced pilots, Bob having been on 245 Squadron for nearly a year and Paddy having completed eighteen months operational flying. Paddy had been posted to 245 from No. 1 Squadron shortly before D-Day when 245 were under canvas at Holmsley South in the Bournemouth area. They had teamed up after Bob's friend, Dennis Lush, had been killed during a rocket attack on the guns of Le Havre. Everybody on 245 had been incensed when Lusho, as he was called, bought it. He had been hit during the dive and baled out, landing in the Channel about a mile and a quarter off the coast. The Squadron saw him waving from his rubber dinghy waiting for the Walrus sea-plane to pick up him. Just as the Walrus took him on board the German guns opened up and blew it out of the water. When the Wing leader, Wing Commander Charles Green, heard about it he immediately scrambled the Wing for a retaliation attack to teach the bastards a lesson. Bob Stanford was particularly upset about it knowing that Lusho's one great ambition in life was to be in on the D-Day operation and he didn't live to see it.

Since that time Stanford and Gray had paired up, sharing a tent together. There were usually two to a tent, except in the case of the CO who had one to himself, and this made for friendships, associations which tended to be on the surface rather than deep rooted because chaps were wary about getting emotionally involved. Nobody knew from one day to the next who might be sharing his tent!

As Stanford and Gray strolled along the edge of the cornfield, on their way to the village, the country road from Creully to Caen was jammed solid with reinforcements going up the line. Soldiers waved to them from the backs of trucks giving them thumbs up and victory signs and they stopped to wave back. Watching all those cheerful characters on their way to the front line made them think and Gray remarked, 'Aren't you glad we're not with that mob, Bob? We're bloody lucky, you know.' Stanford replied that he wouldn't be inside a tank for a fortune and having to sit in those claustrophobic conditions for hours on end wasn't his style. Neither did he fancy the idea of crawling along the ground with a rifle. Flying was the only thing in his life, he said, ever since he had saved up five shillings for a trip with Alan Cobham's circus. He told Paddy that he had been only ten years old when three ancient aircraft had plonked themselves down in a field near Gallows Corner in Essex and he persuaded one of the pilots, whom he believed to be a chap named Turner Hughes, to let him come on a trip.

Paddy thought Bob was in a mood to score points, so he mentioned quite casually that he too had had his first flight with Alan Cobham and so had many thousands of others. 'I reckon', he said in a superior tone, 'that Cobham recruited more pilots for the RAF than anybody else.'

The leafy lane leading steeply down into the village cut off all contact with the strip and the troops moving slowly in the direction of Caen. Overhanging foliage deadened the metallic grinding noise of tanks and the background rumble of gunfire. Half-way down the hill they walked into a powerful and penetrating smell of rich farmyard manure floating up from the village. The stench forced Stanford to light his pipe and Gray a cigarette, in silence. As they emerged from the lane into the brighter light the odour became almost overpowering.

Le Fresne, as it was called, was an ancient little place lying in a hollow and invisible from the airstrip above it. A sprawling village built of local quarried stone and now battle-scarred and boarded up so that it appeared desolate and empty, it wasn't exactly the sort of place that pilots had imagined they would find when they landed in France! When they first landed at B5 there was a rush to go down to Le Fresne to see what it was all about, which was a natural curiosity because the vast majority of pilots had never set foot in France. During this time, however, they were told to stay on the strip because fighting was still going on in the village. In spite of this warning a few pilots made the trip—only to find brown jobs tossing the odd hand grenade through window openings and making a lot of noise. There was no other entertainment so they came back and got a rocket from the CO.

The Germans had long since been winkled out as Gray and Stanford crossed the road and went through an archway into a farmyard where they had made previous sorties for eggs and had always been given mugs of cider. Stanford tapped on the open door of the farmhouse kitchen and the farmer's wife beckoned them inside. The large rectangular kitchen had a low beamed ceiling and smelled of fruit, cider and cheese. She offered them the usual mug and sat down for a chat, a small, thin woman in her forties with sharp features, large brown eyes and a frizzy mop of dark unruly hair. Stanford and Gray hadn't met her husband, who always seemed to be working out in the fields. Grandfather sat in a rocker hidden away in a corner and was barely visible because it was so dark inside.

Both pilots spoke limited French, learned at school, but during their visits they had been able to pick up the gist of the Frenchwoman's conversation, helped by her gestures and expressions.

Paddy had a head start because his father was 'Monsewer' Eddie Gray who was a member of the Crazy Gang. Eddie's juggling act was supplemented by comic fractured French interspersed with English and so Paddy could trot out some of his fathers' lines which had Bob curled up. Patter such as, 'Mesdames et Messieurs, I 'ave 'ere a pack of cards. I cutta de pack in deux, pas in trois, comme à la même chose' or words to that effect.

Listening to her story left them in no doubt that the Normans had had a very rough time under the German yoke. She seemed anxious to talk about those terrible years as if trying to impress upon them how her people had suffered. At first, they didn't really appreciate what she was telling them, the language difficulty was a problem but basically neither of them wanted to be in a serious mood. They were giving the Bosche a good hiding day in and day out and were prepared to leave it at that apart from making jokes about stupid Krauts! Le Fresne wasn't their home and they would probably never see the place again when the Squadron moved up the line. Once they had got to know one another a little better, the farmer's wife had rambled on about the hardships, which bored them. They hadn't been surprised when she told them that there had been an acute shortage of cattle food and that their stock had been virtually wiped out, that German soldiers had come scrounging for milk, butter, eggs and meat if they could get it. They knew that there had been a curfew and had heard that young men had been rounded up for slave labour. It was hardly surprising to hear that she and her family had always been nervous of knocks on the door and that Germans billeted in the village had caused a great deal of trouble with the womenfolk. They sympathized with her but that was all.

Life, as Stanford said, hadn't exactly been a bed of roses at home. London and other cities had taken a terrible bashing from air raids and there had been hundreds of thousands of casualties. Food was very short and throughout the whole bloody war chaps had been getting themselves killed fighting, so he couldn't understand why the Frogs should make such a fuss about their lot.

It was only when they saw German soldiers in the flesh for the first time that they began to appreciate what life must have been like for the Normans. Prisoners were being marched into captivity and they naturally wanted to take a close look at the enemy. Their personal war from the cockpits of their Typhoons had been remote from the physical realities of combat. The only contact they had had with the human side of the affair was when they had been low flying—photographic images of German soldiers running to man their gun positions.

Seeing the enemy in the flesh had brought them up with a jerk when they realized that these were some of the men who had been parading around and laying down the law until a few weeks ago. They looked a sullen, dishevelled second-rate bunch. A few seemed arrogant and aggressive and there were a number of very young men, not much more than boys, amongst them. Stanford had put his finger on it when he had asked Gray how he would have felt if those bastards had taken over Shoreham? The question clarified everything.

The farmer's wife had said that everyone, except the 'collaborateurs' had been waiting anxiously for the landings, not knowing when or where they would come. She told them that shortly after dawn on D-Day the shelling started from the ships and everybody in Le Fresne went into hiding and stayed there. The noise had been terrible and the sky full of aeroplanes. A few miles away, she said, the city of Caen had been destroyed by heavy bombers and was burning. The sound of the shells and machine-gun fire had crept closer and they were all very frightened knowing that they would shortly be in the middle of the battle. All they could do was to keep their heads down, pray and hope that the war would soon pass over them.

She said that when the first wave of assault troops arrived in the area they by-passed Le Fresne, moving south along the high ground towards Bretteville. Nobody had dared to venture outside and it was several days before Germans, barricaded in the village, were cleared out. During this time the airstrip was being bulldozed out of the farmland, while fighting was still going on in the surrounding woods and orchards. It had all been a terrifying experience.

As usual, she produced eggs for them and this time she offered to do some washing, which was very kind of her. They both had a whole pile of dirty laundry packed inside their kitbags, only managing to wash out bare essentials when forced to do so. Walking back up the hill towards the strip, Gray had the bright idea of stirring the eggs into the remains of Stanford's fruit cake which his mother had sent him for his twenty-first birthday and making a kind of sponge mixture. Heated up in a billy-can it should taste pretty good, he said, and it did!

★   ★   ★

Bob Stanford awoke unwillingly; few pilots relished the early show. The morning air was chilly inside the tent and wriggling out of a warm sleeping bag required a real effort. Some pilots waited until they heard the horn of the CO's jeep before crawling out of their tents half dressed, few made any serious attempt to carry out ablutions and Bob Stanford was certain that one or two wore pyjamas under their battledress.

Stanford stretched out a hand and lifted the tent flap to look up into a blue sky so there was nothing else for it but to stagger out and get dressed for the show. The body of his chum, Paddy Gray, didn't stir, with its head covered by a leather flying jacket. A stub of candle, a pack of cards and a cribbage board balanced on an earth-made shelf was a reminder of last night's game when Paddy had maintained that Stanford now owed him the best part of 3,000 francs. In his present circumstances Stanford could not have cared less!

He pulled on his battledress, stepped into flying boots and went outside. Looking across the strip he could see that traces of early morning ground mist were fast being dissipated by the sun and there was no doubt that the show would be on. He would have liked to see a little more cloud which would have given them some cover for the attack but there was still time for it.

There was no sign of life from the other tents so he took the opportunity to stroll over to the field latrine, preferring to perform the vital body functions in private. He hated to sit there in concert, with his bum over the pole, having to listen to coarse chit-chat and often wondered why the good Lord had made him such a sensitive creature in that respect. Cleaning his teeth he spat white froth into the hedge and he was splashing cold water against his face when Nobby appeared through the opening in the hedge bringing mugs of compo tea. Nobby was always a cheerful character and having dumped the mugs on the log table, whistling to himself, he moved down the row of tents to ferret out those who were going on the show.

The first one out was the new chap, Cartwright, grinning all over his face and rubbing his hands as if he was looking forward to going on a day's outing. Cartwright, feeling full of himself, asked Bob if he had any idea where they were going, which was a stupid question as Bob hadn't the faintest clue. At that moment, Jimmy Wilson the Flight commander of B Flight, came over to tell Bob that Cartwright would be flying as his number two and asked him to keep an eye on him.

Bob got that awful feeling that the show was starting off badly for him. He wouldn't be flying his own machine, 'U' (Uncle), and now he would have to look after that stupid sod Cartwright. He knew that he was being unfair to think like that about Cartwright but he couldn't help himself. The trouble was that he never did like flying with a sprog pilot doing his first op. Somebody had told him that Cartwright's flying experience in Typhoons amounted to a grand total of just over six hours—so the chap could barely fly the machine!

His common sense told him to go easy on the chap who would be flying a few yards away from him and could easily do something daft. So he gave him a grin and told him to stick close to him saying, 'Don't worry, it's a piece of cake really. You'll soon get the hang of it.' The horn of Jack Collins' jeep tooted outside and it was time to get moving. As usual, there were stragglers who came out of tents in a trance, still dressing themselves as they piled into the vehicle. Two out of the eight pilots had to stand on the running boards and hang on as the jeep started off on its bumpy journey across the strip towards the Intelligence tent.

Ground crews were busy preparing eight 245 Typhoons for the show and engine noise was deafening as the big Sabres were run up. Dressed in ocean grey and dark green with eighteen-inch black-and-white bands encircling their wings and rear fuselage, the formidable seven ton brutes made an impressive spectacle against the dusty background of the hedge. Piles of rockets and ammunition boxes containing 20-mm shells stacked against it were an awesome reminder of the firepower of the beast. Its eight rockets with 60-lb high explosive heads provided a firepower equivalent to a broadside from a light cruiser. This armament was supplemented by four Hispano cannons each of which spat out 20-mm shells at the rate of 650 a minute or eleven a second.

As the jeep passed a canvas maintenance hangar, erected in an orchard, two 245 Typhoons bearing the Squadron code ('MR') on the starboard side of their fuselages, stood patiently waiting for repair. Petrol bowsers and water wagons were slowly doing their early morning rounds as the jeep pulled up outside Intelligence. Nobody had spoken on the way over and even Cartwright had sat silent, apparently absorbed in his surroundings and the thought of actually going on his first op.

The Army Intelligence Captain was largish, slightly tubby and rather pompous. He had an annoying habit of saying that 'we' need to watch out for flak or 'we' should expect the target indicator at such and such a time as if he was going on the show himself instead of sitting his fat arse in a deck chair after the lads had taken off. His briefings, however, were detailed and efficient and he didn't seem to mind a few wisecracks, which he had come to expect being the only 'brown job' on the scene.

Intelligence was housed in a large marquee. Rows of folding wooden chairs sat facing a platform where large scale maps pinned to boards rested on easels. The remainder of the marquee was taken up with a whole series of large maps covering an area from the east of the River Orne, right across Normandy, and over to the Cherbourg Peninsula. The entire Allied front line was continually being updated on a daily basis with coloured pencils and pilots were able to amend their own maps accordingly. It was vital that pilots had the precise location of the battle line and any area in which our forward troops might be operating during an assault. Air-to-ground strikes often had to be carried out on targets only a few hundred yards away from our own infantry so detailed briefings on the immediate ground situation were essential.

Details and locations of Allied forces and those of the Germans facing them were also recorded. Pilots knew, for example, that No. 1 Corps of the British Second Army holding the line along the northern environs of Caen, was opposed by the 12th SS Panzer Division with the 21st Panzer Division in reserve. They had also learned from experience to expect heavy flak from any area where Panzer divisions were located. This was going to be the case as far as the early morning show was concerned. The target was 'dug-in' tanks which were giving our chaps a lot of trouble at a crossroads a few miles to the east of the outskirts of Caen. Pointing to the red areas on the map with his stick, the Army Captain told his audience that they could expect heavy flak from neighbouring Panzer divisions. He also said that a red marker shell would be fired directly over the target when the Squadron appeared on the scene.

Pilots had already noted that there had been no change in battle lines and both sides were still in a stalemate situation. The projected American push south and east out of the Cherbourg Peninsula was delayed because of bad weather and the British attack, code named 'Goodwood', in the Caen area seemed to be bogged down also. In pilots' language, 'the brown jobs needed to take their fingers out'.

The Army Captain handed over to the Met officer who reported that the Squadron could expect some patchy cloud at about 1,500 feet moving up from the south. The final brief came from Jack Collins who quietly told the chaps that he would do his usual stint of flying round the coast and approaching the target east of the River Dives. The attack would be made from north to south and he instructed pilots to be careful not to undershoot the targets because our troops were on the northern side of the crossroads.

While pilots were busy marking their maps, Collins came up to Stanford and patting him on the shoulder told him to be a good chap and look after Cartwright, 'He hasn't got many hours in' he said with a grin. Once again the boys piled into the jeep, looking at their maps and making note of useful pin-points which would help them identify the area when they approached the target.

There was time for a last smoke and a few words with ground crews before they began climbing into cockpits. Stanford always handed his pipe to either Nobby or Darty who looked after him. Each experienced pilot had his regular team who laid out his straps, handed him his helmet and plugged in his leads before giving the windscreen a final wipe and making sure that he was settled down. Stanford always had a pee against his rudder beforehand. It had become such a ritual that he was superstitious about it. Being caught short upstairs, compressed inside all his gear and straps was not only uncomfortable but could be a painful process. He would never have admitted it to anybody but his subconscious mind urged him to leave his mark on the aeroplane as a final gesture in case he 'went in'. The others used to joke about it, telling him that he was corroding the works and that his tail plane would fall off one day.

He gave Cartwright, who was already in his cockpit alongside, the thumbs up sign and winding a long grubby, sometime white, silk scarf around his neck he put his foot in the step which Nobby had pulled down from under the fuselage and heaved himself up onto the wing. The office (or cockpit) was in apple pie order as he put on his flying gloves and clipped the straps of his parachute into the metal box. Nobby, leaning over, helped him to adjust his harness straps as he put on his flying helmet and plugged into radio transmission and oxygen supply.

Running an experienced eye over his controls and instruments, Stanford clipped on his oxygen mask, checked that his RT was live, and waited for the CO to start his engine. Jack Collins always flew 'MR-?' which stood at the front end of the line and as soon as the CO's Sabre engine hissed and coughed before picking up and breaking into a steady roar, Bob Stanford selected a cartridge, primed his engine and pressed the starter buttons.

Pilots immediately wound their bubble hoods shut to escape from billowing clouds of dust as ground crews, with handkerchiefs covering noses and mouths, pulled away chocks and waved aircraft round. One after the other 245 Squadron Typhoons took up their positions behind Jack Collins and started zigzagging their way slowly to the top end of the wire mesh strip where, with brakes squealing, they came to a standstill.

Having completed a final cockpit check before take-off, pilots revved their engines against brakes, blowing out clouds of black oil from their exhaust stubs, and in pairs taxied onto the runway. The first pair, Jack Collins and his number two, Terry Gray, slowly rolled forwards and then accelerated fast, bumping and bouncing along the uneven wire mesh. Those following had to rely on their gyros to help them keep straight because of the dust blown back from the chaps in front. After a steep climbing turn off the deck to keep well away from German gun positions a mile or so to the south, 245 Squadron, whose call sign was Archduke, climbed hard towards the Invasion beaches, gathering formation.

Stanford glanced across at Cartwright in the climbing turn and was relieved to see him maintaining reasonable station and not darting about as some sprog chaps were prone to do in a tight turn. They had been the last pair to take-off and had some catching up to do to join the Squadron formation. When they came out of the turn Cartwright began edging closer and Stanford waved him out and back. Cartwright appeared to do this reluctantly but he was still too damn close for comfort as far as Stanford was concerned.

Down below, silver barrage balloons, moored to shipping lying off-shore, swung gently in a light breeze, and off to the west, Mulberry, the floating harbour, was busy receiving supplies and equipment from an assortment of boats. The beaches of Lion-sur-Mer, Luc and St Aubin were still cluttered with metal obstacles and burned-out vehicles left stranded from the landings, but despite all this muck and debris the little seaside towns had a holiday look about them, enhanced by lines of white foam marking the shoreline.

Stanford had often thought about that narrow coastal belt occupied by the Allies as he crossed out on ops. It looked no more than a toe-hold of Normandy from the air and an insignificant achievement after a month or more of bitter fighting especially as Normandy was such a large land area. And even Normandy was only a small part of France which made him think that there was an awful long way to go yet before this war would be over.

The Squadron was still climbing when Collins turned east into the sun, flying over the sea with the coast on the starboard side. The lighthouse at Ouistreham, where the Caen Canal and the River Orne empty into the estuary, stood out like a pointing finger. Ouistreham had been a major centre of French underground activity during the occupation and became the hinge of the British and Canadian landings. Thousands of paratroopers of the 6th Airborne Division had been dropped on the night before D-Day to the south of Ouistreham, along the banks of the River Orne and the Caen Canal to capture and hold this strip of land. It measured only ten miles in length and was about three miles wide but constituted the left flank of the entire Allied Invasion Force. Field-Marshal Erwin Rommel, standing on some high ground across the estuary from Ouistreham, made a prophetic announcement just before D-Day when he told his aides that whoever occupied this high ground would hold the key to the gateway into France and finally into Germany itself. Ironically, the landings took place in this very area and the 6th Airborne Division had captured the high ground Rommel had been indicating.

Levelling out at 3,500 feet the Squadron turned south and recrossed the Normandy coastline between Cabourg and Houlgate with Caen a few miles to the south-west. A and B Flights were flying in finger-four formation as pilots switched on and adjusted reflector gun sights, turned cannon buttons to the fire position and flipped down rocket switches in preparation for the attack.

Below, and to their right, was the pockmarked area of the Merville Battery which had been captured by Lieutenant-Colonel Terence Otway and the Paras of his 9th Battalion on the night before D-Day dawned. Pegasus Bridge, which Major John Howard took intact, was clearly visible, as were the tall chimneys of Colombelles just east of the outskirts of Caen. The ruined city was ringed round by gun flashes, and smoke from isolated fires drifted across the landscape.

As the weather man had predicted, a layer of patchy white cloud was sailing over the target area. The Squadron had been flying for about fifteen minutes when Collins called 'Archduke, line astern, GO!' and they circled round waiting for the red smoke shell to burst over the 'dug-in' tanks at the crossroads. The Squadron had previously made several attacks in this area, usually against targets which were holding up the advance of our troops. Consequently, pilots had had an opportunity to look at the terrain. The landscape was Bocage country, closely bordered with hedges and wooded areas, making it ideal for tanks because there was plenty of surrounding cover. The Second Tactical Air Force was able to operate without any hindrance from the Luftwaffe, except for the odd skirmish, and so Typhoons were able to make air-to-ground attacks without having to worry about bandits being in the area. Typhoon squadrons, therefore, could freely comb the countryside looking for anything on the roads or lanes and immediately dive down and attack. Such air superiority ensured that it was a suicidal exercise for Panzer divisions to be out in the open during daylight hours. As yet, rocket Typhoons had never had an opportunity to catch Panzer armour on the move and they had to be content with attacks on very small groups of tanks or those dug in.

Stanford always disliked any delay while waiting for the red smoke shell to identify the target. Circling round in whiplash formation was a trifle uncomfortable especially if one was at the tail end of the lash. Apart from that, it gave enemy gunners time to line up the Typhoons in their sights. He wanted to get the op over and done with, expecting the flak to come up at any second. He became more tense and nervous, and cursed the brown jobs for keeping them hanging about like this. Black splodges of flak began bursting above and to the left of the formation but there was still no sign of the red smoke as they flew round and round. Collins didn't seem bothered because he maintained his height and position and Stanford was beginning to think that they might have to 'abort' when the target indicator was fired. The good old red smoke billowed out and one after the other the Typhoons performed a wing-over into a steep dive. Automatically, the Squadron spread out in echelon, each man firing short bursts from his cannons to keep the German gunners' heads down.

Stanford knew and felt that Collins had made a steeper dive than usual as he looked up at the Normandy countryside through the roof of his perspex bubble hood. Dives always seemed steeper than they actually were and a 60-degree dive felt like a vertical one. It flashed through Stanford's mind that Jack had made this one a steep as possible to keep close on the target to lessen the risk of undershooting. He reminded himself to watch the pull-out because the seven ton machine mushed like hell coming out of a dive and would sink several hundred feet and there was nothing that one could do about it.

Down they hurtled with speed rapidly building up towards 500 mph and controls getting heavy, requiring real physical effort on rudder pedals and stick. German gunners were pumping up tracer shells which came up at them in an arc, slowly at first and then rushing past like shooting stars, carving up the sky in red and yellow hoops. When they appeared to be coming straight for the aircraft instinctive reaction was to kick on rudder and slide or skid sideways out of the line of fire. The Typhoon was a rugged beast and it would take more than one man's physical strength on the controls to break it.

The last few seconds of the dive were crucial. It was the time when the pilot had to keep his head on the target and fly the aircraft without skid or slide which would send the rockets off line. Range was also of vital importance and a distance of 2,200 yards, or a little over a mile, was considered to be ideal because at that point a rocket achieved its maximum velocity.

Out of a corner of his eye, Stanford caught a glimpse of tell-tale puffs of smoke coming from the rocket rails of a Typhoon ahead and to one side of him and knew that the pilot had fired his salvo. Almost immediately he let go his eight rockets and pulled out of the dive into a steep climbing turn. As the force of 'G' clamped down on him he saw a Typhoon, which must have been Cartwright's still in the dive, and he hoped that the poor sod hadn't been clobbered by flak.

Stanford felt intense pressure on his body so that he couldn't lift a hand or even a finger and momentarily greyed out. This happened many times in pulling out of steep dives and he had become so accustomed to the sensation that he never gave it a thought. Rather like flying his Typhoon, which he did automatically, this enabled him to fly, for the most part, with his head out of the office. An occasional glance across the instrument panel was enough to reassure him that everything was in order because he knew, from experience, the exact position and the pattern of the needles and dials recording pressures and temperatures.

As he climbed towards the others, Cartwright appeared out of nowhere and slid into position alongside him, grinning and giving the thumbs up sign. Stanford gave a wave and mentally made a note to have a word with him about pulling out dangerously low. Three times on the way home Stanford was forced to signal to Cartwright to keep his distance and it made him mad. The little bastard had continued to challenge him, tucking his wing inside his own and edging closer and closer. Bob found himself seething at Cartwright's antics instead of being able to relax a little after the attack. It had, however, been a good prang as he had seen one of those semi dug-in tanks burning and smoke billowing up from another.

Stanford was relieved when they landed back on the strip at 7.00 am having been in the air for 35 minutes. He climbed out of his cockpit hot, sweaty and irritable and was even short with Nobby and Gyppo, his ground crew, who asked him, as usual, whether it had been a good show. He strode across to Cartwright, who was all smiles, and told him bluntly that he had pulled out too low and if he did it again he would probably kill himself. Also, that flying in formation on ops was not like taking part in the Hendon Air Display and, in future, he was to do what his number one told him and not play games.

Having got it off his chest Stanford stalked off towards the jeep which would take them over to Intelligence for de-briefing. Simmering down a little he felt a bit of a shit for having a go at Cartwright and Collins gave him an old-fashioned look when he climbed aboard. The CO, in fact, had been tooting his horn for them both to get a move on and must have known that they were having words.

The de-briefing was usually all part of the winding down session after a show with the Army Captain all poised and eager to find out how his op had gone. For experienced pilots it had been just another job and nothing to get enthusiastic about, rather like clocking off after work when one wanted to whizz off and forget all about it. Most of them reported a fair amount of flak and that, in their opinion, the target had been well pranged. The brown job had to dig it out of them that there had been flames and smoke coming from the tanks. But Cartwright, who was the last pilot to tell his story, said in a loud voice that he hadn't seen much flak to worry about and he didn't think that the Squadron had really pressed home the attack.

Everybody stopped talking and looked at him. Nobody had ever said anything like that before and there was an awkward silence. The pilots looked at Jack Collins, expecting him to say something, but Jack just stood there grinning and ignoring the remark. The Army Captain asked Cartwright to be more explicit but Cartwright only mumbled something about getting in closer to the target. Thinking that the CO didn't want to have a domestic argument in front of the Intelligence officer, they all left the tent preferring to walk back and leave Cartwright alone with Collins who no doubt would sort him out.

On the way back, little was said about the incident and Stanford found himself the prime mover in stirring things up for Cartwright who, he said, had no idea how a Typhoon sinks when pulling out of a dive or how easy it was to become mesmerized by the target. Everybody knew that what Cartwright had said at de-briefing was unforgivable but they preferred to forget it. They returned to the log table to find that another sprog pilot had just been flown in—a Flight Sergeant Hughes, who was known as 'Spike'. Somebody said that Spike had once played the trombone in a Salvation Army band. That was all they needed!

Bob Stanford had no sooner sat himself on the ground and reached out for a mug of tea than Ches West ambled towards him. Ches was a big Canadian, standing six feet or more with rounded shoulders propping up a head small for his size and he had a puckered mouth which talked in a distinctly nasal tone as slowly as he walked. 'How ja make out?', he drawled, smoking a Lucky Strike and chewing gum. Stanford told him that he thought it was a good prang but there was quite a bit of flak around. Ches snorted and spat out phlegm. 'Aw, shit', he said, 'I didn't mean that. How'ja find my machine?'. That was all Ches cared about. Even when Bob mentioned the Cartwright incident the big Canadian just grinned and blew out his chewing gum, 'Aw hell', he said, 'That Limey bastard'll soon get his arse burned off, for sure!'

Chapter 3

Life on the strip

It was a nice afternoon and Stanford had made himself comfortable on his camp bed, lying outside in the sun. He had just come back from the village having collected his own washing and some of Paddy Gray's which the farmer's wife had kindly done for them. She seemed quite happy with a bar of soap and a packet of cigarettes and offered him cider plus a chunk of cheese which he brought back with him.

Except for the sound of gunfire the war seemed a million miles away as he lay there reading a Western. Dud Nott and Maxie Maxwell, a few tents down the line, were hammering away at something and had been dragging some poles up the slope towards the field latrine. Every now and then Dud ambled over to Terry Gray's emporium and he could hear them laughing and joking and he knew that something was going on. He heard Dud yell, 'Don't be such a twit, Maxie. You've got to have some bloody holes in the bottom otherwise the water won't come out'.

This was too much for Bob so he went over to have a look. Dud told him that they were making a shower. 'All this strip washing from canvas bowls is not on', Dud said, 'so Maxie and I are going to have our own shower'. Terry Gray had told them how to do it, 'You procure a large biscuit tin', he said, 'and you punch holes in the bottom. Then you flatten the edges of the lid, punch a hole in it and thread through a piece of string. Stand the tin box on the lid and fit it into a wooden frame. All you have to do is to fill the tin with water and pull the string and away comes the lid and down comes the water. Simple, isn't it?'

It wasn't that simple and they had to get Terry to sort it out, grumbling that he was too busy and he didn't want an effing shower anyway. Surprisingly, the thing worked very well and Dud decided that Benny Bennet should be persuaded to take a shower 'on the house', but not in his flying boots. He was saved from a 'rag' when Jimmy Wilson arrived to call some of them off to do an armed recce in the Monts area.

Stanford was down to fly number two to Flight Lieutenant 'Ace' Miron, a smallish cobby French Canadian who hadn't acquired the Ace symbol for nothing! Ace, like the Frenchman de Kerdril, was one of those chaps who liked to fight his war at very close quarters. He told Bob Stanford during the briefing to stick close to him because if the others didn't find anything he bloody well would.

It was like a pleasant Sunday afternoon stroll in the sun until Ace broke RT silence, 'Archduke Leader, there's something down there at ten o'clock, I'm going down'. Jimmy Wilson, who was leading the show called, 'Roger' as Ace did a wing-over with Stanford following. Ace was right because steady streams of tracer were immediately pumped up at them in the dive. Bob Stanford saw one lot coming straight at him and without thinking pulled back on the stick in a desperate effort to get away from it. He felt an agonising pain in his stomach, as if he had been kicked by a horse, and then he blacked out.

When he came to, the aircraft was climbing furiously and instinctively he tried to push the stick forward and throttle back but found that he couldn't move his hands or exert any pressure on the controls. There was a terrible pain in his guts and he thought that he had been hit. His Typhoon was approaching the stall when somehow he managed to put rudder on and slide sideways out of the climb. He could hear Ace's voice on the RT, 'Blue four, where are you? Come in Blue four' as he tried to get his hands to work. His left hand had slipped off the throttle but he couldn't lift it back up onto the bar control.

Any effort to move his limbs produced a stabbing pain in his stomach. He had to grit his teeth to get her flying reasonably straight and level and was astonished to find that he had shot up some 6,000 feet in the climb. His stomach pain eased off gradually and he was feeling life coming back when Ace suddenly appeared out of nowhere. 'Blue four. Are you OK?' came over the RT. He told Ace that he had stomach cramp after pulling out and asked him to take it gently.

He had to be helped out of the cockpit after landing, having no strength and sweating like a pig. Doc Saunders made him lie flat on a stretcher when they got him to the hospital tent and gave his guts a good bashing. 'Nothing serious', he said with a smile, 'You've just left your stomach at the bottom of a dive and it takes a little time to climb back into its original shape, that's all. No flying for a couple of days. I'll check you out then'.

This worried Stanford and he could have kicked himself for not having dragged himself out of the aircraft somehow and then he wouldn't have got himself into the Doc's clutches. His stomach was damned sore and he felt 'a bit flakers' but nothing more. To be taken off flying was a bastard. It had only ever happened to him once before when he couldn't even crawl around then and they discovered he had got pneumonia. Now, he would have to get the Doc's clearance before he could take-off again and no pilot wanted to be in that position.

The Doc drove him back to the tents in his jeep and told him to be a good chap and take it easy for a while. The boys around the log table gawped at him as he got out of the jeep rather gingerly. 'Jesus, Bob', one said, 'We all thought you were shot full of holes when they lifted you out, man'. This made him feel a fraud and Ches West touched him on the raw, 'Aw shit, Bob,' he drawled, 'never knew you was flak happy, did we!'

Bob flushed and Tubby Sago, never one for stirring himself suddenly got up off his arse and said, 'We're all bloody flak happy West. So, shut your Canadian gob'. This started off a good old slanging match and Bob left him to it, disappearing into his tent. His chum Paddy Gray had gone off somewhere with Bill Smith and he was glad to be alone for once. It had been a rough day. He still got painful twinges from his stomach when he walked and he felt weak so he flopped down onto his camp bed and lit his pipe. Maxie Maxwell had told him that Ace's aircraft had been clobbered well and truly by flak so maybe he had been lucky to pull out of the dive when he had. But he knew that he was only fooling himself to think like that. He had panicked and that was all there was to it. It was a wonder, he thought, that he hadn't bent the poor bloody aircraft when he pulled the stick back so suddenly. It was a poor show and he had no excuse but he wasn't going to do it again.

He was dozing off when Benny Bennett put his head in through the flap, 'Get your arse out of that sack, Bob', he said, 'there's a load of booze just come in'. Bob made a miraculous recovery and a little later he had forgotten all about having been flak happy and felt fit and ready to fly.

*   *   *

51

One evening the conversation turned to Winston Churchill's recent visit to the strip. It had come as a complete surprise but when everybody off duty had been summoned to the HQ area they knew something was up. An armada of Spitfires could be seen circling high up over the beach head as a captured German Fiesler Storch approached the strip and nipped into an adjacent cornfield, coming to a stop within about 20 yards.

There was no mistaking the passenger sitting in the back smoking a large cigar—strictly against regulations—and wearing a soft peaked cap and siren suit. A great cheer went up as Winston, who had been flown in by Harry Broadhurst, the Air Officer Commanding, was carefully eased out of the aircraft holding his stick aloft and giving the 'V' sign. A never-to-be-forgotten moment for all those standing and waving under a summer sun, with a light breeze gently rippling the corn husks and barrage balloons sparkling in a blue sky.

The Prime Minister suddenly arriving in a captured German aircraft when the guns were thundering out and the front line was only a mile or so to the south was a gesture of impudence and arrogance which had captivated his audience. His timing had been perfect because the Allied advance was at a standstill and his electrifying personality and presence gave everyone an uplift. Stanford, by chance, had come face to face with Eisenhower and had seen Montgomery at close quarters but Churchill's impact, in his opinion, transcended them all.

It was Warrant Officer Tubby Sago who had brought up the subject of Churchill's visit in the first place when he was binding about the food. This large and plump Australian liked his tucker and was brassed off with a diet of compo stew, tinned bangers and hard tack. 'If they can fly in fresh bread and cakes for Churchill's tea', he had groused, 'then they can bloody do the same for us. Top brass! they get on my wick'. Nobody took much notice of Sago's remarks except to suggest that the shortage of bread should eventually enable him to get his fat arse into a Typhoon more easily. 'All right, you bastards', Tubby retorted, 'but how much longer are you going to sit on your arses and eat this crap?'

This was a challenge from the big Aussie and got everybody going. Winston deserved his fresh bread and cakes if anybody did, they said. The PM had even brought his own bottle of brandy and hadn't drunk the mess booze. The great man had refused to eat the scrawny chicken which somebody had scrounged from a local farm. And Winston had gone around asking questions and inviting them. Sago was reminded that he hadn't said anything when Churchill asked him the breaking strength of the shearing wire which held the rockets on the rails until they built up sufficient impetus to whizz off—because Sago didn't bloody well know, and neither did they for that matter. But Sago had had an opportunity of telling Winston that the grub was piss poor in these parts and he should not have simply stood there wiping his nose with the back of his hand.

Those around the log table were quick to point out that Winston had done his homework and appeared to know more about the technicalities of Typhoons than they did. Most admitted that it might have been bad for their morale if they had known. Ches West made the point when he drawled, 'Aw shit. Who the hell wants to know anyway. Just as long as that fan keeps turning is all right by me. I tell you.'

As the light faded they drifted back to their tents and lit candles to read or play cards. Some time ago, Warrant Officers Terry Gray and Tubby Sago had decided that their tent wasn't too comfortable and also that they would draw their own rations in future and cook for themselves. So they had dug a rectangular hole about four feet deep which they floored with opened-out rocket cases that Terry had procured from stores. Then they put ammunition boxes filled with earth around the sides to make it higher and banked up more earth to ensure that it was blast proof. The metal framework and tarpaulin cover from a three tonner made a roof and they cut four steps up to ground level. The end of the tarpaulin gave them a covered area where they had a little cooker which Terry had procured and a place in which they did their cooking and washing.

At first, their initiative was frowned upon by the others, although some had dug holes in order to sleep below ground without having to worry about the nightly bomber. When Terry's emporium took shape, however, it became the envy of other pilots. Terry admitted that it was bloody hard work building the damn thing but he had been determined to make himself comfortable. Personal comfort was an essential ingredient of life as far as Terry was concerned and he always made sure of it. A born mechanical genius, he had always had a motor car and could be relied upon to provide Squadron transport. He had even sold the CO a duff MG when the Squadron was based at West Hampnett and Jack had quietly ordered him to put it right or else! Anybody looking closely at Terry's cars would find the initials AM (Air Ministry) stamped on various parts and his favourite word was 'procure'. Anything in short supply or impossible to get, Terry would procure. How he got it or from where nobody knew or cared.

Gray and Sago were a strange combination. Unlike Sago, Gray was short, wiry and compact with blonde hair, blue eyes and a Douglas Fairbanks moustache. He had a keen look about him as if he was always sizing up potential opportunities for further advancement in life. A roguish look, perhaps, but for all that the girls found him attractive and amusing and he was never lost for their company. He referred to his chum as Glen and never called him Tubby as he was generally known. Sago, by contrast, was a rather dour and sombre personality whose massive frame was topped up by his Warrant Officer's cap—looking rather like a pimple on a haystack.

One day Terry had been taking a look at the Arromanches area, a mile or so north of Bayeux, and he went out in a DUKW to one of the ships lying off shore where he managed to procure about two dozen loaves of bread. There was a craving for lovely thick slices of white loaf and most of the Squadron enjoyed a small sample. Terry, having Squadron funds, then made his way to the base NAAFI at Arromanches and collected a month's ration for every member of the Squadron which included spirits, beer and cigarettes plus all the little odds and ends which were very handy to everybody. During the next 'stand down' there was a party in the Squadron dispersal tent and all ground crews were issued with a couple of bottles of beer plus extra rations for free. Then, as it happened, supplies came through so everybody got double rations as a result of Terry's excursion.

On the following morning, frothy little white pillow case clouds were chasing one another across a blue sky. The early show had been a recce but there had been nothing to shoot up on the roads so rockets and cannon shells had been fired into a wood supposedly hiding German armour. A most unrewarding affair which even Benny Bennet had failed to liven up with one of his lucky strikes. The pilots concerned had joked about it, reminding Benny of the attack on an oil dump near Flers. The Squadron had already set the dump on fire and shot up the surrounding buildings when Benny, who was the last man in, made his attack. He completely missed the target with his rockets, which by the merest fluke, managed to find their way into an ammunition dump exploding it in a giant ball of orange flame and black smoke. Benny was seen to fly into this inferno and everybody thought that he had got the chop. But no, a charred and blackened Typhoon rejoined the formation with a grinning Benny giving the thumbs-up sign. He had not only found a hidden ammunition dump, which even Intelligence didn't know existed, but had also blown the oil depot into thin air.

Later, Flying Officer George Dakin, a neatly built and good looking Canadian, was sitting smoking a cigarette in company with his chums Dud Nott and Maxie Maxwell, when Jimmy Wilson, B Flight commander, interrupted the conversation. He told George Dakin that he was down for the next show and Stanford would be flying his number two.

A ripple of excitement had gone round the place when Wilson said it was going to be a Wing show and all the squadrons would be taking part. The strip was already beginning to look like Piccadilly Circus with vehicles buzzing about everywhere and blowing up clouds of dust. Ground crews, being inquisitive beings, wanted to know what it was all about and pilots tossed them a few throw away lines which was their usual practice when a big deal was imminent.

The Intelligence tent was packed when the Army Captain briefed the Wing on the general battle front situation and the target. Heavy bomber attacks had been carried out at dawn on areas south and east of Caen in preparation for an advance, code-named 'Goodwood'. The 'Goodwood' plan was to have a hard crack at the enemy and attract his armour to the eastern flank. Caen, as usual, was the pivot around which the action would take place but although the city itself had been taken there were parts of it still occupied by the enemy. These were to be cleaned up as part of the operation to establish firm bridgeheads south of Caen and sap the enemy's strength there. The Army Captain pointed out that the success of the 'Goodwood' operation should make it difficult for the enemy to resist the projected American breakout, code-named 'Cobra', from the Cherbourg Peninsula.

After listening to the Army Captain's assessment of the military scene, pilots were not surprised to learn that their target was to be a Panzer headquarters to the south and east of Caen. Apparently, this particular Panzer division was being held in reserve and had taken over a large château as a temporary headquarters before moving up the line. The job for the Typhoons was to prang the château and give the surrounding woods concealing the armour, a good going over.

The Intelligence officer didn't exactly endear himself to pilots when he said that 'we' can undoubtedly expect heavy flak from tanks and surrounding gun positions in the woods. Even Charles Green, the Wing leader, grinned at the 'we' bit and gave the brown job an old fashioned look. This South African Wing Commander was a big man with close-cropped bushy hair, large luminous dark brown eyes, wide shoulders and a physique which looked as if he had been built out of solid teak. He had an intense hatred of the Hun and wore two Smith and Wesson revolvers around his waist in order to knock off as many Krauts as possible if ever he had to bale out. Green had already established himself as one of the most fearless Wing leaders in the business and everybody jumped to it when he came on the scene.

Flying Officer George Dakin sat smoking a cigarette and listening intently as Wing Commander Charles Green used his pointer on the target map and issued his instructions. Two squadrons would be going in first in an anti-flak role to keep the German gunners' heads down and liven up the surrounding woods and it would be 245's job to blast the château wide open.

There was no doubt in Dakin's mind that this was going to be one hell of a trip and he said as much to Stanford who was sitting next to him. Stanford reckoned that the gunners would be fairly warmed up by the time they went in but he told George not to worry. 'The château's that bloody big,' he said, 'we can't miss it.' In the jeep, on the way back from briefing, Stanford had remarked that every time a major attack was launched he noticed on the map that the Guards Armoured Division had been switched into the front line and it seemed a bit tough on those poor bloody guards. Dakin thought for a moment and laughed, 'You think so,' he said, 'well what about the crappy job they've given us!' Stanford was flying 'R' (Robert) again because his new machine hadn't arrived and Ches West was standing beside it with a sly grin on his face. Patting the fuselage Ches drawled, 'See here, Stanford. This is a good machine and don'tcha go and bend it, you Limey bastard!'

They had a few minutes to go before getting into their aircraft and Dakin pulled out his map from his flying boot and said to Stanford, 'Look Bob, we'll be following the River Orne and we'll pick it up south of Caen. It wiggles about a bit and here's that funny bubble in it by this place Thury Harcourt. That's where we'll turn to port and make for the target so watch out for it because Green is likely to put us into line astern a bit sharpish.'

Ches West had sloped off so Stanford enjoyed his usual pee against the tailplane of 'R' (Robert) and hauled himself up into the cockpit with Nobby's help. He settled himself down and remembered to ease off the throttle nut a little because Ches, being such a ham-fisted bastard, had it screwed up too tightly. He pulled on his flying gloves and helmet, adjusted his tinted goggles and fastened his oxygen mask, checking that his RT was live. Gyppo had signalled to him to give the Sabre one and a half strokes on the primer and having selected a starter cartridge he waited to press the button.

Nobby would be giving him the signal as soon as the three-bladed prop of Jack Collin's Typhoon started to rotate. Bob always found himself keyed up during these moments of waiting, probably because he was locked into a situation from which there was no escape. Sitting there tightly strapped in, gloved and goggled with an oxygen mask across his face, gave him a claustrophobic feeling and an urge to get going. In the old days, Bob had always hated to sit in his cockpit standing off the end of the runway and waiting for the signal to scramble. He couldn't stop his mind triggering off all kinds of morbid thoughts. Some chaps were so relaxed that they could even read a book while they were sitting there and he thought that they were lucky bastards not to have his kind of imagination. It had often occurred to him that he was too highly strung to be doing this kind of job but as soon as the action started he wasn't bothered.

Thumbs-up from Nobby and he pressed the starter buttons, hearing the hiss as the cartridge exploded and turned over the big Sabre engine, which cleared its throat and coughed once or twice before breaking into a steady roar. He could feel the Typhoon vibrating underneath him as he gently opened the throttle to clear the engine. The air was dry and dusty under patchy cloud as Gyppo and Nobby, half bent, moved forward to pull away the chocks and wave him round. He squeezed the hand brake lever inside the spade grip of his control column and, applying full left rudder, turned the Typhoon and began to roll forwards behind George Dakin in 'N' (Nuts).

The whole strip was boiling up into a gigantic dust cloud when 121 Wing squadrons lined up for take-off with brakes squealing and wings vibrating as engines were opened up. Squadron call signs, 'Crayfish', 'Quebec', 'Landlord' and 'Archduke' crackled over the RT as those who were left behind on the strip stood there watching. As the dust settled the Wing was climbing hard over the Normandy beaches and gathering formation before turning east into the sun.

Stanford looked around him thinking that the whole bloody sky was filled with Typhoons and it made him feel good. So did flying in finger-four squadron formation. There was a closeness about it, as if the whole thing was a family affair, because one knew the personalities behind the goggles and masks and they were all in it together. He had to watch George Dakin carefully in order to keep formation but, out of the corner of his eye, he could see Jimmy Wilson who was leading the Flight and Spike Hughes, the new man, formating on Jimmy.

The ruined area around Caen, pockmarked with bomb craters,

was alive with flashes of gunfire and a curtain of smoke which had drifted across the battlefield. To the south the countryside unfolded in a pattern of greens, rich browns, yellows and a sprinkling of poppy reds here and there. On their right, the sluggish waters of the River Orne wound their way towards St Remy where a main road from Caen bisected the forests of Grimbosq and Cinglais and crossed the river on its journey south to Condé. Over to the left the road from Caen to Falaise cut through the countryside like a knife until it reached Potigny.

Dakin gave Stanford a thumbs-up sign and pointed down where Bob could clearly see the strange loop in the River Orne and, as George had predicted, Charles Green ordered his formation into line astern. This time Bob really had to concentrate on his flying because he was at the end of the lash and skating all over the sky. He wasn't conscious of the flak, although there was plenty of it, until he was into the dive when he saw what appeared to be a white cloud over the target area. It didn't match up to surrounding clouds which were like dollops of whipped cream and then he realized that he would be diving through a curtain of flak. He could see George Dakin below him and off to his left as George fired his rockets. There was no mistaking the château, conveniently set in its own grounds and surrounded by lawns and an adjoining lake. It presented a perfect target and Stanford let go a salvo of eight rockets before pulling up into a tight climbing turn.

The first thing he did, after going through the 'G' barrier, was to look around for George expecting him to be somewhere up above him but there was no sign of his aircraft. Other Typhoons were milling about over the target but George seemed to have disappeared. He called up Jack Collins, Archduke leader, over the RT and told him that he had lost his number one, so Jack circled the target but there was no trace of Dakin. Stanford could hear the RT jabbering away—apparently somebody had got clobbered and had baled out, but it was a pilot from another squadron.

Stanford felt badly about losing George because as Dakin's number two his job had been to look after him. He consoled himself with the thought that there was nothing he could have done in the circumstances and he remembered that Bill Reynolds had gone the same way. They had dived through cloud and Bill had just vanished without trace like George. On the way home, Stanford was still thinking about poor old George and what he was going to say to his particular chums, Dud Nott and Maxie Maxwell. He told the Wing Commander at debriefing that he had seen George fire his rockets and disappear into the smoke. A couple of hours later the mystery was solved when Charles Green took a call from the Americans.

Apparently, Dakin had been hit as he climbed through the smoke billowing up from the château. There was an almighty bang, something slapped him across the side of his head, and he had passed out. He vaguely remembered coming to and finding his aircraft climbing steeply out of control. Somehow he managed to push the stick forward and ease back on the throttle as the Typhoon dropped its nose and built up speed. He couldn't see out of one eye and blood was running down his face and chest. During moments of consciousness he endeavoured to get his aircraft flying straight and level by using the trimmers but had no idea where he was or where he was going. His perspex hood had been shattered and he was cold from the blast of air rushing into the cockpit but felt no pain. During one of his more lucid moments he was able to read his compass with his good eye only to discover to his horror that he was flying south into enemy territory.

It was too much for him to manipulate the joystick but he managed to turn his aircraft round into a north-westerly direction by easing back on the throttle and pushing the rudder pedal. Although the Typhoon skidded and slipped all over the place he succeeded, by trial and error, in making a split arse turn and then flaked out. He regained consciousness every now and then and did his best to trim his machine which had been gaining and losing height as if in a drunken stupor.

He was losing a lot of blood and getting weaker all the time when he saw an airfield. Through a red haze he could see the strip ahead of him and he made one final effort to try to get his aircraft down. On the point of collapse, his reflexes took over and subconsciously he throttled back and managed to get some flap down as, losing height, he pointed the aircraft in the direction of the runway cutting his switches as he neared the ground alongside the wire mesh strip. The last thing he heard, before he passed out, was a metallic tearing noise as his body was buffeted about and pain flooded through his system.

Dakin's phenomenal luck and courage saw him through. He had crashed on an American strip and within minutes they had erected an oxygen tent over his cockpit and given him blood transfusions which saved his life. A little later he was on the operating table. Within a couple of weeks he came to visit the Squadron, seeming as good as new except that he had a glass eye and flak scars down his face. Dakin's war was over and he was on his way back to Canada where he belonged.

Stanford had been relieved to hear that Dakin had made it but still found it difficult to understand how George had vanished. Then he realized that as he had come off the target into a climbing turn, George must have climbed straight ahead in his unconscious state. Their speed must have been approaching 500 mph at the bottom of the dive, he thought, and with George flying in the opposite direction it was obvious why he had lost him.

Shortly after the château operation the Squadron was airborne again, this time to attack a brickworks in the vicinity of Caen on the eastern flank. The 'Goodwood' push was hotting up and apparently this brickworks, a heavily defended German position at a cross roads, was giving the brown jobs a lot of trouble. Armoured vehicles which had attempted to run the German blockade had been shot up and the Army had called up the Typhoons to demolish the chimney and buildings and also to give the close perimeter area a good bashing.

Bob Stanford wasn't on the show but when the Squadron came back he counted only seven Typhoons in the circuit so it looked as if someone must have bought it. Bob's chum, Paddy Gray, followed his usual pattern of behaviour after an op by coming into the tent and sitting on the edge of his camp bed loosening his shirt and battledress blouse. Then, folding back his cuffs he flipped open his cigarette case and lit up, blowing out clouds of smoke and staring straight ahead lost in thought. After a while he said very quietly, 'Cartwright's had it.'

Most pilots experienced a kind of numbness after the excitement of going on a show combined with a feeling that once again they had 'made it'. Few had an urge to fool about because there was no point, as the next op might be coming up sooner than later. It came as no surprise to anybody that Cartwright should have written himself off. As Gray told Stanford and Bennet, 'There was an enormous orange and yellow explosion. This bloody great chimney seemed to hang upright in mid air. Then it crumbled slowly like a pack of cards. Cartwright pressed home his attack and tried to pull out at the very last moment and, of course, the stupid bastard mushed straight into the base of the chimney.'

Benny Bennet wasn't paying much attention to Paddy's remarks but was engrossed in trying to open a parcel from home. Gray and Stanford watched eagerly as Benny, with a cigarette drooping out of the corner of his mouth and chewing at the same time, was fumbling around with the string. In the end he gave up and took a sheath knife out of his flying boot, slicing open the cardboard outer. 'Jesus

Christ', he said, as half-a-dozen coat hangers fell out, 'What the hell is going on?' His mum in Toronto had written him a little note telling him to be sure to hang up his best blues and not get them too creased. The boys were still laughing when Spike Hughes poked his nose through the tent flap and looked at the coat hangers in astonishment. 'Yesh', he said, 'Very nishe but there'sh no hooksh in the tentsh to hang them on!' Although he had only done a couple of ops, Spike already had the makings of a sound and reliable Squadron pilot and was becoming a popular chap. He didn't drink, smoke or swear and had played the trombone in a Salvation Army Band, hardly qualities which one would have expected in a rocket Typhoon pilot. He came in for a good deal of ragging but was always cheerful and never lost his temper. Spike was a well built young chap with a rather prominent nose and fleshy pursed lips which the boys thought were the result of his trombone blowing.

One afternoon, Stanford and Gray thought it would be a great idea to send Spike to buy eggs in Le Fresne. The poor chap didn't speak a word of French and with his lisp they reckoned that the outcome would be very funny. They explained that in French, one egg was 'ern erf' but half a dozen was 'sees er' and Spike trundled off, with a haversack over his arm, muttering 'seese erse'! They hadn't even told him about their own particular farm but left him to make his own way and try his luck.

When Spike reappeared, he solemnly walked up to the log table and opened his bag. 'Yesh', he said with a grin, 'I didn't know cheesh wash fromage,' and he proceeded to unload a dozen eggs, a hunk of cheese and some strawberries! He even put Terry Gray's nose out of joint. Terry, the procurer of everything, wasn't particularly amused and stalked off saying that he could have got all that stuff with no bother!

Apart from Terry Gray's activities using Squadron funds to procure extra rations and other goodies there had been a few refinements on the catering front and these had coincided with engine changes. When Typhoons began operating from the strip, fine particles of top soil were sucked into the Sabre engine and they began to score the cylinders, cutting engine life down to a few hours. This problem suddenly became a disaster when engines started to seize up and immediate action had to be taken. It seemed extraordinary that Typhoons had been allowed to operate from temporary airstrips in Normandy, which were bulldozed out of farmland, without fitting air filters, particularly as this trouble had been solved in North Africa. Panic measures were taken and a suitable air filter, incorporated in the air intake, was designed, manufactured and tested within 24 hours. Within a week, the entire Typhoon force in Normandy had been fitted with the new filter but a number of aircraft had to be flown back to service bases in Southern England for engine changes. This provided a few lucky chaps with an opportunity to fly back to the old country and have a night out, but there was more to it than that.

It only took about thirty minutes to fly back home across the Channel—an exciting trip during which one was looking forward to the prospects of a hot bath, a change of clothes, female company, decent grub and plenty of booze. A couple of bottles of warm NAAFI beer, the weekly ration on the strip, bore no comparison to a foaming pint of good old British draught bitter and, as most pilots were beer drinkers, the thought of sinking a few jars was uppermost in their minds.

Turning their backs on the war, if only for a short time, gave pilots a holiday and a carefree spirit. There would be no ops for a while and, providing the old Sabre engine kept going over the sea, they could actually take a breather and make plans. Never in these circumstances did the Sabre engine sound so sweet and physical control of the machine feel so satisfying.

The Channel was never free from a lifeline of ships bucketing their way across to the Mulberry harbour and back to home ports. Air corridors were seldom empty of gaggles of fighters, streams of bombers and transport aircraft so one was rarely alone when crossing the expanse of water. The maintenance depot at Needs Point was the Typhoon hospital, and a crowd of giant hangars surrounded the strip. Having delivered the body, those with squadron funds would fly off in a replacement machine to bases where they could do a deal with friendly catering officers who were most co-operative. Flying Officer George Wharry of 245 Squadron returned to Normandy with over 150 freshly-baked loaves of bread stuffed into his gun bays, and his two 45-gallon long range drop tanks, which had been flushed out, were filled with beer. Tea, sugar, butter, whisky, cigarettes and other essentials were somehow packed into his Typhoon which staggered off the deck and made for Normandy like a flying NAAFI wagon!

Chapter 4

Crash landing

Bob Stanford had managed a non-operational trip over the other side on only one occasion since D-Day but not because he had to fly over for an engine change. It happened on 18 June when the Squadron was operating from the strip in Normandy during the day and then returning back to base at Holmsley South, outside Bournemouth, during the evening because of shelling. The Germans still hadn't been cleared out of surrounding woods and were making a nuisance of themselves.

The first show, after take-off from Holmsley, was an armed recce south of a line between Bayeux and Caen. The Squadron found nothing on the roads and eventually fired their rockets and cannons into forests and woods giving cover to German armour and then landed on the strip. Life wasn't particularly pleasant there because shells whined over at regular intervals which meant jumping into slit trenches.

The next op was an attack on an SS headquarters to the east of Caen. A blue sky with a touch of fair weather cumulus was soon disfigured by splotches of brown flak bursting around the Squadron as pilots winged over into the dive. Stanford was following Dud Nott down through layers of the stuff and, as he pulled out there was a bang from underneath the engine and he knew that he must have been hit. His immediate reaction was to check his instruments but everything appeared to be normal. He kept taking sidelong glances at the dials and throttled back a little in case it was anything serious. There was nothing else he could do except to call up Archduke leader saying that he had been hit and would find his own way back. His number one, Dud Nott, dropped out of Squadron formation and flew alongside giving him a thumbs-up sign. Suddenly he noticed the needle of his radiator temperature gauge flickering towards the danger mark and he throttled back further, gliding gently, hoping to cool the engine. They had cleared Caen and were in reach of British territory when the needle went off the clock. Bob could feel sweat running down his back and prayed that she wouldn't blow up, trying to convince himself that maybe the instrument was faulty because everything else seemed to be OK. Then, he felt the scorching heat blowing back from the engine and was dead scared of going up in flames so he switched off.

There was a horrible empty feeling inside his stomach when he realized that he was going to have to make a forced landing and there was no emergency strip within range. He hadn't belly landed a Typhoon on rough ground before but he supposed that there was always going to be a first time. Everything had suddenly gone quiet as he feverishly looked around for a convenient field. The Typhoon was losing height rapidly as, without power, it had a gliding angle like a brick. He knew that he had to maintain a speed of at least 200 mph and be ready to pump down some flap if necessary. It all happened very quickly as he jettisoned his hood, let his seat right down, pulled out his plug leads and tightened his harness straps until they bit into his body. Tracer was coming up at him and he was conscious of Dud Nott diving at the German gunners to give them a squirt.

To make matters more complicated a Spitfire, streaming glycol vapour, suddenly appeared alongside him obviously trying to get into the same field—which looked bloody small. With a hand clenched tightly on the spade grip of his control column, he levelled out and pushed the nose of his Typhoon into the ground and kept it there to avoid the aircraft ballooning. The aircraft shook and rocked from side to side as the fuselage tore along the ground so he put an arm across his face and kept his head down.

Pressure on his body pinned him back against the metal seat as the aircraft came to a grinding halt. Instinctively, he pulled the safety pin from his harness and struggled out, falling on the ground as he was still wearing his parachute. Half bent, he waddled rapidly away from the aircraft expecting it to blow up at any second. His heart was pounding like mad when some brown jobs appeared out of nowhere and forced him to duck down and crawl to the hedge. Bob got the message when a Company Sergeant Major told him that Jerry was only a few hundred yards away and if he didn't keep his head down he might be shot.

Above A rocket Typhoon takes off from the landing strip as a gun crew watch proceedings.

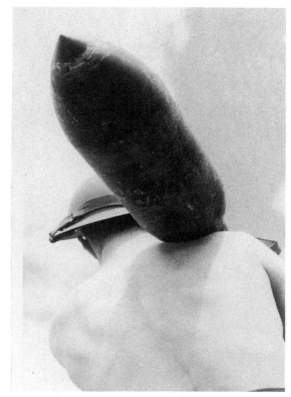

Right An armourer, stripped to the waist, carries a 65 lb rocket head *(Imperial War Museum)*.

Left Tents were erected over holes dug into the ground for protection against shelling and bombing *(Imperial War Museum)*.

Below left Rocket tubes with fins being stacked alongside the hedge on the strip *(Imperial War Museum)*.

Above Plugging in rockets ready for the attack *(Imperial War Museum)*.

Below Armourers and fitters working on a Typhoon. Note the Typhoon in the background camouflaged by trees *(Imperial War Museum)*.

245 Squadron off to a briefing session. On the bonnet are Paddy Gray and the author, at the back, Al Dellar, Tubby Sago and Roly Temple. Inside, Jack Collins is at the wheel and Jeff Jeffries sits behind him.

Left The author outside his tent.

Below A 245 Squadron Typhoon being re-armed—note the Squadron letters 'MR' and the aircraft taking off.

Right Squadron Leader Jack Collins DFC and Bar, the commanding officer of 245 Squadron *(Imperial War Museum)*.

Top 121 Wing leader, Wing Commander Charles Green (South Africa) DSO DFC *(Imperial War Museum)*.

Above Wing Commander C. S. (Tim) Morice MC (later Group Captain DSO MC), the airfield commander, watching the Wing take off *(Imperial War Museum)*.

Below A 245 Squadron wedding at the Osterley Arms. Left to right, the bride's brother, (an air gunner); Jeff Jeffries; Dud Nott; the bride; the groom, Doug Martin (not to be confused with 'Which' Martin); Maxie Maxwell and Ken Dickie.

Bob Stanford must have looked a little weak and watery because the CSM produced a flask saying, 'I should have a drop of this, sonny, if I were you. It'll do you good.' Being called sonny made Bob mad, so to prove a point, he took a couple of good swallows which seemed to blow his head off, making his eyes water. The Spitfire had flopped into the far corner of the field and the brown jobs escorted Bob crawling towards it. The pilot, a Frenchman by the name of Jean Maquis, solemnly shook hands although they were both on their knees at the time and waved a hand towards both aircraft with a 'kaput' expression on his face which said it all.

The two pilots were then bundled along hedges and across ditches with the brown jobs carrying their parachutes for them. From time to time, machine gun fire forced them to hit the deck but eventually they arrived at a crossroads and were able to take a breather. The CSM then told Bob that he would send for a truck to take them to the nearest airstrip which was about one and a half miles way.

Other brown jobs gathered round while they were waiting and much to Bob's delight they seemed genuinely enthusiastic about Typhoon operations and asked him all kinds of questions about the aircraft. This rather made his day because nobody bothered about the Spitfire and poor old Jean Maquis was left out of it. All this glory plus the effects of the whisky had put him a cocky frame of mind and he was still carrying on about the virtues of his favourite aircraft when the truck arrived at the strip.

Bob explained to a rather pompous and officious Squadron Leader, a wingless wonder who appeared to be running the show, that they had belly landed and needed to get back to England and report to their squadrons as soon as possible. The chap seemed to regard them as a bloody nuisance and told them curtly that they would have to wait until after 17.00 hours when Dakotas would be coming in to pick up wounded. 'You can get a lift in one of those', he said, and before they could ask him about food or anything else he stalked off.

Spotting a Flying Fortress parked off the far end of the strip they decided to go and have a look while they were waiting. There didn't seem to be anybody around and the fuselage door at the far end was open so they climbed the steps and went inside. To their astonishment they were confronted by a small kitchen containing a fridge with several crates of Coke stacked beside it, so they helped themselves. Beyond the kitchen there was a curtained-off saloon with comfortable arm chairs and tables. Obviously, Bob thought, this was a special machine for top brass and they had better get out fast.

As he ducked under the roof and put a foot on the steps the first thing he saw was a pair of highly polished brown cavalry boots and he slowly looked up to see the Allied Supreme Commander, General Eisenhower, standing in the middle of a group of high ranking American officers. Instinctively, he saluted and froze. There was an awkward silence before the General smiled and beckoned them both over. It was too late to hide the bottle when the General said, 'What are you boys doing drinking my Coke? Where are you from?' Bob explained that he was a Typhoon pilot and had had to make a forced landing after rocketing an SS headquarters and Jean also told his story. Eisenhower beamed and wanted to know more about the targets the Typhoons had been attacking. Eventually, he patted them both on the shoulder and told them that they were doing a fine job and to go ahead and enjoy his Coke! Several of the other Americans had been grinning at them and obviously treating the whole thing as a joke but there was an American Major, at the far end of the group, who appeared to be less than enthusiastic. He looked daggers at them and Bob reckoned that he was the one who should have posted an armed guard on Eisenhower's machine.

As they walked away, the Squadron Leader came running up and asked what they had been talking to General Eisenhower about. 'I'm afraid it's confidential', Bob replied, trying not to laugh. 'He gave us a drink, of course, and suggested we now go and eat. By the way, where is the mess tent?' The Squadron Leader looked nonplussed and simply pointed a finger across the field and took off without saying a word. The mess tent was quiet when they walked in because most people had had lunch. Surprisingly, bacon and egg was dished up but there was no bread, only hard biscuit. Bob was convinced that the strip was used mainly by Transport Command to fly in supplies and collect the wounded. 'I don't suppose they get many ops types like ourselves dropping in here', he said to Jean, 'because that bloody Squadron Leader wouldn't last five minutes on our strip. He's got the wrong attitude. Think's he's a tin god he does. I felt like telling him to get stuffed!'

Jean Maquis was a quiet and rather reserved Frenchman whose home was in Paris. A year or two older than Stanford he had escaped when France fell and joined the Free French Air Force in England. He was a member of a French Spitfire Squadron and had been on a sweep over the beach-head when his engine developed a glycol leak forcing him to switch off and make a forced landing. He spotted Stanford's Typhoon and decided to follow him down.

Bob told him that they had a French pilot on 245 Squadron by the name of Michael de Kerdril or DK, as he was called. DK, he said, had won a Croix de Guerre as a soldier when the French Army was fighting a rearguard action during the German advance. The story went round that de Kerdril had rescued his Captain under heavy shell fire but nobody really knew the exact circumstances because DK wouldn't say much about it. DK had escaped like Maquis but had joined the RAF and trained as a pilot in England and America. He told Jean that DK, underneath that reserve of his, was quite the reverse when he was on ops. 'Most of us', Bob said, 'are quite content to blow a railway engine off the track but DK wants to put his rockets down the funnel'.

It was a hot afternoon and after their meal Stanford and Maquis lay down on the grass beside the wire mesh strip using their parachutes as pillows. Too excited and wound up to doze they chatted to one another. Bob insisted that Jean should come home with him for a bath and a kip when they got back. 'We can nip up to London and you can phone your squadron from home, Jean', he said, 'and I'll do the same.'

The Dakotas finally arrived at about 18.30 hours but there was still no sign of the wounded. They sat in a Dakota, crewed by Australians, talking to four WAAF nurses while they waited for patients. The fuselage was fitted out with stretcher bunks from floor to ceiling, illustrating the flexibility of these rugged, well-proven twin-engine transports. The C-47 Dakotas, or 'Daks' as they were called were mass produced in their thousands and had become a workhorse of the air, comfortable to fly and free from any particular vices. Although somewhat ponderous and slow, from a pilot's point of view, they were capable of taking a great deal of punishment and carrying on flying.

Bob had a word with the pilot, Flying Officer James, and suggested that he might consider making a right hand turn after take-off instead of the customary left because of German flak positions in the area. The look on the Australian's face left him in no doubt that he should mind his own business so he shut up. It was just after 22.00 hours before the Dak got clearance for take-off, still without any wounded on board.

Bob had been making great headway with a WAAF called Joan as they took-off and did a climbing turn to the left. Everything went well and the pilot was just straightening out when heavy flak burst around the aircraft. The crump, crump of the flak was followed by metallic rattling noises as fragments of shrapnel struck the fuselage. One shell must have burst directly under the aircraft, which was lifted bodily by the explosion, and the pilot began to take evasive action.

Bob Stanford was scared but he dared not show it. He experienced a claustrophobic feeling being bottled up inside the Dak, knowing that they had been clobbered, and having to sit there as a passenger. The girls looked anxiously at them as Jean Maquis put on a French face of resignation and gestured with his hands. The aircraft returned to normal flight after weaving about to escape the flak and things were beginning to settle down when the navigator appeared and told them that the hydraulics had been shot up but not to worry.

They crossed the coast and a little while later were informed that the pilot was going to make a precautionary landing at an airfield called Blakehill Farm, in the direction of Swindon. Both Stanford and Maquis had had a fairly hectic time and were too tired to start worrying about it. They assured the girls that the precautionary landing would be just 'a piece of cake' after being shot up by flak. 'Routine stuff', Bob said, 'just to make sure that the old wheels are locked down. Nothing to it!'.

After the excitement the chatter died down and, making themselves as comfortable as possible, they began to doze off. It was getting late when the Dak began circling the airfield in the half-light and the navigator appeared again to prepare them for the landing and told them to hang on. Bob held his WAAF's hand tightly as the pilot gently lowered the Dak onto the grass and with a few squeaks and groans the aircraft came to a standstill. Tension had evaporated and they came out as if nothing had happened.

The two pilots wanted to get up to London as quickly as possible and were given a lift into Swindon to catch an early morning train which arrived at Paddington Station as commuters were making their way to work. They must have looked rather odd walking along the platform carrying parachutes and helmets, wearing flying boots and covered in Normandy dust, but nobody paid much attention. Some gave a sidelong glance and turned their heads the other way pretending not to notice, others overtaking looked over their shoulders for a second or two and hurried on. Stanford, who had been bubbling over with jollity now that he was back in civilization, turned to Jean, 'If that couple of Red Caps over there say anything about the way we look, we'll give them the old 'V' sign. I hate the bastards!'.

The idea of going by tube to Waterloo didn't appeal to them but there was a long queue for taxis and they stood there wondering what to do. However, the policeman in charge beckoned them over and bundled them into the first taxi and off they went. The driver never stopped asking them questions about how things were going for us over in Normandy and Bob told him that nobody on his squadron had any doubts about the outcome so there was no problem! Neither did they have a problem when it came to paying the fare because the cab driver said it was on the house.

Bob lived in south-west London on the outskirts of Raynes Park in a road called Parkway which overlooked Cannon Hill Common, appropriately named because it housed a large anti-aircraft gun site covering twenty acres and whenever the guns went off the house jumped up and down as if built on springs. Number 66 Parkway had sustained bomb damage on several occasions, like many others in the surrounding area, and there was more of an open view across the slopes from the back because an odd house here and there in the adjoining road had been completely demolished during the blitz.

Jean Maquis had been concerned about them dropping in out of the blue in such a filthy state but Stanford explained that he had four sisters and there was usually a flying type or a brown job hanging about the place so he could forget it. When they arrived there was nobody there except his mother who suggested, in her own inimitable way, that they should pop upstairs and have a bath before doing anything else.

Their squadrons gave them 24 hours before having to report back so Bob reckoned that the form was to press on down to the local for a lunch-time session after they got cleaned up. They could have a quiet 'zizz' in the afternoon, he said, and then he would organize some female talent for the evening. When it came to the point, they were both flaked out after lunch and didn't surface until late in the evening so there was only time for a beer or two before going back to bed.

Sitting in the train on the way back to the Squadron, Stanford wondered how the boys were getting on. They must be flying off the strip in Normandy, he thought, and wouldn't be back at base at Holmsley South until evening unless the weather clamped. His girlfriend Sylvia in flying control at Holmsley would probably be able to give him the gen so it might be a good idea to go over and see her. Come to think of it, he would ask her for a date. They would cycle over to the Cat and Fiddle for a few beers and he might as well make the most of a touch of female company before the Squadron was permanently based in Normandy, which could happen at any moment.

He had enjoyed his few hours off in London because it was always exciting to go back there. There was nowhere in the world like it for him, not even when he had regular operational leave and friends used to say, 'Not on leave again Bob, surely!' Even his own family didn't really understand why he got ten days off every six weeks when there was a war on! Typhoon operations were getting a lot of publicity and his mother enjoyed telling people that her son flew a Typhoon but she blamed the RAF for not making him an officer. Sometimes, she would ask him in a roundabout way why he was only a Flight Sergeant and this used to irritate him. It touched a raw nerve and he reacted strongly, telling her that flying a Typhoon on ops was all that mattered to him. He liked being a Flight Sergeant and there was no rank discrimination on the Squadron. Reminding her that he was now a bloody sight more experienced pilot than many officers on the Squadron and, moreover, he was still alive didn't seem to satisfy her because she broached the subject on several occasions.

The truth was that Bob would have jumped at a commission. Dud Nott had got his a month or two previously and Bob envied him but Dud had been on the Squadron for at least six months longer than he had and Bob was sure that he would get his eventually if he survived. He hadn't been honest with his mother because he wasn't going to admit that a commission meant anything to him. After all, he had got his wings and joined a fighter squadron which wasn't a bad effort by any standard. The fact that he had made the grade as an operational pilot was also in his favour and he considered himself to be one of the 'elite' which transcended everything else. But he wasn't a Pilot Officer and this niggled him a little especially when he was taken out to clubs and restaurants.

He remembered the panic when Dud Nott went up for his commission. Dud had just taxied in to dispersal after a dive-bombing op and Wing Commander 'Tim' Morice, the airfield commander, came running up to him and said that he was frightfully sorry but he had forgotten to tell him that he was due to see the Air Officer Commanding, Air-Vice-Marshal Harry Broadhurst, that day and he was due at Redhill in an hour and a half. Dud pointed out that he couldn't possibly go in such a filthy condition and there was no time to clean up and put on best blues. Tim thought for a moment and told him to take his car and driver right away, 'I'll walk back', he said, 'and don't forget to tell Harry that you've just come off an op. He'll appreciate that, old boy!'

Paddy Gray once told Bob Stanford that he had gone up for a commission but didn't get it. At that time he had only been with Number 1 Squadron, which was then stationed at Lympne near Hythe, for a matter of a few weeks and the recommendation came right out of the blue. The evening before his interview he had dinner with his father, 'Monsewer' Eddie Gray, and the rest of the Crazy Gang. The Gang used the Hungaria restaurant, which was very famous, and had a regular table there. It was a hilarious party with Flanagan and Allen, Nervo and Knox and Nauton and Gold with Will Hay and a girlfriend at an adjourning table. During the frivolity Paddy had noticed an Air-Vice-Marshal sitting quietly in a corner but thought nothing of it. The next morning when he marched in and saluted he found himself facing the same officer. He was turned down for lack of experience but Paddy always thought that it must have had something to do with that riotous night out at the Hungaria.

Chapter 5

Carpiquet Abbey, Rommel, and barges on the Seine

Returning to the Squadron after a break, however short, always gave Bob Stanford an uneasy feeling. As he grabbed his parachute from the floor of the three tonner which had been sent to pick him up from Hinton Admiral station he couldn't help wondering whether he would be 'down' for the morning show. He supposed that some of the other chaps must have felt a bit anxious about returning to ops when they came off leave but nobody ever mentioned it.

The first thing they would want to know would be how he had got on when he crash landed in Normandy. He wasn't going to tell them that he had been shit scared only that he had got the bloody thing down in a field and then had a piss-up with a Company Sergeant Major with bullets flying over their heads. He thought that the bit about meeting Eisenhower and drinking his coke would make their day. They would also like to hear about the Aussie Dakota pilot doing a rate one turn over German flak positions and wondering why he got the arse knocked out of him. It cheered him up thinking about it and made him feel glad to be back.

Stanford's story went down well. Ches West's mouth dropped open, 'You mean to tell me you actually drank Ike's coke', he said nearly swallowing his gum, 'Stanford, you're full of bullshit, you are, you line shooting bastard!' They weren't terribly interested in Bob's belly landing because Paddy Gray, Bill Smith, Ace Miron, George Wharry and one or two others had either crashed or forced landed in Normandy before and it was hardly original. Bob's stock, however, went up in the telling and it was all a 'good show' as far as they were concerned.

The thing was to adopt a nonchalant air about such matters and never to get excited about anything, which was difficult for a man like Stanford who was more sensitive and highly tuned than most of the others. Bob liked to explode and found it hard to dampen down his enthusiasms and fears. Everybody had their own particular fears which were personal and not for publication. Being burnt alive or disfigured and maimed for life, trapped in a cockpit with no chance of baling out, moments before the final explosion and getting shot up were only some of the horrors which flashed across pilot's minds from time to time. Things which they dreaded but pushed aside.

There was no future in worrying or getting stewed up as one or two chaps had done and found themselves posted off the Squadron with a label round their necks, 'lacking in moral fibre'. LMF it was called, and the RAF regarded such cases as cancerous growths in the body of the Squadron which had to be cut out immediately they were diagnosed. Nobody said much about such chaps who disappeared off the scene because they had 'a touch of the nadgers'. It could happen to them and, anyway, most people felt bloody sorry for them.

The RAF weren't being particularly ruthless and cold blooded about such cases. Any pilot with shattered nerves was dangerous. One pilot literally went berserk in close flak and darted about all over the place endangering others and finishing up by flying a couple of hundred feet above or below the Squadron. Another started to chop the tail off the man in front when taxiing out which he did on three occasions, pleading brake failure, before he was twigged.

Any bloke who had genuinely 'gone round the twist' or become 'flak happy' left without bad feeling or recrimination. It was quite the reverse, in fact. When the Squadron did a rocket firing course at Eastchurch on the Isle of Sheppey there was an LMF camp adjacent to the airfield. It was full of ex-NCO aircrews who had been stripped of their rank and flying badges. They were a pitiful looking crowd easily identified by the faded spaces on their uniforms where their stripes and brevets had been.

245, being off ops during the rocket course, took the opportunity of having as many Squadron piss ups as possible in the town and made their presence felt in their usual cocky and arrogant way. Seeing those poor bastards sitting around in corners of the bar was an excuse for quietly moving a few jars of beer in their direction with a very positive 'cheers' and 'down the hatch, mate'.

Benny Bennet couldn't help staring at them, usually with a fixed expression on his face as if he couldn't really believe what had happened and one evening he came out with a profound statement, 'It's

OK for the officers', he said, 'They don't lose their rank. Nothing like that. They get found desk jobs, don't they. Not like those poor bastards over there. They have to clean out the shit houses'. Benny was right but he needn't have worried, the Canadians eventually commissioned all their aircrews, including Benny!

After several months of being on ops Stanford had few illusions about himself. The truth was that he had been very scared indeed on a number of occasions—seconds of terror when he shouted into his oxygen mask ordering himself to steady down and talking all the time until his heartbeats stopped thumping. If his Sabre engine coughed it sent a spasm of fear through his body making him stare at the fuel, temperature and pressure gauges. Hearing and feeling heavy flak bursts, which were obviously close, or seeing tracer coming straight at him increased his blood pressure, forcing him to keep himself under control. On those occasions he recognized that his working parts were doing maximum overtime and sometimes wondered how much longer they could keep going at that rate.

These were only odd moments which he disregarded when he got back to base feeling relieved and on top of the world because he had chalked up another op. He had never been depressed about it and convinced himself that it was perfectly natural for anybody to get worked up on Typhoon ops.

*   *   *

Warrant Officer Paddy Gray wandered over to Flights to find out what was cooking and whether he was down for the next show. Stanford had already taken off on the first op which had been delayed because of the weather but now it looked as if it was going to be a fine day. Paddy's Flight commander told him that he wouldn't be on call for at least another two hours so he drifted back to the tent not being keen to sit around chatting. He had long since become accustomed to waiting, which he found a boring business. Most of the others whiled away the time in idle conversation, playing cards or generally fooling about but he preferred his own company. This morning, he decided to wash out some socks in his canvas bowl, write home and perhaps take a stroll. At least, he thought, he would be doing something positive and not wasting his time.

The guns were thundering away in the direction of Caen as he walked down through the cornfield towards the perimeter of the strip. The never-ending line of tanks and vehicles was still grinding its way towards the front and the thought struck him that the brown jobs would soon run out of parking space up there because the battle line hadn't moved much for some time. There were some tanks standing in the woods which he hadn't seen before and he went over to take a look. The crews were sitting around outside their vehicles and he asked an Army Captain why they had stopped there and what was going on. The Captain quietly informed him that his tanks were staying right here because they were the rearguard if the Germans broke through the line. It suddenly struck Paddy that if this should occur then these tanks were really the last line of defence and he wondered what would happen to the strip. But when he asked, the Captain simply threw his hands in the air!

When he got back to the tent he found Bob Stanford, Ches West and Benny Bennet, who had landed back after their op, gathered round the log table drinking mugs of tea. He told them what the Army Captain had said and this was regarded as a huge joke. They were still laughing about brown jobs when Paddy was summoned to Flights. He was the last one into the jeep as the CO, Jack Collins drove over to Intelligence. The Intelligence officer said that he had a rather special brief for them concerning the abbey at Carpiquet. The Germans had dug in a number of mortar positions along the moat and outside walls and these were giving a lot of trouble to our forward troops who were only about a hundred yards or more away. The job for the Typhoons was to rocket the mortar positions without hitting our chaps or damaging the abbey which was an ancient monument.

The abbey was in the village of Carpiquet, adjacent to a large airfield which had been the scene of fierce fighting since shortly after D-Day. This airfield was situated on the western outskirts of Caen and would have been a rich prize if the British had been able to capture the city within 48 hours—as per schedule—and penetrate further south. Such an advance would have enabled them to use its runways for bombers and transport aircraft. Temporary make-shift strips, like Le Fresne, could only accommodate fighters and, as yet, there was not one substantial air base in Normandy.

The pilots could see from the maps and photographs that this was going to be a very difficult show and there were a few wisecracks about the importance of not damaging the abbey. Then they were told that the operation was going to be a 245 show and no other Squadron would be involved, which put them on their mettle. Talking amongst themselves they regarded the brief as being something of a challenge to the accuracy of their rocket firing and the efficiency of their Squadron.

Warrant Officer Paddy Gray pointed out, 'Well, it's obvious isn't it,' he said, 'they've given us the job because they know we're the only Squadron capable of doing it'. This remark went down well but one wag who had been measuring distances on the map made the comment that the abbey was only about five miles away in a direct line, 'So why bother to get airborne', he said, 'we can poop off from here'.

The laughter subsided when the CO said, 'All right chaps, let's get down to business shall we?'. He explained that the plan was to make four separate rocket attacks, firing rockets in pairs. Aircraft would be approaching the target from over our own lines which was an advantage, he said, and he would position the Squadron to enable pilots to press home their attacks and get in 'real close'. The moat and the walls provided guidelines and he reminded pilots that our own chaps were dug in on the outside of the moat only a short distance away so there was no room for any undershooting. And if they did overshoot then rockets would hit the abbey. Finally he reminded everybody to keep a good look out to avoid mid air collisions.

Pilots were confident and enthusiastic about the op as they drove over to dispersals. The idea of shooting up German mortar positions appealed to them because they had been under mortar fire on the strip themselves and found the experience most unpleasant. Now they had an opportunity of getting their own back on those bastards and were going to make the most of it. Before getting into his Typhoon 'O' (Oscar) Paddy Gray told his ground crew to watch out for the Squadron. 'You'll be able to see us attacking from here', he said, 'Carpiquet's just up the road'.

Weather conditions were perfect with a very high cloud base as they climbed over the beach-head gathering formation. The CO kept well away from the coast giving his pilots time to prepare for the attack and also to keep the Germans guessing as to his intent. Then came the order, 'Line astern. Go!' and they re-crossed the coast and began circling the target area. The Germans responded with a variety of light and medium flak as the CO made a wide sweep over the Allied lines. There was no problem in picking out the abbey alongside the large expanse of Carpiquet airfield which appeared to be the centre of a firework display. The CO's voice came over the RT, 'Archduke leader. Going down in six seconds, five, four, three, two, one—now!' and one after another they winged-over into the dive and fanned out in échelon.

The abbey loomed larger in the dive and along the hollow of the moat German mortar positions were clearly identified, exposed in naked fashion from above. Tracer curled its way upwards and white puffs of flak peppered the air below as they fired short bursts of 20-mm cannon shells, feeling their Typhoons shudder and shake with the recoil. In the closing seconds all eyes were glued on the red dots of their ring and bead sights lined up on targets and automatically they fought to keep their aircraft steady before letting go the first pair of rockets. Fragmentary pictures of gun crews firing, tracer spitting from the moat, the abbey walls and the edifice itself flashed through their minds as they pulled out of dives and broke away into steep climbing turns feeling the clamp of 'G' on their bodies. Aircraft banked and heads turned back to see clouds of earth and dust blown high by exploding rockets.

All eyes were on the target as they swept round in a tightish turn, looking out for each other, as they positioned themselves to make the second run in. This time the Squadron was spread out as each man picked his target and came in for a second attack. The Germans firing frantically faced another hail of cannon fire and sixteen more rocket projectiles as the eight Typhoons, strung out in line, dived on to them.

After the fourth and last attack they joined Squadron formation and within five minutes had landed back on the strip, having been airborne for less than half an hour.

At debriefing Squadron pilots reported that they were confident the target had been well and truly pranged and Jack Collins, the CO, was well pleased with his team. There had been little chatter over the RT except for the odd, 'Watch out Red Three—on your right', 'Roger, I see him', and of course their instructions from Archduke leader. The show had been a professional job of work and apart from a few Typhoons receiving superficial flak damage there had been no casualties. Later, the brown jobs reported that the op had been highly successful and only a couple of rockets had hit the abbey.

During the early evening when they were gathered round the log table drinking the inevitable compo tea, Squadron Leader Robin McNair turned up to see Jack Collins. They had been personal friends since Robin joined 245 as Flight commander of A Flight back in the old days when the Squadron had been based at Lydd and West Hampnett. Robin now commanded 247 rocket Typhoon Squadron based in Normandy and the two men had a lot to talk about. The 'old hands' knew Robin and gave him a wave but the others kept watching him talking intently to Jack and obviously didn't like the idea of a strange Squadron Leader suddenly arriving in their backyard. They acted like a bunch of old women asking questions, 'Who is that chap?' 'What's he doing here?' 'Is he going to take over from Jack?' 'Aw hell, Jack's not going is he?'.

Stanford loftily announced to those around him that Robin McNair used to have his ground crew always polishing his aircraft with a special kind of mixture which was supposed to put at least another 15 mph on the machine. 'He always flew "MR-G",' he said, 'and took it away with him when he left the Squadron'. Nobody paid much attention to Stanford's remarks thinking that he was only trying to prove how long he had been around. Ches West ambled across, 'You're full of bullshit, you are Stanford. If you know this McNair guy so well why don't you get your arse off the ground and ask him what the hell goes on?'. Stanford said nothing but got to his feet and walked over to McNair, who was still talking to Jack, and tapped him on the shoulder, 'Hallo Sir,' they heard him say, 'nice to see you again'.

*　　　　*　　　　*

One morning word had filtered through that 193 Squadron had clobbered Rommel in his staff car out on the open road. The general reaction was that 193 were a shower of jammy bastards and had all the luck! Time and again 245 had scoured the roads looking for anything to shoot up but had never found a Field Marshal! That Rommel should have chanced his luck and taken to the road in daylight surprised them. They had a sneaking admiration for him because he was obviously a good General and he didn't appear to be a Nazi. He was reported to be a good chap as far as prisoners were concerned and played a relatively straight bat. Not that any 245 pilot would have had second thoughts about giving him a squirt and blasting him off the road, because that was all part of their game, but it was a pity that 193 should have had the privilege and not them.

Apparently, Rommel had driven via Falaise to visit the 276th and 277th Infantry Divisions and found that the 2nd SS Panzer Corps was too far in the rear and not providing sufficient back-up for the infantry. The Squadron had recently attacked a château in that area which was believed to be the temporary headquarters of the Panzer Corps concerned. Rommel, at this time, was trying to regroup his Panzer divisions and hold them in mobile reserve. When he visited the command post of the 1st SS he was told of an enemy attack in the Saint-Lo area and he decided to get back to his headquarters, some forty or fifty miles north-west of Paris, as quickly as possible.

His driver was used to taking side roads and using cover whenever enemy aircraft were about but on this occasion was forced to join the main road approaching Vimoutiers. On that afternoon there was a cloudless sky and two low-flying Typhoons of 193 Squadron spotted his car and immediately attacked. They pumped 20-mm shells into the vehicle as it gathered speed in a frantic effort to escape and Rommel was thrown out and lay unconscious on the roadside. The driver was mortally wounded and other occupants badly injured. The Field Marshal received a fracture at the base of his skull and three other fractures of the skull as well as shrapnel splinters in his face. He had been knocked out of the battle and would never be the same man again.

While pilots of 245 Squadron, gathered around the log table, were feeling pleased that Typhoons had got Rommel, Flying Officer Roly Temple pointed out that 609 had very nearly nailed the Field Marshal on another occasion. It had happened a month or two before D-Day when they attacked his headquarters at La Roche-Guyon. Roly said that the front of the château had been practically demolished and Rommel himself had left only about five minutes previously. Ches West drawled, 'Aw shit. They sure had it in for that guy.'

Later that day Flight Lieutenant Bob Monk provided some amusement. Bob was a member of the 'toffee-nosed' bridge playing school and he and a few cronies were 'stood down' and managed to borrow a jeep for a local recce. During their run around they came across a crashed Dakota and climbed inside the wreckage to look it over. It must have pranged recently because everything inside was relatively intact. Normally, the locusts would have descended and stripped it of anything worthwhile but Monk discovered a flak suit which an American crew member must have left behind. Flak was a subject uppermost in most Typhoon pilots' minds and Monk, thinking it might come in handy, brought it back to the strip giving rise to a lot of ribald comment about the Yanks being afraid of flak and having to wear armour.

Nobody thought that Monk would actually go ahead and wear the damn thing but he got dressed up in it for the next show. He waddled towards his aircraft like an armour-plated duck and his ground crew heaved him up and levered him into his cockpit amidst general laughter. His tall, slim and gangly frame made him look all the funnier especially as he had a very serious expression on his face and this experiment was no joke as far as he was concerned. Some were beginning to think that Monk might have something but Dud Nott reckoned it was a load of bullshit, 'It's purely psychological', he said, 'we've got armour-plated sides to our cockpits and under our seats, so that we don't get our balls blown off, and I can't see that getting wrapped up in that thing will do any good'.

All eyes were on Bob Monk as the Squadron taxied in but Monk's Typhoon remained stationary after landing so something was wrong. It didn't take long to find out that the poor bastard had collected a flak packet and was in great pain. Shrapnel had penetrated his joints, parts his flak suit couldn't cover. But he managed to bring his aircraft back safely and the flak suit might possibly have saved his life. Shortly afterwards it disappeared and so did Bob Monk with Blighty wounds.

Monk's departure for home raised the question of leave. Nobody around the log table seriously expected to get any in the foreseeable future but it was nice to talk about it. Sago told the new chaps that before the D-Day thing started they used to get ten days leave every six weeks. 'And, what's more,' said Terry Gray, 'being on ops we collected an extra thirty bob whenever we went on leave. Up to the rank of Flying Officer, that was. The extra money was supposed to have come from Lord Nuffield, bless him! We also got three eggs a week, oranges, vitamin pills and chocolate, apart from the booze ration which you could get from the mess.'

Nobody knew more than Terry about one's rights as far as privileges and perks were concerned. He was always quick off the mark to make certain that he got more than his fair share of anything going. There had been talk about him running two pay books when the Squadron was at West Hampnett and when challenged he was quite open about it. He hadn't actually run two pay books, he said, that would have been impossible. What he had done was to collect an advance from the Flight hut before going on leave which was common practice. Then he would come back off leave for regular pay day and collect his week's money from Station headquarters and buzz off again. A simple formula which he had worked out himself knowing that the powers that be would eventually catch up with him. He wasn't particularly worried, he said, because all he wanted to do was to make life as comfortable as possible before the Invasion.

Terry Gray was nobody's fool and knew perfectly well that experienced Typhoon pilots were at a premium and it was unlikely that the establishment would court martial him. Even if they had, he wouldn't have shed any tears because flying a Typhoon was a bloody dangerous occupation. The fact that the RAF had taken a gamble that he would live long enough to pay off the balance owed, he said with a grin, was their affair.

Bob Stanford's day was brightened up when he was told that his new machine had arrived. He had been flying 'R' (Robert) and 'T' (Tommy) on the last four ops and he was looking forward to having his own aircraft again. It wasn't only for psychological reasons that he was happier being in 'U' (Uncle) but he would be able to air test and trim the machine to his liking and make it his personal property. The letters 'MR-U' painted on the fuselage were symbolic, as far as he was concerned, and it always pleased him to see his machine in the Squadron line up. Childish, perhaps, but he wasn't alone in that respect.

The trouble with testing a new machine from the strip was that the air space was clogged up and there really wasn't room to put the aircraft through its paces. One simply had to fly out over the Channel and get right away from air corridors and keep a close eye open for Spitfires who always maintained a top cover over the beach-head. Apart from that, the Navy became very trigger-happy when aircraft attempted to perform aerobatics or dived suddenly out of cloud.

One of the advantages of flying a Typhoon, however, was that one was able to cover a lot of ground very quickly and Stanford flew north and east to get out of the traffic before he started to play around with his new toy. He liked the feel of the controls when looping and rolling from 8,000 feet and she handled well in steep turns and dives. All the instruments inside the office were behaving themselves as he opened her up and dived down towards the clouds.

A patchy layer of summer cloud in bulbous shapes, like round buns with rolly tops, sailed across the sky in majestic style and provided him with a playground at 3,000 feet. Chasing the contours and skimming across undulating vapour he shot skywards in a full power zoom climb back up to 8,000 feet. Then he firmly pulled the stick back and roared into a loop watching the clouds through the roof of his perspex hood as the earth tumbled upside down. Glued into his seat by pressure he throttled back into a dive and picked a cloud to aim at, feeling the controls heavying up as he rocketed down and shot through the frothy white vapour like a bullet.

There could be nothing more exhilarating in flying, Stanford thought, than chasing clouds in a fast single seater; feeling the power and sensing the speed of the aircraft as one roared through a world of fantasy, billowing cloud in watery colours; watching the silhouette of the aircraft ringed by the sun chasing across an eiderdown of foamy shapes and glancing upwards to see great fermentations of moisture like mountains in the sky; twisting and turning through a jungle of clouds stretching out like a sea of icebergs and going hell bent for the peaks. Climbing until the aircraft falls away into a stall and then sliding down a mountain side of froth with mist tearing past like gossamer on the wings; leaving behind no trace of imprint after those ecstatic moments in the virgin sky.

Flying back to the strip Stanford was confident that he had a good machine and he called up 'Flashbang Control' for permission to land. He came straight in over the barrage balloons throttling back to lose height, and putting his undercarriage down. Automatically, he adjusted his mixture to rich and pitch to fine, giving his engine a good burst to clear it before landing. Then in a curved approach he put his flaps down and straightened up as he crossed the airfield boundaries. The controls were sweet and sensitive to the point of touch down, at about 75 mph, when the wide tracked undercarriage took over and he rumbled down the wire mesh strip.

This machine was Stanford's fourth 'U' (Uncle). His first one disappeared on 7 June, the day after D-Day, in rather strange circumstances. The Squadron was due to carry out an armed recce over the Normandy battle area and Stanford was down to fly as 'spare man'. This entailed taking off with the Squadron and keeping station at the rear of the formation until the Squadron was well over the Channel. If nobody had to drop out then the 'spare man' was told to return to base having played the role of an extra man in reserve.

By a quirk of fate, a new ground crew had put Stanford's gear in 'V' (Victor), Flight Sergeant 'Tubby' Noakes, aircraft, and there was no time to change over so Tubby took 'U' (Uncle). Stanford returned, as spare man in 'V' (Victor) and was told later that Tubby had gone down in his aircraft. The boys reckoned that Tubby must have had a fuel blockage because his fan suddenly stopped and he crashed in enemy territory south of the Cherbourg Peninsula. Irrationally, Stanford had felt a guilt complex over poor old Tubby knowing that it really should have been him on that op in 'U' (Uncle). But Tubby hadn't been the only casualty because Flying Officers Ken Dickie and Greeners Greenhalgh had also gone down. Only the day before, D-Day, Flying Officer Scottie Gordon had just managed to get back with serious head wounds while Flight Lieutenants Bill Smith and Bill Reynolds were being picked up out of the Channel.

*   *   *   .

After mid-July a series of depressions grounded the Typhoons for a day or two. Heavy rain and gales lashed the strip turning everything into a quagmire. The weather was so bad that the American 'Mulberry' harbour had been wrecked and many boats damaged and driven ashore. Drainage ditches had to be dug around the tents and everything inside was wet and uncomfortable. Playing cards and rolling the bones eventually became a boring exercise and there was little else to do other than 'brew up', smoke and chat. Despite Terry Gray's talent for procuring things there wasn't enough booze to have a really good piss-up and nobody was enthusiastic about doing a local recce for liquid supplies in that weather.

Somebody thought it would be a good idea for the Intelligence officer to give the pilots a talk on the current military situation so they were all summoned to the Intelligence tent in the pouring rain. A military lecture on a wet afternoon wasn't exactly what they had in mind and they weren't particularly concerned how the brown jobs ran their war only that 'they took their fingers out' and got on with it.

They listened in reasonable silence and stared at the maps while the Intelligence officer pointed to the build-up of German forces and the disposition of our troops. It was obvious that the British were holding the bulk of the German armour. There were no less than seven Panzer and two SS divisions identified on the map around the Caen area while the First US Army had only a single German armoured division opposing its southern flank. This gave rise to some ribald comment about the British having to take the stick, as usual, and carry the can! The Intelligence officer couldn't avoid overhearing a few comments about 'bloody Yanks' and he went on to explain that this was all part of Monty's strategy of drawing as much German armour as possible towards the British Second Army around Caen leaving the Americans the job of breaking out south and east of the Cherbourg Peninsula. Most pilots only became interested in the situation on the ground when it directly concerned their day-to-day operations. They lived in a world of their own doing what they were told and making the best out of life. They were 'chuffed' that Monty, a British General, had been made boss of the entire show and it was up to him to make the bloody thing work.

A short break in the weather gave Terry Gray and his friend Tubby Sago a chance to do a recce for essential supplies. Terry had recently procured a most interesting motor cycle which was an Italian machine called a Guzzi. It was a huge thing with two lots of handlebars and could seat three quite comfortably. This acquisition was by courtesy of a chum who happened to be a Regimental Sergeant Major in the 7th Armoured Brigade Workshops. Terry was always a great one for making useful contacts! They went off together on a BMW motor bike and sidecar and found the Guzzi in a derelict barn. A bullet had gone through one side of the petrol tank and knocked the top of the centre part of the frame on its way out.

The RSM had got one of his blokes to start welding it without having drained any petrol or oil so Terry had decided that the best place for him was round the other side of a three tonner until the job was finished.

Terry's excursions often took him close to the front line where there were more opportunities to acquire useful things but sometimes he was forced to pass through military police check points. This required some nerve and ability to bluff one's way through. Apart from his khaki battledress, wings and flying boots Terry wore an officer's peaked cap which he said he had inherited from Squadron Leader Hordern who had commanded 245 before Jack Collins took over. Plastic goggles from his gas mask kit completed the headgear but he displayed no sign of rank. Tubby Sago inevitably sitting on the Guzzi behind him wore a warrant officer's badge so it was reasonable for a military policeman to assume that Terry might be a Squadron or Flight commander. That wasn't enough for Terry who, in his clipped and precise speech, would say 'Air Commodore Gray' to anybody who signalled them to halt. Normally the MP would salute and wave them through but on one occasion they weren't so lucky.

They had been drinking Calvados with red wine chasers in Crepon when they were asked for identity cards. Both were fairly hammered at the time, particularly as Calvados is a strong and fiery liquid even without being topped up with vino! Terry could tell by the look on the Sergeant MP's face that prompt evasive action was required so he opened up the throttle and skidded round, but army vehicles blocked all immediate escape routes so the pavement was his only way out. People leapt for their lives as he and Tubby rocketed up and down curbstones before finally disappearing up a side street to find themselves on a tiny country road leading to Bazenville.

This had been a close shave and Terry crossed Crepon off his list for the time being. During the break in the bad weather he decided to nip over to the American sector—which proved to be a fruitful exercise. He met a bunch of Yanks 'brewing up' in a ruined house south of Carentan. They were on their way up front and told him that their own Air Force had bombed their own forward troops only a day or two previously. That and the weather, they told him, had 'sure as hell made them drag their arses for a while'. What they had to say about the bombing was unprintable but words to the effect that whenever US bombers showed up everybody ducked.

Terry thought it might be a smart idea not to mention that he was engaged in providing air support close to forward troops so he said that he was a Spitfire pilot which got him off to a splendid start. When one of them said that he would give anything for a bottle of Scotch right now, Terry knew he could do a deal. He would provide the whisky in return for one of their jeeps, he said, shooting a line about his Squadron pilots desperately needing some form of transport and a jeep would be just the job. Having carefully hidden his Guzzi motor cycle Terry arrived back at the strip in the American jeep, creating quite a stir. Everybody wanted to know how the hell he had managed to get it but all he would say, with a grin, was that he had procured it with the aid of some of his American friends. He told his friend Tubby Sago later, 'they can ask all the questions they like but I'm not going to bloody well tell them'.

Soon after Terry came back the weather closed in again which was a little depressing because pilots wanted to get going and not be kept sitting around. Since D-Day the Squadron had lost about one third of its pilots. Scottie Gordon and George Dakin's wounds had ended their flying careers but Monk would be back. Tubby Noakes, Cartwright, Ken Dickie, Les Greenhaulgh, Bill Reynolds and Sam Slaney had gone down. Bill Reynold's departure had been a mystery because he disappeared in cloud when the Squadron dived on Villers Bocage and nobody saw any sign of a Typhoon going in. There was a chance that some of them might have been lucky and would turn up eventually but once a pilot had vanished from the scene he was forgotten except, perhaps, when people were talking about the old days with a glass in their hands.

One miracle was big Bill Waudby's return from the dead which was talked about as a bloody miracle. It had happened long before D-Day when the Squadron was based at West Hampnett on the outskirts of Chichester. Bill, a large raw-boned blond and blue-eyed Yorkshireman, saw a Junkers 88 while on a sweep, and he immeddiately attacked it, but the rear gunner got him. He was seen to go down and blow up and was reported to have had it. This was a natural assumption because the chaps had seen the explosion down below when he hit the deck.

Several weeks later he walked into the mess at Holmsley South during breakfast time and gave everybody a shock as if they had seen a ghost or the time machine had gone haywire. The first question he had asked was where was Terry Gray because parts of his kit were missing. It took a few seconds before anybody could speak because they thought Bill just had to be dead. But there he was very much alive and in a rage. Apparently, Bill had been blown out of his aircraft when it dived into the ground and found himself in a hedge amazingly unhurt. He remained hidden for several hours before being contacted by the Underground. He wouldn't say much about his journey through France to the Spanish border except that he had cycled all the way down there with a girlfriend. Bill had had the most fantastic luck and had been very clever to get away with it. Most pilots believed that they would survive because this was the only way they could look at life. Any fears they might have were never discussed openly with anybody but were swept under the carpet and never allowed to surface.

Only Michael de Kerdril, the French pilot, had admitted in private that he wouldn't survive. His confidants didn't want to know and changed the subject. They weren't being rude but they simply couldn't bring themselves to talk about it. DK was a strong character and never displayed any signs of nervousness. His arrogance when attacking targets was well known and he came so close to disaster at times that some pilots got the impression that he was trying to write himself off for some reason or another but in the end his luck did run out.

The bad weather dispersed as suddenly as it had blown up with the sun boring holes through the muck and the wind dying down. Responding to the brightness and warmth the airfield tidied itself up and clicked into gear. The first indication that the brown jobs had got their backsides out of their 'bogged down' positions in the mud came from a call requesting help to knock out some Panzer tanks south of Caen.

It was a great feeling to climb back up into the old cockpit again and have some excitement. Anything to get away from the mud and squelch of the strip and out of the tent atmosphere into the open air. The show was to back up the Second British Army at a point south and slightly east of Caen where a group of German tanks were creating a spot of bother. Flying time would only be about thirty minutes including the attack so it was only a question of whizzing straight over there and back with a short sharp interlude in between. The usual smoke shell would identify the target. The steep climb off the deck and circling round over the beaches while the Squadron gathered formation was exhilarating. Breathing oxygen always enlivened the senses but flying was also an addictive drug for which they craved. From the moment the undercarriage wheels retracted in their casings with soft thuds one broke physical contact with the earth and became free.

The Squadron shot through a thin wad of mist into dazzling light and skirted clouds which looked like ice cream cornets with white frothy tops, glistening in the sun against a blue background. Flying in two finger-four formations the Typhoons gobbled up the few miles to the target for the attack. Below, to the north, the ruins of Caen, propped up by mountains of rubble, looked like an elongated and shattered graveyard whose stones stepped up in échelon to the crest of the hill dominated by an ancient and unscathed fortress. The environs of the stricken city had been churned into a sea of brown mud erupting with a rash of twinkling yellow flashes from the guns.

The customary dark brown puffs of bursting flak smudged the sky around them as the Typhoons circled, waiting and watching for the red smoke shell. These were irritating and anxious moments for pilots keyed up and concentrating hard to keep formation with one eye on the chap in front and with the other searching for the red smoke trail. It always came as a relief when they turned the world upside down in the wing over and could see the red ball of smoke through the roofs of their canopies.

As they hurtled down with hands and feet hard on the controls, the landscape opened out like a fast growing photographic enlargement. The ground seemed to rush up at the windscreen as they eased out of the steep dive searching for the target. They had only seconds to spot the long snouts of 88-mm guns on three tanks hiding amongst some ruins before firing their rockets, leaving two burning and the other smoking. It had been a fair prang!

Landing back at the strip they saw other squadrons moving out of dispersals and it looked like being a busy day with plenty of trade about. The war, thank goodness, had got going again.

After the early show, Squadron Leader Jack Collins told Nott, Jeffries, West and Stanford that they were 'stood down' for the rest of the day which didn't appeal to any of them and they made noises about it. But Jack was firm and in his quiet way reminded them that they had each done two ops yesterday plus the one this morning and he wanted to give some of the less experienced chaps a chance. Jimmy Wilson, their Flight commander, couldn't pull any strings so they had no alternative but to leave Flights and go back to their tents.

It was sunny and warm as they sat round the log table drinking mugs of compo tea and watching the others take off. Nobody said very much as they were all feeling a little 'brassed off' and at a loose end. Suddenly, Dud Nott came up with a great idea. 'Why don't we go swimming', he said 'we can borrow Terry's jeep and nip down to the coast'. Jeff Jeffries, the little Welshman, was all for it and so was Stanford who had visions of leaping into the briny but Ches West, the Canadian, wasn't so keen. 'Aw shit', he drawled, 'you guys must be crazy or something. You'll get your arses blown off, for sure, on those goddam beaches'.

Studying the map, they decided to go via Fontaine Henri and Reviers and then make for Lion-sur-Mer and have a swim. 'Afterwards', Dud said, 'we can stooge around the coast and see what cooks'. Taking off in Terry's jeep they had one hell of a job getting across the road from Creully leading to Caen because it was congested with trucks and armour nose to tail. One man leaning out of the back of a truck asked them where they were going and Stanford yelled, 'We're off on our 'olidays'. 'Gotcha buckets and spades, ave yer?' came the reply with grins and victory signs. When they got near the coast the place was practically deserted and the little seaside town looked battered and war-torn with everything boarded up. The sea was gentle with lines of foam breaking on the shore but there were nasty looking bits of metal poking out of the water and the beach itself.

The party was in high spirits, however, and couldn't care less about the debris. While Ches parked his behind on a concrete block, chewing gum and smoking a cigarette, they stripped off 'starkers' and fooled about as they tiptoed down the beach avoiding the obstacles. Dud kept shouting, 'Achtung Minen', and pointing to sinister objects in the sand which set them all off into fits of laughter. Bob Stanford was the first to dip a toe in, 'Christ', he said, 'it's bloody cold' as he started to wade out slowly, half bent, and staring into the sea searching for the nasties. Ches's Canadian drawl boomed out from the shore, 'Jesus, Bob. I sure can see yore ass winking at me from here, boy'.

Some of the bravado dissipated when they were up to their knees in water waiting and watching to see who would be first to take the plunge. They knew that it was all bloody stupid but nobody was going to chicken out. Jeff Jeffreys took a header just as a brown job came running down the beach frantically waving his arms and shouting at them to get out at once. This gave them the excuse for an honourable retreat so, splashing themselves all over as they waded back, they gingerly and somewhat sheepishly approached the Corporal who had been swearing and cursing at them. 'You stupid bastards', he roared, 'Don't you know these bloody beaches are mined. You could have got yourselves blown up, you could'. The Corporal's manner changed appreciably as they got dressed and he saw their wings. A 'Sir' crept into his conversation now and again and he was good enough to recommend a certain café in St. Aubin which his lads frequented and he told them that there was 'a nice bit of stuff behind the bar'.

They found the cafe on a corner of some old buildings. It was dark inside, especially after coming in out of the sun, and it had a small bar, stone floor and a few old tables and chairs. Half-closed curtains led into another room but there was no sign of anybody. Stanford lit his pipe, studying the dusty old bottles on the shelf containing coloured liquids which meant nothing to him. The others sat down in a bubbly mood feeling fresh and invigorated after the cold salt water.

Dud Nott had everybody convulsed telling them a story about a Canadian called Sheep Milne who had been with 245. 'Sheep's greatest ambition in life', he said, 'was to light a fart'. The laughter subsided when a good looking French girl came in to serve them and they stared at her thinking that the Corporal could have been right and this place might have something after all. She had longish dark hair swept back in a bun, brown eyes, a pale complexion and wide sensuous lips. Ches whistled, 'Geeze', he said, 'I sure would like to give that bird a few flying lessons'. Smiling at them, she held up a glass but they were speechless for a moment trying to think of what to order in French. Dud mumbled 'Calvados' and held up four fingers. Nobody failed to notice her low-cut dress, the saucy look in her eyes and the slight swaying of her hips as she came over with the tray.

After more Calvados they began talking about the old days; the time when they did a recce around the local pubs in Selsey Bill searching for beer which was scarce in those parts and one landlord told them that he had plenty, more than they could drink, he said. As they left the landlord came up to Terry Gray to tell him that the six of them had drunk sixty one pints. Terry looked at the lads and said, 'Who's the bastard who drank the extra one?'.

The stories flowed but the one about poor old Tubby Sago was a gem. Tubby had a bout of sleep walking and one night got out of his camp bed, opened the flap of his kit bag, and had a pee carefully shutting the flap and getting back into bed still fast asleep. Everything, by now, sounded terribly funny and the French girl watching from behind the bar laughed with them although she didn't understand a word. It was when they started to air their French that she really began giggling. Stanford asked her, 'Voulez-vous, madamoiselle, promenez avec moi sur le sea front after dark?'. But it didn't get him anywhere! She began calling them 'er peelottes' and when they mentioned 'manger' and that they were 'faim' and needed a 'repas' she shepherded them through the curtains into a

97

small dining room. Chips and some kind of mince were washed down with rough cider before they staggered out and snored off on a grassy bank beside the jeep.

That evening the airfield commander turned up at the log table. Wing Commander Tim Morice was always welcome, not only because he happened to be the boss who looked after everything on the ground, but he had been a pilot during World War 1 and therefore was one of the fraternity. Everybody stood up when he arrived and then settled down for a chat. It was a friendly, easy-going atmosphere and he said that according to Group, the Wing was doing well. 'I stuffed the signal somewhere in my pockets', and he fumbled around for it. This made them laugh and then Tim told them that he had acknowledged the signal with thanks and had promised Group that 121 Wing would be the first Wing to set foot on German soil. The new chaps, like Spike Hughes, were a little over-awed by Tim's commanding presence and stood somewhat rigidly in the background not knowing quite how to react. Dud Nott whispered to Spike, 'Don't get worried, Spike. He's the boss but the sun shines out of that man. You can always go and see him if you're in trouble'.

During the chit-chat, Squadron Leader Jack Collins told Stanford that he would be flying as his number two on the early show. 'Just the pair of us', he said, 'and we'll be taking a look around the area south of the Cherbourg Peninsula to find out what's going on'. Bob was pleased because he liked covering the CO who was a damned good pilot and always looked after his number two. It was getting late by the time Tim left and the group gradually broke up. Bob wasn't feeling in top form as his stomach seemed to be doing a few rolls and he had a touch of the grumbleguts.

His friend, Paddy Gray, had already lit the stub of candle and was ready with the cards and the cribbage board. After a couple of games he was forced to make a hurried exit to the field latrine thinking that it must have been something he had eaten at the café, perhaps. Finding his way back with the aid of a shaded torch he passed Dud Nott who was on a similar mission but thought nothing of it. A little later he was on his way out again to find Ches, Dud and Jeff sitting on the pole. As he pulled his trousers down and did likewise he heard Dud say, 'For Christ sake, Ches. Don't keep starting each sentence with "aw shit".' They agreed that it had nothing to do with the booze and 'must have been something they ate'. Jeff said it was the mince and so did Ches who was a little more positive and reckoned that the goddam stuff must have been the popsie's little old cat.

They all had several more reunions on the pole that night during which the vulgarity dried up because it started to drizzle. Bob was relieved to find when he woke up that the weather was 'Harry Clampers' and the early show postponed indefinitely. He was still feeling slightly 'off the beam' and the thought of greasy, fatty tinned bacon with hard tack was nauseating so he boiled an egg and ate the last remaining biscuit from the tin his mother had sent him.

The cloud gradually lifted off the deck and after breakfast he was called to Flights. Squadron Leader Jack Collins told him that Maxie Maxwell was about to do an air test and if the weather was OK they would take off in about half an hour. When Maxie landed he reported a cloud base of 400 feet which was acceptable and the trip was on. Bob wasn't exactly thrilled when Terry Gray popped his head into the Flight tent and said, 'Jesus, Bob. You're not going off in all this shit are you? Rather you than me, cock!'.

Bob, like the others, had done a certain amount of cloud flying but not in a concentrated sense and it looked as though he was about to remedy that situation. He wasn't anxious because he knew the CO wouldn't perform any sudden manoeuvres in cloud without thinking of the poor bastard formating on him. Even if he lost Jack he could always call up 'Flashbang Control' for a homing so there was nothing to worry about.

He had his usual pee against the tailplane before climbing into his cockpit hoping that his stomach would behave after last night. Gyppo and Nobby, his ground crew, had looked up at the low cloud and whistled but said nothing as they helped him with his straps and leads. Jack, as usual, was flying 'MR-?' and gave him a wave before starting up. They took off together and circled the strip low down under the cloud base as Jack set course and told him to switch on navigation lights. Within seconds he was tucked in behind Jack in a white blanket of mist concentrating hard on Jack's nav lights and flying by the seat of his pants. The air was surprisingly smooth allowing him to be light on the controls and he could easily see the underbelly of Jack's aircraft in his windscreen. He was relaxed and happy thinking that the trip was going to be 'a piece of cake'. The altimeter showed him that they were still climbing although he hadn't been conscious of it. An occasional glance across his instruments told him that 'U' (Uncle) was in good form and he sat back enjoying the experience.

Suddenly the white blanket turned grey and there were a few bumps which made him sit up and take notice. A preliminary warning of things to come, he thought, as he tightened his control on the aircraft. The dirty grey mist turned several shades darker as they climbed through turbulent air and he was forced to stare straight ahead at Jack's nav lights without taking his eyes off them for a second.

The vague outline of Jack's aircraft disappeared as he fought to control his Typhoon, feeling the pressures but going with Jack all the time. He was completely disorientated and had no sense of direction only a ruthless desire to keep those nav lights above him in focus. Every nerve and sinew in his body was working overtime to make absolutely bloody certain that he stayed glued to Jack's arse. He had no idea now long they had been airborne but it seemed an awful long time and he hoped like hell that Jack would soon start going down out of this filthy bumpy muck.

The only time that they broke cloud was over the strip and it happened quite suddenly because he had been concentrating so hard that he hadn't sensed the gentle descent or been aware that the cloud had been getting brighter. A feeling of well-being and achievement flowed through him as he broke cloud and followed Jack in tight formation, landing only a few feet away from him as they plonked down on the wire mesh of the strip.

He was full of himself walking into Flights with the CO who told him that he had put up a good show and he was astonished when he learned that they had been airborne for 45 minutes. The boys were sitting around in the tent waiting for an ops call and he could see by the look on their faces that they knew he must have had a fairly hairy trip. When Jack came over and asked him to fly his number two on the next show it made his day. But he knew very well that the recce had achieved nothing except as an excercise for him in cloud flying.

*   *   *

With the coming of August, the Intelligence officer had a busy time updating his maps. The battle line in the American western sector was suddenly moving south towards Avranches and pilots could see that the Yankee war machine was rolling. After the hiccup of the bad weather and the long stalemate situation it looked as if the long awaited breakout was now firmly under way. The name of General 'Blood and Guts' Patton and his Third Army showed up on the maps for the first time so mobility would probably be the name of the game.

It was disappointing for pilots to note, in contrast, that the battle line of the British Second Army still remained fairly static and some of them couldn't understand why our chaps weren't getting a move on. However, the Intelligence officer reiterated that the plan was for the British Second Army to draw off German armoured divisions by repeatedly making attacks which the Germans were forced to block. 'This, as you can see', he said pointing to the map, 'is now paying off and allowing the Americans to advance here, here and here'. Most thought that it was 'bully' for the Yanks who would get all the glory but 'tough tit' for our boys. At least the Yanks would be giving everybody a bit more elbow-room in Normandy, as Terry Gray said and he'd covered most of the ground, 'The place is so clobbered up with troops, tanks and gear that if they bring in any more I reckon Normandy'll sink!'.

On 4 August, 245 Squadron was briefed to attack barges on the River Seine. This was going to be a rare opportunity for them because hitherto the Germans had not used river transport, to any extent, during daylight. The Krauts were now forced to cross the river in order to move troops and supplies over from the eastern sector in the Le Havre area. This had now become vital in order to back up German Panzer and SS divisions which were moving west into the centre section of the Allied line covered by British Second Army.

The Seine attack was going to be a longer trip than usual with twenty minutes or more flying time to the target area. The plan was to break formation and make section attacks, firing rockets in pairs rather than salvos. It was going to be every man for himself with his number two covering him. Other squadrons in the Wing would be joining in the party and pilots were warned to keep a good lookout to avoid mid-air collisions.

Stanford was in good form. It looked like being a fairly juicy target and he had Flying Officer Roly Temple as his number two. He had seen on the Intelligence map, from the red dots indicating gun batteries, that they would be getting quite a bit of flak as they flew across country towards the river but it didn't bother him. He had had skirmishes with those batteries before, especially the one on the top of Mont Cassigny outside Deauville, and he had come through all right so why should he bother!

After having a pee against his tailplane he had a few last puffs of his pipe before handing it over to Nobby to look after. Nobby always took it rather gingerly, carrying it carefully towards the hedge and placing it alongside his forage cap. Taking a final glance at his map to familiarize himself with the flight plan, he stuffed it inside his flying boot and with one foot in the step heaved himself up onto the mainplane. The cockpit was in apple pie order, as usual, with his helmet draped over the spade grip of the control column and his parachute and harness straps laid out ready for him to clip in and adjust. Nobby told him that the engine only needed one and a half strokes of the primer and within a minute or so he had settled in and checked everything. Winding his bubble hood shut because of the dust, he adjusted the throttle setting, primed the engine, selected a starter cartridge and waited for the signal to push the buttons.

It was rapidly getting hot under the perspex hood and he started sweating a little as he watched the three-bladed prop of Jack Collins' Typhoon, waiting for it to rotate before he could start up. For him, these were always odd moments of suspense being all wrapped up in a tight little world and just having to sit there while the seconds ticked away. It came as a relief to press the buttons and hear the big engine cough and splutter, making the airframe shudder and vibrate, as it picked up with a little help from the throttle and broke into a steady roar.

There was something about taxiing out with the Squadron which never failed to uplift him. The boys were helmeted, goggled and their faces covered by oxygen masks, so that one could only identify them by the letter on the side of their aircraft, but they shared a feeling of camaraderie which no words could convey. This was also the case in the air when flying in finger-four formation; perhaps even more so because pilots were close enough to recognize the shape, style and form of each other.

245 Squadron had to wait at the end of the strip while 175 took-off which made Stanford curse because he didn't like hanging around and having to keep giving his engine a burst to clear it. Whenever he opened the throttle, holding the Typhoon against the brakes, the Sabre engine spat back globules of oil which splattered all over the sides of his windscreen. Also, he had to keep an eye on the radiator temperature which gradually started creeping up.

The wind being from the north, they took-off and did a climbing turn over the beaches. Looking down on the barrage balloons and seaside towns Stanford had a quiet laugh thinking about their swim at Lion-sur-Mer and tried to pick out the café at St Aubin. Roly Temple was comfortably tucked in beside him and he felt relaxed and confident as he joined formation with Jimmy Wilson, his Flight commander, and Spike Hughes who was flying Jimmy's number two.

The morning was sunny with about four-tenths cloud at 3,500 feet, not the heavy stuff but small pillow-cases of light, frothy cumulus sailing along like an armada of little ships. The rest of the sky was a beautiful blue with no sign of an approaching front and Stanford thought that some really good weather was on the way at last. Down below, through patches of cloud, he caught glimpses of the River Dives winding from the south and the long straight road pointing like a finger towards Falaise. He was just beginning to think that German gunners had taken the day off when they obliged by sending up boxes of flak which burst above and to the left of the formation. Having put up a marker they then peppered the sky around with flak bursts but the CO held his course seemingly oblivious to all this action. Bob wasn't particularly concerned because he knew from experience that the Germans were way off target but he was relieved when the CO altered course and dived down a few hundred feet to hoodwink the bastards.

The estuary at Le Havre began to show up way off to their left and the sky ahead seemed to be full of flak bursts. He could hear 175 pilots, whose call sign was 'Quebec', talking to one another and it sounded as if they were having quite a party, excited voices clogging up the air. 'Look out Blue four, on your right', 'Come in, Red two, Red two—are you receiving me? Over. Red two—are you receiving me?', 'There's more of the bastards under the trees. Ten o'clock Ronnie, just in the bend', 'Roger, I see em'. This went on until somebody called out, 'For Christ sake, wrap it up'.

Squadron Leader Jack Collins put 245 into line astern following the river, leaving other squadrons to their own patches. The area was thickly wooded on both sides of the Seine which writhed round in great loops like a snake. He had only to pin-point flak positions which the Germans had installed to guard crossing points and stores depots to find the streams of heavy river traffic he was after.

Stanford, like the others, adjusted the rheostat of his gunsight, turned his cannon button to the fire position, switched on his camera, flipped down two rocket switches and tightened his straps ready for the dive. These things he did automatically without thinking or having to grope, although on this occasion he was more excited than usual, perhaps because they were going to catch the enemy out in the open on the water and he was leading a section. Even the flak, and there was plenty of it, didn't give him an uneasy feeling as he heard the CO count down for the wing-over, 'Six, five, four, three, two, one, zero—go!'.

The Seine, which Stanford could see as a narrow winding ribbon of water through the roof of his perspex hood, widened out considerably as they hurtled down through the flak. The river traffic, encircled by wash began to take shape and presented ideal targets. Easing back on the spadegrip handle of his stick, Stanford came out of the steep dive and picked out a large craft whose funnel was belting out smoke. He got a bead on it and touched his cannon button feeling the aircraft shudder and shake with the recoil. The boat was enveloped in pillars of foam as his shells bit into the water and he fired his first pair of rockets straight into the steaming cauldron. He knew that he must have scored a bulls-eye as he pulled back on the stick and shot up into a climbing turn telling himself that he had been bloody daft to get in so close. He heard Roly Temple's voice over the RT saying, 'You blew the bottom out of that one—good show'. Peering over his shoulder he caught a glimpse of the front and back end of the boat sticking up out of the water. The middle section had disappeared, leaving only a mass of floating debris, and as Roly came up alongside he waved a victory sign.

He felt pleased with himself as he climbed up at full throttle towards the flak bursts and bubbling with confidence stall-turned his aircraft, allowing the nose to fall away into a dive. On his way down he found it difficult to find a clear run into the target because Typhoons seemed to be appearing out of nowhere and shooting across his sights. Rocket trails down below hung suspended in the air looking like smoke cornets as he veered this way and that trying to fix a bead on one of the long flat-bottomed barges.

He could see his cannon shells carving up the water and cutting right across a barge as he let go another pair of rockets and pulled back on the stick. He powered up through smoke feeling the 'G' slide off his body and pulled the aircraft into a tight turn to get round quickly for another attack. This time he nearly bought it as another Typhoon flashed across his windscreen and his aircraft jumped up and down hitting its slipstream.

It had been bloody close and it took him a few seconds to be himself again. But the near miss had dampened down some of his over-confidence because he started screwing his head around taking a good look for any Typhoons in the vicinity before he went down into another attack. This time he caught a barge drifting broadside on and was certain that he must have got close enough with his rockets to have knocked it out. As he climbed away he could see the Squadron high up above him circling round waiting for the others to join up.

'Archduke Leader, Blue Three, am going in again, over', he called. 'Roger Blue Three, Archduke Leader, out' came the reply. Jack Collins never wasted words over the RT! Stanford decided that after his last pair of rockets he would make a low fast run over the stretch

Above Terry Gray on his Guzzi.

Above right Dudley Nott just before he got his DFC.

Right The author after receiving his commission.

Left Terry Gray 'at home'.

Below 245 Squadron after dive bombing a 'Noball Target' (flying-bomb site) when the Squadron was based at West Hampnett. From left to right are Bob Lee, John Hampson, Roly Temple, 'Which' Martin, the author, Sheep Milne and Nobby Clark *(Imperial War Museum)*.

Above right Chalking a message on a five hundred pounder. Note the open roof flap denoting that the Typhoon is a Mark 1A; also the 'Northern Rhodesian Squadron' legend painted on the engine cowling.

Right Dennis Lush never realized his ambition to be in on the show on D-Day.

Below right The author's ground crew, Gyppo and Nobby with 'char and wads'.

Above Cleaning the gun barrels on a Typhoon 1A at West Hampnett.

Left Tim Morice in August '43.

Right Robin McNair DFC with his famous 'MR-G' at West Hampnett. Note the Austin 7 doors on the Typhoon 1A.

Below Paddy Gray (far right) with members of No 1 Squadron just before he joined 245.

245 Squadron on Strip B5 Le Fresne Camilly. On the back row from left to right are Paddy Gray, the author, Spike Hughes, Roly Temple, Archie Lamb (standing), Ches West, Al Dellar, Doug Martin, Jeff Jeffries and one unknown. On the front row stand George Dakin, George Wharry, Jack Collins, Bob Lee, Dud Nott, Ace Miron and Jimmy Wilson *(Imperial War Museum)*.

Top NAAFI wagon at West Hampnett—note the Sabre engine's overcoat against the cold wet weather.

Above Bombing up for a dive-bombing attack on a 'Noball Target'—a Typhoon 1A. Note the Austin 7 door and the roof flap.

Below Jimmy Wilson's 'M' for Mike. 'The only thing that ever worked on that aeroplane was the brake on the control column'. Who said that?

of river using up his remaining cannon shells. The flak was getting uncomfortably close but Stanford was too busy positioning himself from the target in order to make his dive to worry about it. He heard somebody say over the RT on the way down, 'Get on with it for Christ sake, why don't you?' and it made him laugh.

He knew that they were the last pair in on the target and was determined to make the most of it. Excited, over-confident and eager, he fired his rockets at a supply depot on the river bank knowing instinctively that he had over shot but he couldn't look back because he had opened the throttle wide and eased the nose down. His Typhoon was going very fast indeed now and he clenched the spade grip on his control column tightly to keep her steady as he dived towards the surface of the water.

The Seine was littered with half-sunken barges lying at drunken angles and masses of floating debris. He was conscious of the white upturned faces of troops still on board, some of them firing rifles and machine guns, half-submerged trucks and men struggling in the water as he flashed overhead firing odd bursts of cannon into the wreckage. Running out of cannon shells surprisingly quickly he pulled back on the stick and climbed to join up with the Squadron.

Flying back to base in finger-four formation Stanford waved to Roly Temple alongside, grateful that throughout the show Roly had stuck with him like a leech. Roly was a good chap and it had been a terrific prang. He felt very pleased with himself at what he had done. Roly, no doubt, would confirm that he had definitely sunk one bloody great barge and damaged several others. It didn't sound particularly devastating, he thought, not like bagging a tank or a train but it was big stuff! Those barges had been full of troops and trucks so God knows how many Krauts he must have knocked off.

Flying Officer Roly Temple was rather a quiet and reserved character who was married and had a baby daughter. A shortish, slim figure he had dark hair, brown eyes and a small clipped moustache giving him an almost dapper appearance. He spent quite a lot of time writing letters to his wife alone in his tent which he shared with Flying Officer Al Dellar. Nobody ever bothered him when he was engrossed in his epistles because they understood that life must be difficult for a married man. Bob Stanford liked Roly, not only because he was a bloody good number two, but he was a nice man to have a quiet and more serious chat with.

After the Seine show, when they were both 'stood down' for the day, Roly had suggested that they might cadge a lift down to the coast and take a look around. He wanted, he said, to visit Courseulles, an old

Norman fishing village where he might find something or another to send home as a souvenir. Bob had managed a shower that morning and found a clean shirt at the bottom of his kit bag which made him feel good and ready for anything. To improve matters, Terry Gray told Roly that he could take the jeep, asking him, in return, to procure anything in the food line which might come in handy. The sun came out as they started off in high spirits setting course for the ancient little village of Fontaine Henri. Bob was a little taken aback when Roly stopped the jeep to have a wander round Fontaine because Bob knew that apart from the old buildings there was nothing of interest and usually nobody to talk to.

Roly left him standing in front of the old church and disappeared inside saying that he was going to take a look even if Bob wasn't keen. Bob was slightly annoyed and lit his pipe waiting impatiently. Lounging against a wall in the warm sun, he found it almost impossible to believe that a war was actually going on all around them. The place could have been a Devon village, lying deep in the natural contours of rich soil smelling of cowsheds and muck, except for the distant rumble of gunfire and the sight of barrage balloons along the coast turning in the wind. He half wanted to go into the dark interior of the church and join Roly but was frustrated because time was slipping away. It wasn't often that one was 'stood down' for the best part of a sunny day and here they were wasting time. He thought it was too bad of Roly to go off and he got so mad that he blasted away on the jeep's horn.

Roly finally emerged giving him a thumbs-up sign and waved some faded old picture postcards saying that they were just the job to send home. Bob didn't say a word but climbed into the jeep and sat without comment as they drove through Reviers and on to Courseulles. Roly appeared to take no notice of Bob's surly behaviour but chattered on about the beautiful countryside saying that after the war he was going to bring his family over to Normandy and take them round some of these lovely old villages. Bob couldn't keep 'steam up' for long and reminded himself that Roly hadn't really been long and it was stupid to get worked up over nothing. He was ashamed and tried to excuse himself by saying that he had no idea that Roly was that damned religious. Roly laughed, telling Bob that he had looked like a bridegroom waiting at the church for his bride to turn up, and the incident was forgotten.

They arrived in Courseulles to find the old fishing port choked with vehicles and trucks. A multitude of brown jobs, carrying their weapons, and a sprinkling of naval types had taken over the place which was vibrating with activity and basic British humour! Bob had regained his best form and they both enjoyed walking through the narrow streets and taking a look at the harbour. Roly had acquired a rag doll and some more postcards when they fought their way into a local café for a noggin.

Apart from the décor and the absence of good old British draught bitter it was just like barging one's way into a crowded pub back home. When Roly told an Army Corporal that they were flying Typhoons it created quite a stir and they became the centre of attention. The Army blokes asked lots of questions and were genuinely enthusiastic about the job the Typhoons were doing, apart from one or two caustic remarks about rockets which had clobbered them by mistake.

Drinks were 'on the Army' and Bob found himself verbally flying a Typhoon in the bar, aware that he was line-shooting but too carried away to stop himself. Even Roly, normally rather shy, was busy explaining how the Typhoon taxi service worked and how quickly they could go straight down on a target once they got a call from the scout car, or light armoured vehicle, and could see the marker shell burning over the target. The interest in Typhoon operations displayed by the brown jobs had caught them completely by surprise and they enjoyed it.

After the party they went back to the jeep stimulated by the Calvados and feeling 'dead chuffed' by their reception. It had been bloody nice to know at first hand that they had baled out those particular chaps from a number of dicey situations and that the Krauts were shit-scared of rocket attacks. Listening to a mortar platoon Sergeant, who had been up front when the 21st Panzer Division had attacked his unit, convinced them that they were bloody lucky to be up in the air and not crawling around on the ground.

Both agreed that it had been a worthwhile experience and it was fun to get away from the strip and meet other chaps. Bob suggested that it might be a good idea to 'do a Terry Gray recce' and take a wander across to the American sector to find out what was going on with the Yanks. So they decided to move along the coast and then head towards St Lo which they knew had been the scene of some fierce fighting. Terry Gray had warned everybody going on excursions to keep to country roads because the main ones were bunged up with traffic going up and down the line so Roly gave Bob the job of map reading his way around Bayeux and cutting across country towards Pont-de-la-Hoderie a few miles to the north of St Lo.

They were stopped a few times by military police at crossroads and asked for their 1250s, or identity cards, but when Bob explained that he was going over to meet an American cousin they were let through. The countryside changed rapidly as they got well away from the flat areas behind the coast and into the wooded valleys and hills in the American sector. Nipping along the little country lanes was like taking a spin in Cotswold country with only shattered buildings here and there to remind them that the war had passed that way.

Both of them were excited because it was thrilling to drive through a battlefield not knowing what to expect around the next corner. Reaching the other side of Villiers Fossard they could see American trucks and vehicles moving up the line and quite suddenly the sun disappeared and it started to rain. The countryside melted away leaving a vast expanse of barren land torn up by vehicle tracks with here and there a ruined building and a few stunted trees. All at once they had emerged from green fields and foliage into a clay coloured quagmire.

Bob asked a couple of Yanks parked in a jeep off the road if they were all right for St Lo. 'Straight ahead, bud', they replied. 'You can't miss it, fella'. They drove on but there was no sign of a town looming up and he was beginning to think that the Yanks were 'having him on'. They were edging closer all the time to the main road from Carentan which was choked with traffic. Not wishing to get caught up in that lot, Roly pulled off the road before they came to the junction and they both got out to take a look around.

Beyond the road junction the land dropped away and as they got nearer they looked down into a huge waterlogged crater with some old stone walls and battlements standing out of the water near the bottom. Masses of rubble had obviously slid down the slopes into the morass leaving a grotesque assortment of ruins stuck into the sides of the enormous hole. They could see that the entire town of St Lo had disappeared into an abyss and it left them speechless for a moment. It was a scene of utter desolation made even more hideous by the dirty greyish watery bog which covered the remains of what had been a large community. Stanford, who had been accustomed to London blitzes, turned to Temple, 'Good God', he said, 'I've never seen anything quite like this'.

Bob had often seen Caen from the air and knew that the city had taken a terrible pasting but the sight of St Lo was something quite different. His revulsion, he thought, was not only because the town had sunk into a hole but was heightened by the fact that he was standing there looking at it and had physical and mental contact with the scene. Big droplets of rain were now falling fast and the damp and depressing atmosphere seeped into him forcing him to turn away and make his escape. He could see by the look on Roly's face that he felt much the same and without saying anything they began to walk back to their jeep. A truck had spilled out a small group of GIs, who were standing beside it smoking, and as they passed, one of them waved a cigar in their direction and called out, 'Hi'. Roly responded and the Yank, looking over to St Lo, grimaced and said, 'Pretty— ain't it!'.

There was no point in them hanging about in the rain so they decided to go back the way they came and try to find a café some- where on the outskirts of Bayeux. Driving along in the jeep Bob said how different the Yanks had looked from our chaps. 'They seem bigger altogether, somehow Roly', he said, 'broad shoulders and narrow hips. By the way, did you notice their arses? They looked to me like bloody great hard conkers. And that bloke with the cigar must have been nearly seven feet tall'.

*   *   *

A hard core of experienced pilots, who had been on 245 for a year or more, formed the backbone of the Squadron. Operations like the Seine attack called for a high standard of flying skills and experience in carrying out air-to-ground rocket attacks. The Squadron flew as a team and there was no place for misfits or those wanting 'to go it alone'. Although discipline in the air was strict, it rarely had to be enforced because pilots were dedicated to the job and totally integrated when doing it.

It was very hard on those replacement pilots, who had only a few hours Typhoon flying experience and had never been on ops, to be suddenly pitchforked into the war. They were, of course, mad keen to get going but by Squadron standards they could barely fly a Typhoon. An experienced combat pilot could fly his machine as though it was 'strapped to his arse' without having to think about it. But there was no time or opportunity in Normandy for a new pilot to go up and thoroughly master his aeroplane or be given Squadron ops training.

Replacement pilots were sent over to France having completed a short course at an Operational Training Unit. They did a few hours flying in Typhoons including a little formation and low level prac- tice but that was about all. Few pilots could honestly admit that even their first solo in a Typhoon had been 'a piece of cake'. Unlike the ladylike 'Spit' and the dear old 'Hurribus', the 'Tiffy' was like a fast bucking bronco which had to be reined in quickly and firmly. The cockpit was more complex with over one hundred tits, switches, knobs and gadgets; a pilot had to breathe in oxygen before starting the engine; she swung viciously on take-off and then she went like an express train adding another 100 mph to the standard performance of other aircraft. Although pilots' confidence in the machine built up quickly during the first few flying hours most of them treated their aircraft with the greatest respect.

Pilots who had joined the Squadron well before D-Day and gained operational experience had considerable advantages. There had been ample opportunities for them to aerobat their aircraft and practice dog fights, Squadron formation, low level cross-countries and to fire at targets on the practice range. These exercises gradually enabled them to fly 'by the seat of their pants' in that man and machine became totally integrated.

Most of the 'old hands' had been engaged in a variety of operational work including, Channel patrols, sweeps, armed recces, anti-shipping strikes, dive bombing and low level 'rhubarbs'. These operations not only capitalized on the speed, toughness, heavy armament and the stability of the Typhoon as a firing platform but gave pilots a chance of realizing the full potential of their machines. One of the major tasks for 245 Squadron was to dive-bomb flying bomb launching sites or 'Noball' targets as they were code named. The Squadron would cross the Channel at wave-top height to get under German radar and when in sight of the French coast climb furiously, putting in the 'blower', up to a height of about 10,000 feet. Targets were along the flak belt in the Pas de Calais area. The Germans immediately responded with heavy flak and the idea was to get in and out fast letting the bombs go between 4,000 and 5,000 feet to keep away from the light flak. The steep dive was a little uncomfortable on one's first trip because the tailplane seemed to be leaning over the vertical and the aircraft clattered and vibrated a great deal. This vibration wasn't simply a slight shuddering but shook the pilot's body quite violently, making him feel that something must be wrong and that the aircraft was likely to break up at any moment.

Unfortunately, the Typhoon had experienced a history of tails breaking off before the fault was eventually discovered and rectified. This had been due to 'flutter' induced in the elevators which built up to such an extent that it tore apart the rear fuselage. Metal fatigue in a bracket and the positioning of the mass balance within the elevator had been the cause of the trouble, resulting in some 28 Typhoons suffering massive failure of the rear fuselage and diving into the ground. There had been little or no chance of any pilot getting out alive. Word soon got around that the Typhoon was a death trap for the poor bastards who had to fly it. Although tail failures hadn't occurred during high speed dives and other manoeuvres which put the greatest strain on the fuselage, it took some time before pilots were able to forget all about it.

Apart from excessive noise and vibration in steep dives pilots had to become accustomed to the controls 'heavying up' and the effects of 'G' (the pull of gravity) when pulling out. With seven-and-a-half tons of machine hurtling down at speeds in excess of 400 mph, the pilot had to exert considerable pressure on the controls to keep her steady and generally blacked out when he pulled the stick back to come out of the dive. To help him with the 'G' problem, Hawker Aircraft had installed upper and lower pedals on the rudder controls which were adjustable for length. Using the upper bars or pedals enabled a pilot to get his knees up in a hunched position thus protecting his stomach and arresting the blood flow—giving him more resistance to 'G' forces.

Continually blacking out didn't appear to have any physical effect upon pilots but there were complaints that the excessive vibration in the dive was causing virility problems! Hawker Aircraft responded by installing a sprung seat which certainly made life more comfortable. Pilots reckoned that resistance to 'G' varied according to a chap's physical make-up but had no doubt that after a few late night piss-ups it deteriorated rapidly.

Most of the 'old hands' on 245 had done a few 'rhubarbs', which were not obligatory so there was fierce competition to go on them. Two pilots could select a target for themselves and submit their plan for approval. Such targets included goods trains, airfields, troop concentrations, ships, army vehicles and supplies depots. These low level attacks were usually carried out during winter months when the weather was suitable. There had to be sufficient cloud cover for protection against possible Luftwaffe attacks and enough visibility to navigate at high speed flying at a height of two or three hundred feet. A 'rhubarb' was a highly exciting project for any pilot in that it allowed him full scope for his initiative and aggressive spirit. Apart from that, low flying a Typhoon across Northern France was terrific fun. Everything whizzed past so quickly and often one had to get right down on the deck below tree tops and roofs to escape ground fire. It gave pilots a superior feeling being able to flash over enemy-occupied territory and catch glimpses of German soldiers diving for cover; then to shoot up the target with cannon fire and let go a couple of delayed action bombs as a *'coup de grace'*!

These excursions proved to be very effective in many ways. Successful attacks were made on hundreds of goods trains and other targets and 'train busting' became a popular and competitive pastime. So much so, that train drivers in Northern France were top of the league as far as pay was concerned! Rhubarbs were also of great psychological value both to the French who waved and doffed their caps to the Typhoons streaking overhead and to our people who saw them as embodying a spirit of relentless aggression.

There is no doubt that in carrying out these low-level attacks over Northern France, the Low Countries, the North Sea and the Channel pilots developed powers of leadership, increased their navigational efficiency and their low-flying techniques. Also, the Typhoon itself proved beyond doubt that it could take the sort of punishment that would have finished off machines of lighter construction. Apart from being severely clobbered by flak, pilots brought back aircraft with bits of trees and telephone wires embedded in radiators and gaping holes in fuselages; badly dented air scoops and spinners were not uncommon after low-level attacks.

There was another side to the story, as far as 245 was concerned, because the Squadron lost several pilots on these operations. They were highly dangerous and any pilot was rather pushing his luck when he took-off on one but this didn't dampen down enthusiasm for 'having a go'! The spirit of the game was to outdo the other chaps and build a reputation as a specialist in trainbusting or some other activity.

Pilots who survived the months of 1943 and 1944 leading up to D-Day had gained invaluable experience in all aspects of Typhoon operations including its ultimate role as a cannon and rocket-firing fighter in air-to-ground attack. They had been lucky but undoubtedly possessed the kind of flying ability which ops demanded. But they wouldn't talk about it, not even amongst themselves. One or two might unbend a little and say something about split-arse turns to confuse German gunners but nothing more, probably because they didn't really know the answers. There was no book on the subject of, 'how to fly on ops', only Squadron discussions on tactics, formation and discipline in the air.

Plans were usually marked out on bits of paper or chalked up on blackboards in 'Flights' and accompanied by understatements in Squadron jargon which assumed that everyone knew what the form was. All this was an entirely new world for replacement pilots who had suddenly arrived on the scene and they quickly realized that their only salvation lay in following their number one.

The number one would usually confirm this by saying, 'Stick close to me, chum, and do everything I do and you'll be all right.' The net result was that the poor chap would survive his first few ops, if he was lucky, concentrating so hard on the arse end of his leader that he was oblivious to the action. He had fired his cannons and rockets into something or another but his eyes had been glued on his leader who was his only hope.

It took time and luck for most new chaps to be able to relax a little and take note of what was going on around them. This usually came about when they were finding the feel of their machine and not having to concentrate on flying it and keeping station. If they could survive their first few ops and begin to settle down without becoming over-confident then they stood a chance of staying the course.

On 6 August 1944, 245 Squadron found itself with a basis of 'old hands', a number of less experienced pilots and a few new arrivals before it was about to fight the biggest battle since it was formed during the First World War.

Chapter 6

The Battle of Mortain

There was a chill in the evening air on 6 August as pilots gathered around the log table. Moisture trickled down tent walls and guy ropes were wet and taut to the touch, making one's hands grateful for the warmth of a hot mug of compo tea. It was a time for fur-lined flying jackets to be carelessly draped across shoulders and a chance to make an early trip to the field latrine before the long grass became sopping wet and the light faded.

Guns were still grumbling away in the distance and behind the hedge the Squadron's Typhoons stood side by side waiting patiently for their nightly run up. A thin film of mist from the woods below began to creep steadily across the field as a pale moon showed itself in a darkening sky. Those around the log table immediately stood up when Wing Commander Charles Green, accompanied by Squadron Leader Jack Collins, suddenly appeared through the gap in the hedge.

The big South African took off his cap and told them to relax, saying that he had just dropped in for a chat with nothing serious in mind. For most of them a Wing Commander was a dizzy rank and Green, a tough and powerful character who never minced his words, was always received with the utmost respect and attention. One or two of the 'old hands', who had known him for some time, usually got him going by referring to a particular show which had been a good prang.

As the Wing Commander's prime object in life was to knock off as many Krauts as possible, he warmed up to the subject. There was no bullshit in what Green had to say about Typhoon operations and he made it crystal clear that the Wing's job was to root out the enemy and destroy him. He wasn't being melodramatic because he often led the onslaught and had already built up a reputation for being one of the best Wing leaders in the business in company with Roland Beamont, Dennis Gillam and Erik Haabjoern of Norway. Standing there wearing his two Smith and Wesson .38 revolvers he looked every inch the part when he told his pilots that the only good German was a dead one. He was probably the only man who could have got away with such a remark without a few raised eyebrows or backhand whispers. Later, he was to bale out over the lines and arrive back with a load of German prisoners so his guns came in handy after all!

The Wing leader was in very good form that evening telling the chaps about General Patton's Third American Army break-out south and east of the Cherbourg Peninsula. This advance had been very rapid and there was a chance that the American forces could threaten the rear of the German Army in that area. If all went well, Charles Green thought that there should be some excellent trade around for the Typhoons. Before leaving, he took Warrant Officer Paddy Gray on one side to tell Paddy that he would be flying his number two on tomorrow's early morning recce. 'We'll take a look over the general area and see what's going on', he said.

Paddy Gray had flown number two to the Wing leader on a couple of previous occasions and enjoyed it very much. Green was a first-class pilot, who was thoroughly professional in everything he did, and Paddy had plenty of ops experience to be able to stay with him in any situation. A few of the chaps around the log table made facetious remarks to Paddy about 'sucking up to the Wing CO' or 'it's all right for some' and Ches West drawled, 'Aw shit. Better you than me, brother! You wanna keep a good look out. Sure as hell, there'll be some fireworks around, I tell you'.

The night was damp and cold when Gray lit the candle and got out the cards and the cribbage board. Bob Stanford's luck was in and after a few hands, Paddy Gray who always kept a meticulous count, announced that Stanford now owed him 'only two thousand, seven hundred and three francs'. 'Apart from that, Bob', he said, 'it's about time you bought some more matches for that pipe of yours. My lighter's nearly had it'.

When Gray pulled back the tent flap in the early morning of 7 August he could see the tents down the line shrouded in mist and there was no sign of a break up above. Everything was dripping wet, clammy and cold, so knowing that the recce would be postponed he pulled his flying jacket back over his head and kipped down again. He was vaguely aware that Sabre engines were being run up as he drifted off and it seemed only seconds later that Nobby shook him and handed over a mug of hot compo tea. The little leading air-craftsman said that a jeep would pick him up in half-an-hour and that was all he knew.

He could hear ground crews shouting across to one another as he had a quick wash in the canvas bowl outside. The mist had lifted a little but was still draped over tree tops and tent roofs and he knew that they wouldn't be able to take-off for some time yet. The cosiest and warmest place in these surroundings, he thought, was in the cockpit of a Typhoon now that engines had been run up. Ground crews usually took it in turns to thaw out in the cockpit and he didn't blame them because they had to stagger out during the night to start up the Sabres. Thinking about it reminded him of those times when he had spent hours in his cockpit parked beside the runway waiting for the signal to start up and scramble. He had been with Number One Squadron then and they had been carrying out 'hit and run' raids on seaside towns. The Typhoons used to operate in pairs, flying up and down the Channel waiting to be vectored onto the Focke Wulfs, and the boys nicknamed these patrols 'Gert and Daisy's', after the comediennes Elsie and Doris Waters. It all seemed a long time ago now!

The jeep was late in arriving and there was still no sign of any break in the weather with the dirty grey mist still clamped down over the strip. He could see his own ground crew working on 'O' (Oscar) and they gave him a thumbs-down sign and pointed up at the muck. He was wondering what the Wing Commander had in mind as they drove up beside the Intelligence tent. The tall, broad figure of Charles Green was pacing up and down looking up at the murk. Paddy Gray could see by the look on Green's face that he was impatient and brassed off with the delay but he smiled at Paddy, slapped him on the back, and told him that the stuff was going to clear and they would get going as soon as there was enough 'vis' to take-off.

Tea and biscuits were produced which Paddy thought was one consolation for flying with the Wing Commander. He liked sweet things but wasn't a big eater and only took enough fuel on board to keep his engine going. While waiting he studied the ops map and marked his own up accordingly. There was nothing difficult about the trip. They would be flying south-west crossing the American sector and making a wide sweep around Avranches and then back to base. It looked like being 'a piece of cake'.

The cloud base was slow to lift off the deck but when visibility reached a few hundred yards the Wing CO said they might as well get cracking and rendezvous at the top end of the strip. Checking his watch Charles Green told him to start up his engine in fifteen minutes and join up at the top end of the strip with navigation lights on. Coming back to dispersal in the jeep, Gray looked up at the muck still hanging about and hoped the met man was right about it clearing because if it clamped down again they might be diverted back home to Southern England.

As soon as he heard the hiss and crack of Green's engine exploding into life Gray pressed his starter buttons and was a little relieved when his own Sabre settled down into a steady roar. He wasn't bothered or even slightly keyed up at having to fly with the Wing Commander but in very damp weather conditions the Sabre engine might have misbehaved and he didn't want to keep Charles Green waiting. As his ground crew waved him round he caught sight of the Wing CO's machine taxiing slowly towards the top end of the strip.

When Gray felt the dull thuds of his undercarriage wheels bumping into their casings both aircraft were enveloped in thick grey mist and Green held a steady course allowing Gray to tuck in behind him in line astern formation. As they turned gently in the climb the grey cloud lightened up and quite suddenly they broke through white vapour into dazzling light, forcing Gray to pull down his tinted goggles. Below them, a carpet of mist and cloud stretched out on all sides as far as the eye could see making an undulating pattern of frothy white and grey brown vapour against a background of deep blue sky. Behind them a blazing sun was burning into the mantle of moisture but there wasn't a glimpse of the ground or any sign of a hole in the cloudscape.

Green continued on a rough heading of 230 degrees weaving about gently, searching for any gap in the cloud but there was nothing but undulating ridges of vapour. Then, he made a wide sweep round turning in an easterly direction and Gray was beginning to think that the show would turn out to be an 'abort' when he heard the Wing Commander's voice. 'There's a hole down there at two o'clock. I thought I saw something moving. Going down in five seconds—now!'

It was a difficult dive because the cloud base was only a few hundred feet and there were patches of mist all over the place. They pulled out of the dive having only seconds to look around and Gray told the Wing Leader over the RT that he had seen what looked like some vehicles but he wasn't sure what they were. Green's voice came over, 'Let's take another look. Going down again—now!'. This time Green really went in low and there was no doubt about it. The vehicles were tanks and there appeared to be a number of them. They pulled up and climbed through the cloud and Green called, 'They are tanks all right. Let's find out whose they are', and for the third time the pair of them shot down through the hole in the cloud and streaked low over the column of tanks. This time there was no doubt in either of their minds, the tanks were German and there seemed to be hundreds of the bastards.

Green had pin-pointed the position of the armour as being eight or ten miles east of Avranches and south of Vire and headed back towards the strip at full throttle knowing that there was no time to be lost. He couldn't believe his luck in spotting a whole army of Kraut tanks out in the open like sitting ducks and was impatient to get at them before they could reach cover. The Krauts would know for certain, he thought, that the Typhoons would be back and he called base for emergency action.

The sun had already burnt up great holes in the cloud as minutes later they landed on the strip and Green jumped out of his aircraft at the end of the runway and ran over to Intelligence, map in hand. Group had already been on the line having received a call for help from the Americans and every serviceable rocket Typhoon in Normandy was to be thrown into the attack. The situation was serious and the flap was on!

★   ★   ★

The flap was the result of a personal directive from Adolph Hitler himself when he gambled on driving a wedge between the American and British Armies by committing four Panzer divisions to an all-out counter-attack from which there would be no retreat. The battle centred around a small town called Mortain which lies on the southern base of the Cherbourg Peninsula some ten miles to the east of Avranches, the gateway into Brittany. Just off the coast near Avranches is the familiar landmark of Mont-Saint-Michel and roads to the south lead to Saint Malo and Rennes, then the headquarters of the German 7th Army. The insignificant little town of Mortain was in ruins and had been taken by the Americans a few days previously, its population of 3,000 having gone into hiding in the surrounding countryside.

But, Mortain wasn't just another small Norman town to suffer the ravages of war. It became the centre of one of the fiercest and most important battles of the Normandy campaign and there were reasons for this. The town was right in a line dividing the Americans and the British Second Army running north through Caumont and on to Bayeux. Built on high ground, Mortain dominated the surrounding landscape with heavily wooded areas and forests to the west right across to Alencon and Argentan. These woods provided vital cover for German infantry and armoured divisions almost to the outskirts of the town. The area made a perfect base for the Germans to counter-attack the American advance, cut off Patton's forces to the south and wheel north towards the Normandy beaches and so isolate the Americans.

Before Rommel had been badly wounded in his car by a Typhoon squadron, the Field Marshal had warned Hitler that it was becoming increasingly difficult and would probably be well-nigh impossible to hold the line south of the Cherbourg Peninsula. Since then, the port of Cherbourg had fallen and during the first week in August the Americans were breaking out in all directions. American infantry divisions had learned a great deal since they fought their way off the beaches of Utah and Omaha and advanced through the close bocage country surrounding St Lo. Experienced German infantry divisions opposing them had been well dug in and the Yanks had had to fight inch by inch through difficult terrain. Now, in the first few days of August, the American war machine was really rolling and General Patton's mobile Army which had recently entered the fight was now going flat out. It was against these events that the Americans suddenly found themselves confronted by four Panzer divisions and having only anti-tank guns and no tanks to counter the German attack.

During their morning recce on 7 August, Charles Green and Paddy Gray had had phenomenal luck in being able to locate and pin-point the German tanks on the road to Saint-Barthélemy on the outskirts of Mortain. The hole in the cloud over that particular spot can only be described as an act of divine providence! Also, the tanks of 1st SS (Leibstandarte Adolph Hitler) Panzer Division, which were on the road, had been delayed for several hours by a lead vehicle which had broken down and blocked the track in the forest. Had this not occurred, the division would have been in position to attack the American lines under cover of mist and hidden from air strikes. Furthermore, it was the sudden arrival of this division heading straight for Saint-Barthélemy which had made the situation critical.

Immediate back-up for the American infantry divisions facing the advancing German armour had to come from air support alone. It was going to be a formidable task, however, for air-to-ground attack fighters to create sufficient mayhem amongst some 300 tanks in order to bring their advance to a standstill. Apart from that, a Panzer division did not consist solely of tanks but included armoured vehicles, lorries, infantry and all the paraphernalia which made a complete mobile army. Also, its various marks of tanks were equipped with the most formidable general-purpose gun of the war, the 88 mm. Such an army could pump up tremendous firepower including small arms, light, medium and heavy flak. Panzer gunners had a high respect for rocket-firing Typhoons and were well aware that when tell-tale puffs of smoke emerged from under the wings rockets were on their way and they lost no time in opening up with every gun in their possession. The big question, as far as German commanders were concerned, was whether the Luftwaffe would show up to cover the counter-attack now approaching its crucial stage. Luftwaffe General Bulowins, with Hitler's personal authority, had promised 300 fighters but there had been no sign of them as yet.

Soon after Charles Green and Paddy Gray had taken off on their recce the weather at the strip showed signs of clearing up. The grey mist suddenly started lifting fast and becoming white and little patches of blue sky began to appear. The air was warming up considerably and after a late start it looked as if it was going to be hot and sunny. Some 245 Squadron pilots, who were down for the next show, had walked over to Flights to find out what was cooking and others were either lazing about or doing odd chores. Nobody could really settle down and relax until they knew the ops position for the day.

Bob Stanford had been writing a letter to his mother when he heard the familiar whining growl of Sabre engines in the circuit and nipped outside the tent to watch the recce pair come in. They didn't waste any time in getting down and he thought no more about it until he heard a jeep draw up on the other side of the hedge with its horn blasting away. It was the CO, Jack Collins, who told them that there was a flap on and everyone was wanted in Intelligence immediately.

A truck arrived to pick up the rest of the pilots after Jack Collin's jeep had raced off. The sun had burst through and cleared up what remained of the mist as pilots grabbed maps and personal gear and piled into the back. The fact that every pilot was being rounded up left no one in any doubt that something really big was brewing. Nothing like this had happened before and excitement mounted as the truck bumped and rolled its way across the strip.

When the 245 truck arrived at Intelligence the tent was already packed solid with Typhoon pilots and the steamy atmosphere inside was full of cigarette and tobacco smoke. Most pilots were in shirt sleeves and some sported silk scarves and wore dark glasses. The buzz of conversation was interrupted only by the sound of Sabre engines being run up and the noise of passing vehicles. Despite the jocularity there was an air of expectancy and tension as they waited for the Wing Commander.

When the burly figure of Charles Green, accompanied by his squadron commanders, came striding onto the platform all chatter ceased abruptly. He looked hard at the gathering in a challenging and aggressive manner, standing rigidly erect. 'This is the moment we have all been waiting for, Gentlemen', he said, 'the chance of getting at Panzer tanks out in the open. And, there's lots of the bastards'.

Green got an enthusiastic response which he quickly waved down. This spontaneous reaction from his pilots was not triggered off by his somewhat theatrical presence but was a genuine desire to have an opportunity to attack Panzer armour 'en masse' which had so far eluded them. Up until now they had shot them up in small groups either dug in or hidden away in woods or behind walls. The Wing Commander pointed out the exact position of the Panzer divisions on his large scale map. 'They are moving along this road', he said, 'from Mortain towards Saint-Barthélemy and the job for 245 pilots, who will be first in, is to concentrate on the lead tanks and jam the road'. He emphasized that aircraft would not fly in Squadron formation but would take off in pairs and attack as individual units. Flying time to the target, he said, was about fifteen minutes. Aircraft would fly back to base to refuel and re-arm and then return to the attack. In this way there would be a continuous cycle of Typhoon sorties until the Panzer armour was destroyed. Other Typhoon Wings would be joining in and he warned pilots to watch out for mid-air collisions.

After leaving Intelligence they drove across to dispersals aware of the frantic activity going on all around them. Piles of rockets and boxes of 20-mm cannon shells were being stacked up off the end of the strip, all ground staff had been brought in to provide back up for the operation and the airfield commander's jeep was dashing from one group to another as the tall figure of Wing Commander Tim Morice leapt out to issue his instructions. He had addressed all his men beforehand and every person knew exactly what he had to do and the importance of the forthcoming battle. His problem was to refuel and re-arm the Typhoons as they came off the end of the runway and get them off again in a continuous rotation.

Most of the cloud had been burnt up by the sun as 245 pilots got into their aircraft and it was obviously going to be a scorcher. Cockpits felt like hot greenhouses and dust was being blown about all over the place. Groundcrews, stripped to the waist, wore handkerchieves covering their noses and mouths. For the first time, every aircraft lined up at dispersals would be taking off on a show and these men were stretched to the limit. The crews didn't say much but pilots were conscious of receiving just that extra little bit of attention as they settled in and waited for the CO to start his engine. Nobody had any illusions about what lay ahead. They had attacked Panzer tanks before and knew what to expect but this time there was going to be an entire army of them and they were going to have to keep on rocketing them until it was all over. Any personal fears had been contained and camouflaged behind a few jocular remarks on the way back from Intelligence. They had been chuffed that their Squadron was going to be first in. Paddy Gray had been the Wing Commander's number two when they found the tanks so 245 naturally got the privilege. Now, all they wanted to do was to get going, knowing that in twenty minutes or so they would be diving on those tanks.

Wing Commander Tim Morice stood off the end of the strip surveying the scene. Fuel lines were in position and huge piles of rockets and cannon shells made ready for the action. He was satisfied that every flyable Typhoon on 121 Wing would be taking part in the show and that his back-up team to service the aircraft as they landed were ready and standing by. Everybody had worked bloody hard and efficiently and he was proud of them. He had told his chaps many times that the sole reason for their existence was to get the Wing's Typhoons, fully armed and refuelled, into the air and then to keep them flying.

He had wished many times, with all his heart and soul, that he could be flying with them. He was a very good pilot and had flown a Hurricane, apart from numerous other machines, but the boys wouldn't let him fly a Typhoon. Once, not long ago, he had actually been in the cockpit of a Typhoon ready to go but somebody's tail fell off in the circuit and they yanked him out saying that it wasn't a good day for him to make his first solo. At the age of 44 he realized that many of the pilots around him could be his sons but he was still determined to fly the bloody thing before the war ended.

Tim had been a fighter pilot in the First World War and had won a

Military Cross flying Bristol Fighters at the age of eighteen. He lived only for aeroplanes and to be in the company of men associated with them. Whenever an aircraft took-off or flew overhead he would glance up at it and was always present to watch 'his' squadrons, as he called them, go off and land back after a show.

He could see the dust storm created, over to his right, as 245 Squadron started up and slowly began taxiing out towards the top end of the runway. One after the other the remaining squadrons did likewise until the air resounded with the roar of Sabre engines, obliterating the noise of gunfire from the area around Caen.

The ground personnel stood there in the hot sun, shading their eyes, gazing at the seemingly never-ending stream of Typhoons thundering towards them and then lifting off over their heads in pairs and climbing steeply before turning south-east for Mortain.

*   *   *

The 1st SS (Leibstandarte Adolph Hitler) Panzer division was slowly making its way towards the fork in the road at Saint Barthélemy as the Typhoons of 121 Wing were on their way from Le Fresne Camilly. Panzer tanks and vehicles, numbering almost a thousand, were spread out along the straight road leading out from Mortain. The terrain was flat and the road was hedged. There were ditches on either side, and here and there groups of trees were the only break in the landscape. On their right, in wooded areas, the tanks and infantry of the 2nd SS (Das Reich) Panzer Division were embedded under foliage, confronting the American 30th, 9th and 4th Infantry Divisions equipped only with automatic weapons, grenades, mortars and anti-tank guns.

The task for the 1st SS Panzer Division was to smash through the American lines at Saint Barthélemy, held by the 30th US Infantry Division, leaving a gap for the others to exploit as part of the plan to drive towards Avranches. It was approaching midday and the Division was still on the open road under a cloudless sky desperately trying to reach the cover of wooded areas. They knew that they had been spotted by the Typhoon recce (of Charles Green and Paddy Gray) and were left in no doubt that rocket Typhoon squadrons would shortly be arriving on the scene.

Behind the Panzer Division, the rocks of Mortain rose high out of the plains making a shelf along which straggled the ruins of the town. This rocky plateau overlooked the wooded countryside where the battle had been raging for several weeks and the Americans had a precarious hold on what remained of the town. The inhabitants had fled into the surrounding country before artillery had pounded it into ruins. La Grande-Rue de Mortain, the main street, was a shambles, piled high with debris. Only a few walls were left standing like rows of decayed teeth. L'Abbaye Blanche had escaped intact because it had been an important German military hospital and Dr. Buisson's house, L'Angevine, which was relatively undamaged had been transformed into a blockhouse by the GIs during the previous evening. Three German soldiers had been buried in shallow graves in the front garden and bombs from a Heinkel 111 attack had straddled the building. Doctor Giles Buisson, later to become the mayor, was in the fields delivering babies when the battle of Saint Barthélemy reached its crescendo.

Behind the ruins of the town, a hill rose sharply. Upon it was La Chapelle Saint Michel de Mortain. Some units of the 30th American Infantry Division had been cut off and were dug in around the wooded slopes of the little chapel. They had been there for several days and were running out of ammunition when the Typhoon attacks took place on the morning of 7 August. The people of Mortain, at great risk, had managed to smuggle food and water supplies through the German lines to keep them going.

The Americans had called for help earlier that day because of the sudden appearance of the 1st SS Panzer Division heading directly towards their lines. They had been able to contain the German attacks of the 2nd SS Panzer Division in the wooded country where the battle was at close quarters but simply did not have firepower enough to stop Panzer armour on the move.

A schoolmistress from Saint Barthélemy was at the crossroads as the tanks of the 1st SS Panzer Division slowly rumbled towards her on the road towards Juvigny. Hearing the noise of aircraft she looked up to see Typhoons circling and immediately ran towards a farm lying back off the road where she joined others taking refuge in the cellar.

There was no problem for 245 pilots in identifying the target because the Panzer Division was stretched out all along the straight road. The Squadron flew parallel to the long column in line astern, then winged over and started to dive from about 4,000 feet, heading for the lead tanks which were their prime objective. Simultaneously, Panzer gunners put up a curtain of medium flak and began firing a barrage of light flak and tracer. In the dive pilots could see an eiderdown of whitish cloud creeping across the target as the light flak built up to form a protective screen. Tanks and vehicles, although

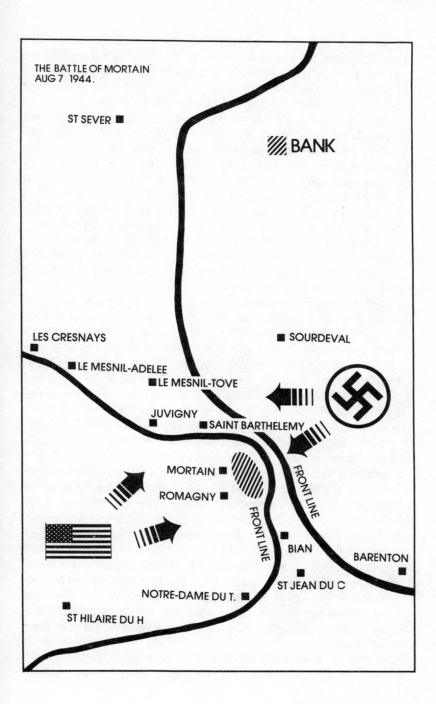

THE BATTLE OF MORTAIN
AUG 7 1944.

ST SEVER ■

BANK

LES CRESNAYS ■

SOURDEVAL ■

■ LE MESNIL-ADELEE

■ LE MESNIL-TOVE

JUVIGNY ■

■ SAINT BARTHELEMY

MORTAIN ■

ROMAGNY ■

FRONT LINE

FRONT LINE

BIAN ■

BARENTON ■

ST JEAN DU C ■

NOTRE-DAME DU T. ■

■ ST HILAIRE DU H

camouflaged with foliage, presented clear targets on the road, which itself provided guidelines for sighting and holding targets. There was no sign of the Luftwaffe and no military support for the Typhoons. It was going to be a straight fight between Panzer Division and rocket Typhoons under a scorching sun.

245 Squadron hurtled down on the leading vehicles, raking the road with cannon fire before letting go pairs of rockets and then breaking away to climb hard over the high ground of the plateau. German soldiers leapt out of trucks, taking cover in ditches as 20-mm cannon shells scissored up the road. The rolling momentum of the 1st SS Panzer Division had been reduced to a crawl as the first wave of attacking Typhoons circled round to come in again. By this time more Typhoons were arriving on the scene and pilots were forced to take a good look around before committing themselves to the dive. There was also another problem in that some Typhoons were taking different lines of approach to the target and so increasing the danger of mid-air collisions.

Neighbouring Panzer divisions began opening up, creating box-like patterns of bursting flak in a deep blue sky crowded with Typhoons on the rampage, like swarms of angry hornets. Black columns of smoke from burning vehicles spiralled upwards and rockets left vapour trails like ice cream cornets hanging suspended in the air over the target. Streams of tracer shot across the scene and down below the atmosphere was riddled with small arms fire as the 1st SS Panzer Division began fighting for its life.

Almost an hour after they had taken off, the first 245 Typhoons began arriving back over the strip in pairs. Everybody down below had been listening and waiting for them, wondering how the battle was going on. Aircraft taxied off the end of the runway and lined up behind one another to be refuelled and re-armed. The Intelligence officer ran from one Typhoon to another taking notes as a swift debriefing. Ground crews handed up mugs of tea and biscuits to their pilots, wanting to know how it was all going. Most pilots had carried out four separate attacks and had been stimulated by the action which had made them excitable and impatient to get back. They were hot and sweating and it had been a relief to open bubble hoods, unclip oxygen masks and take off helmets if only for a few minutes. Even pulling off gloves was a luxury which gave pilots a free and more comfortable feeling after having been confined in their close cockpits.

After taking off for a second series of attacks pilots could identify the target area from a considerable distance. Dark brown puffs of bursting flak left smoke trails in the sky and clouds of reddish brown smoke pulsating into the air were creeping across the landscape. The RT was jabbering away with pilots calling others to watch out or yelling when they hit a tank and saw it burst into flames. The air was full of Typhoons milling around the target and others diving down from various directions and at all angles. Those breaking away after attacks had to fly blind through thick smoke as they climbed up and over the plateau. Without knowing it, pilots were screaming low over the heads of men from the 30th US Infantry Division dug in on the slopes and surrounding countryside.

This Division had suffered heavy casualties in holding the line from north of Saint Barthélemy to south of the town of Mortain where they had been engaged in close combat with the 2nd SS (Das Reich) Panzer Division. It was the Yanks' forward units which had spotted the advancing tanks of the 1st SS Division in the mist when visibility was only about 25 yards and had sent out the call for help. Therefore, the GIs of the 'Old Hickory Division', as they were known, had every reason to be enthusiastic about the Typhoon onslaught. Sergeant Wendell Westall, from Illinois, made the point standing up in his foxhole when a Typhoon flashed overhead, 'Geeze', he said to his buddy, 'Sure as hell, that one damned nearly parted my hair!'. His chum alongside retorted, 'All I can say, bud, is those guys are sure saving our butts. I'll tell you'.

The battle was beginning to enter its crucial phase. The lead tanks of the advance had been blown sideways into the ditches and were now blocking the road, bringing the Panzer Division to a halt. Several tanks down the line were in flames and others put out of action. Many trucks and light vehicles were ablaze but Panzer gunners were still keeping up a murderous rate of fire. More Wings of Typhoons had arrived on the scene to maintain a relentless cycle of attacks. Aircraft were diving down from all quarters and it was almost impossible for gunners to hold a bead on any particular Typhoon. Conditions for those locked inside the German armour were becoming intolerable from the heat generated by the sun and the incessant firing from within. The Germans also knew that their ammunition would be in short supply if rocket firing attacks carried on at this rate.

Pilots landing back at the strip following their second wave of attacks reported that the German armoured column had been halted but there was no sign as yet that the Germans were going to call it a day. If anything, the flak was increasing in its ferocity and some pilots said that they had seen Typhoons going down and mid-air collisions when great balls of orange fire had exploded high over the target. Most of them had completed eight attacks and were returning to carry out four more. They had been airborne for two hours or more and in combat for half of that time. Some had lost their number twos but had no idea what had happened to them because of the chaos and confusion during the attacks. Waiting to be refuelled and re-armed gave them another few minutes break which they needed. Bottoms were becoming a little numb and limbs a trifle weary from yanking the brute around the sky but they were ready and eager to get back on the scene.

The battle had been raging for two-and-a-half hours by the time 245 pilots had returned to start their third wave of attacks. There were more burning tanks and vehicles than before, the smoke had got thicker and more widespread and some of the pilots sensed that at last the tide was turning. The light flak had thinned out and they could see for themselves that the column below, which stretched out down the long road, had taken terrible punishment. Panzer gunners were running short of ammunition and had been forced to curtail their rate of fire knowing that it would not be long before they would have to give up the fight. It was almost impossible and certainly suicidal for ammunition parties to get the stuff up front. They had had to withstand non-stop Typhoon rocket and cannon attacks for some three hours and still there was no sign of a break. Their only consolation had been in seeing a number of Typhoons going down but most Panzers realized by this time that their counter attack and push towards Avranches lay in ruins on the road from Saint-Barthélemy to Juvigny-le-Tertre.

There was no respite as the Typhoons continued to savage the column until the firing from the ground began to peter out. By four o'clock in the afternoon it was all over. The last remaining Typhoons flew off into the sun leaving behind them a scene of utter devastation. Many tanks were still burning, with orange flames licking into their vitals; others lay at grotesque angles in ditches or slewed across the road with turrets and tracks blown off and the long snouts of their 88-mm guns bent and twisted; hundreds of vehicles were burned out skeletons and fresh fires from the last attacks were pumping up billowing smoke into a great pall of black cloud which hung menacingly over the area.

121 Wing Typhoons landed at intervals on the sunbaked strip of Le Fresne Camilly creating clouds of dust as pilots taxied slowly into dispersals. The Americans had already been on the line congratulating and thanking the Wing 'for saving their butts' and word had

got around. Ground crews were in good form and feeling chipper about the news as they stood waiting and looking out for their own particular Typhoon. Usually, 245 Squadron landed and taxied in '*en masse*' but this time machines were arriving in pairs and at intervals. Pilots were tired and although they responded to the enthusiasm of their crews, they weren't particularly looking forward to having to go over to Intelligence for a debriefing session.

Nobody said very much as they waited anxiously for others to arrive. As time went on, the CO looked at his watch and said that they had better get going. A number were still missing including Bob Lee, Jeff Jeffries, Roly Temple and Benny Bennet and by normal standards the Squadron looked 'very thin on the ground' when pilots went wearily into the Intelligence tent to give their accounts of the last show and make their claims.

After the debriefing they returned to the log table to relax, knowing that they had done a good job and wanting to forget about it. It was still hot in the sun and they sat around not saying much, only casting an eye at anybody appearing through the gap in the hedge. When Benny Bennet turned up they wanted to know where he had been. Looking a bit sheepish, he said that he was a little confused after the last attack and his engine sounded a bit 'duff' so he had plonked his aircraft down on the nearest American strip and had a good time. In other words, they thought, Benny had got himself lost—the stupid bastard!

Chapter 7

Aftermath

It soon became apparent that those missing weren't going to turn up and they had either 'bought it' or force-landed somewhere. Most survivors were conscious that the Squadron had lost a third or more of its total strength and realized that they had been bloody lucky to get away with it themselves. Some of the new pilots thought that the Squadron would be put on rest after such losses but the 'old hands' ignored such comments and said nothing. The Mortain battle, as far as they were concerned, had been 'just another show' and they knew perfectly well that the Squadron would be operational as from first light. They were certain that their Squadron commander, Jack Collins, would ensure that 245 would be the first Squadron in the Wing to be airborne on the early show particularly after what had happened today.

Extra booze was handed out in the mess tents at dinner, not enough for a Squadron piss-up, but sufficient to 'iron out a few creases' after at least three hours in the saddle! Later, Wing Commanders Tim Morice and Charles Green, who were in tremendous form, called in at the log table just before dusk. 'You know, chaps,' Green said quietly, 'this has been THE DAY OF THE TYPHOON and no bastard can take it away from us'.

Although no official figures had come through, Green reckoned that well over 150 tanks had either gone up as 'flamers' or been knocked out, apart from hundreds of supporting vehicles which had been left as charred hulks. The Panzer Division, he said, which was to have been the spearhead of the German counter attack in the drive to Avranches had been paralysed and then destroyed. It had been a splendid show on everyone's part and now was the time, he suggested, for congratulations all round. Both men were hugely enjoying themselves, especially Tim Morice who had obviously had a few nips beforehand. Tim stood there, elegant as ever, in battledress and spotted scarf, smoking a cigarette, beaming at everybody and wrinkling up his eyes from the rays of a dying sun. Occasionally his gravelly soft spoken voice would command attention and he would have all the pilots laughing. Green, by contrast, some fifteen years Tim's junior, was the big, tough and aggressive Wing leader whose power and vitality was reflected in his large dark brown eyes which had a kind of luminosity about them. Nobody in the company of these two men that night could have failed to appreciate that they made a great team.

It was getting cold outside and Warrant Officer Paddy Gray had had a busier day than most. Apart from flying number two to Charles Green on the recce he had flown four sorties and made sixteen attacks on Panzer armour. As soon as Morice and Green had departed he turned to his chum Bob Stanford and said, 'Let's go inside for a game of crib, shall we?'

On the following day it was announced that rocket Typhoons of the Second Tactical Air Force had fought a major battle against German tanks. The communiqué went on to say that 162 Panzer tanks had either been destroyed or put out of action, 81 completely, 54 seriously damaged and 26 had gone up in flames.

The day of 7 August had been a fairly hairy one for the Wing but for the inhabitants of Mortain the past 48 hours had been a terrifying experience. The vast majority had fled the town and disappeared into the countryside on Sunday 6 August, before German and American artillery had pounded it into ruins. About sixty of them had been killed in the process and many of those hiding in the fields found themselves in the middle of battles. The young ladies of L' Ecole du Sacré-Coeur de Mortain who had camped out in a ditch, for example, had no idea that they had spent the nights of August 6th and 7th in the middle of a Battery of the 2nd SS (Das Reich) Panzer Division! Despite the battle life went on and during the Typhoon attacks Doctor Giles Buisson delivered five babies in the fields. His young brother had managed to get into the ruins of the town to find a GI mortar platoon 'brewing up' in the cellar of their house. The American occupation, however, was short lived because the Germans retook the town a couple of days later.

In the early morning of 8 August, 245 Squadron was in action again—as the 'old hands' had predicted on the previous evening after the Mortain show. This time the Squadron was back on its old familiar battleground attacking SS Panzer formations a few miles south of Caen. Squadron Leader Jack Collins led the attack as they dived on a Panzer HQ through the usual layers of flak. He was well aware that his Squadron was severely depleted when he took off and that he couldn't afford to lose many more pilots without having 'to come out of the line'. Group had promised a batch of replacement pilots to fill the gap but he knew that it would take time for those chaps to get 'clued up'.

The replacements arrived while the Squadron was airborne; they piled out of a Dakota, some of them in their best uniforms. Having reported to the HQ area, at the back end of the strip and signed in, they were driven across to the Squadron Flights tent. It was empty and having dumped their bags they stood there wondering what the hell was going on. Ground crews in the vicinity couldn't believe their eyes, seeing a bunch of Flight Lieutenants and South African officers all dressed up.

Captain Cook, a South African, called out to a Corporal fitter working on a nearby Typhoon and asked him for the officers' mess. The Corporal waved his spanner towards a tent in the middle of the field and ducked down behind his engine. Cook tried again and this time asked where their quarters were. A Leading Aircraftsman rigger pointed to a gap in the hedge and said, 'Through there'. Cook was astonished that the man hadn't even called him 'Sir' or offered to look after them.

The replacements party had been unlucky to find nobody around. The Squadron adjutant, Flying Officer Tommy Thomson, was somewhere over in HQ and the remnants of 245 pilots were taking it easy in their tents. It was natural for the new pilots to have assumed that somebody from the Squadron would be there to receive them. Warrant Officer Paddy Gray didn't appear exactly enthusiastic when one of the Flight Lieutenants came into the tent, dumped his bags on Stanford's bed and asked him which tent was his. Paddy was tempted to tell him to go over to stores, sign for one and pitch it his bloody self but Tommy Thomson, the adjutant, arrived at that minute and took him away.

Sprog Flight Lieutenants joining the Squadron usually ruffled Paddy a little. As far as he was concerned they were 'needle, ball and airspeed merchants' who had opted out to instruct rather than get stuck into the war. He had been on one of the first pilot training courses to be held in the southern states of America. The USA had been a neutral country then and had to abide by the rules governing neutrality. British cadets wore KDs (khaki drills) and sported only their blue forage caps with white flashes and black ties as part of their RAF uniform. Their flying instructors were civilian pilots and upon graduation the British cadets automatically became Second Lieutenants in the United States Air Force as there were no non-commissioned pilots in the USAF. The training programme was extremely rigid, being a full US officers' graduation course, and upon completion the RAF offered them commissions if they remained behind as RAF instructors. Thus Paddy could have stayed on the station, living off the fat of the land and risen to the rank of Flight Lieutenant in due course without any problems, but that wasn't his style. The rank of Sergeant Pilot on a Fighter Squadron based back in southern England was much more to his liking! Perhaps he was feeling a bit 'up tight' after the Mortain show but he knew that he had been rather rude and short to some of the new arrivals, only waiting for one of them to pull rank or say something out of turn. Sitting on his camp bed, Paddy stared at the kit which one of them had left on Bob Stanford's bed, without asking, and in a fit of temper carted it out and dropped the lot alongside the hedge.

The South Africans, Captain Cook and Lieutenants Cluelow and Gale, in their brown uniforms with shiny pips, eventually got themselves organized and carried their gear into tents. They looked and sounded an odd trio; Cook was short and wiry; Gale stood six feet four inches and Cluelow was somewhere in between. Their South African accents were pronounced as they shouted across to one another and acted as if they had taken the place over. Paddy saw a look of resigned amazement on Dud Nott's face, and heard him say, 'Well—er. I suppose so. Yes, you could be right', to a barrage of questions from little Cook who had him cornered and was trying to pump him for the gen.

Paddy was beginning to think that the new brigade were all officers when he caught sight of a Flight Sergeant, sitting on his kit bag beside the log table smoking a cigarette and apparently oblivious to the hectic activities going on around him. He was small, compact and had light blue eyes and sandy hair. Paddy was about to go over and have a word with him when Stanford, Ches West, Benny Bennet and Terry Gray appeared through the gap in the hedge. They had just been debriefed after rocketing an SS headquarters south of Caen. Stanford strode over to his tent and asked his friend Paddy Gray what the hell was going on.

Not since several weeks before D-Day had the Squadron received such an influx of pilots and even then, when based on home territory, it had taken some time before Squadron atmosphere returned to normal. Pilots accepted that losses had to be replaced and that there would always be new faces suddenly appearing within their tightly knit group. This had been going on for a considerable period and they were acclimatized to the process but being confronted by a whole mob of fresh talent in one go was a little hard to digest in their present circumstances.

It was particularly difficult for those NCO pilots, who were experienced operators, not to resent sprog officers who hadn't been on ops at all. This feeling was enhanced by the aggressive behaviour of some officers who suddenly found themselves in the front line and adopted a spirit of bravado in order to boost their confidence. An experienced Squadron pilot, for example, wasn't particularly interested in hearing how many times they had tried desperately hard to get a squadron posting and how thrilled they were at having finally made it!

There had been talk amongst the 'old hands' that Jack Collins himself and Jimmy Wilson, B Flight commander, were due to be sent home as 'tour expired'. Jack was on his second tour of operations and had constantly been in action leading the Squadron for some eighteen months. They recognized that he would be leaving a large gap when he left but there was no sense in their being concerned about it.

Unlike Dud Nott, Maxie Maxwell, Terry Gray and a few others, who had served in 245 under Squadron Leader Hordern, Bob Stanford's total ops career had revolved around Collins whom he regarded as the absolute lynch pin of the Squadron. Any Squadron commander to a young man like Flight Sergeant Bob Stanford was a god-like figure but Jack, in his quiet way, had encouraged Stanford and given him confidence from the time he did his very first op. The boys occasionally talked about Jack's leadership, usually when they were arguing amongst themselves and proving to one another that 245 was the best rocket Typhoon Squadron in Normandy. Inevitably, they agreed that it was Jack Collins and his personal example which had made the Squadron.

Jeff Jeffries was one of the first of the missing chaps to arrive back on the strip after the Mortain show. He jumped out of the back of an American truck with sticking plaster all over his face and crinkling up his little Welsh beady eyes. Jeff had crash landed out in the countryside and been picked up by the Yanks who gave him a great time. One of his first comments was that he had been fed on a diet of orange juice and ice cream, which made everyone pretty mad, especially as their staple diet was still tinned stew and hard tack enlivened only through the activities of Terry Gray and his ability to procure more attractive fodder. Fortunately, Jeff had only sustained facial scratches which hadn't bothered him as he was a tough little Welshman. He had come from a mining valley and had a pronounced accent, sprinkled liberally with 'is it's', 'fair do's' and odd remarks like, 'down I go then, see!'. He said that he would have been back sooner but the Americans had insisted on 'getting him back in shape' before letting him go.

Flight Lieutenant Robert Lee's experience was quite different. He had only been on the Squadron for about three months, having joined at Holmsley South a few weeks before D-Day, when he was shot down. Bob was a big man, weighing over fifteen stone, with a round red face and a small gingery moustache. The boys used to call him 'the Colonel' because of his somewhat Blimpish looks and rather off-hand and slightly pompous manner. He and his cronies had formed a bridge school playing innumerable rubbers behind the closed flaps of his tent which he designated 'out of bounds' to intruders.

Lee's aircraft was damaged by flak when he dived on the Panzer tanks at Mortain. He was severely injured and losing blood but somehow managed to pull out of the dive and veer away from the target area. After the explosion when the flak hit him, he had only seconds in which to regain control of his aircraft and somehow get down. He passed out as the ground came rushing up at him, losing control of his Typhoon which flicked over onto its back and dived into the ground inverted. The one-and-a-half ton Sabre engine buried itself several feet down into the earth leaving Lee unconscious and hanging upside down in his straps.

Momentarily he came to, managed to pull out his harness pin and dropped head first into the hole in the ground made by his aircraft. He had crashed in no-man's-land between the German and American armies and there was nobody around to find him. Lee lay crumpled up, bleeding from his wounds, and with hot oil dripping onto his back and burning his skin. From time to time he would partially regain consciousness, experiencing waves of nausea and pain, before drifting off again into oblivion. He had no sense of time and only craved for a drink. He couldn't tell whether it was night or day lying buried alive, compressed and trapped under his cockpit and only knew that he must have been down there for a very long time. He had nothing to revive him and relief from physical pain came only when he fainted. Vaguely, he was aware that if help didn't arrive he would surely die.

Lee had been lying, caked with oil, excreta and blood for a couple of days or more when he heard voices which even in his present state he recognized as being German. Some soldiers wandering about the area had come across the wreckage of Lee's Typhoon with its tail sticking up in the air and the rest of it buried in the ground. They thought that nobody could possibly be alive down there and setting up some ration cans on the fuselage began potting away at them for a bit of sport. Bob Lee collected some of their rifle bullets in his legs but he couldn't call out because his throat was too constricted and he was so weak.

Having had their fun, the Germans disappeared and Lee continued to hover between life and death. However, he had one great advantage, apart from his will to survive. He was a big man carrying surplus fat and liquid which kept him alive for five days and nights although he was so badly wounded. Sheer courage and a ruthless determination not to give up prevented him from sinking into the abyss while his body shed over six stones.

An American unit which was clearing the battlefield eventually discovered him. They saw the Typhoon and brought one of their big machines to pull it out of the ground thinking that nobody could possibly be alive in it. To their horror they saw the emaciated form of Bob Lee barely alive and unconscious in the bottom of the hole. Their medics saved his life although he was crippled in both legs from bullet wounds. Bob Lee's war was over but for his courage in staying alive in the most appalling circumstances he was awarded the DFC.

*　　　　　*　　　　　*

The Squadron had now been operating from Le Fresne Camilly for over six weeks and life on the strip, except for the excitement of ops, had been boring and uncomfortable. Having to wear the same clothes for days on end and eat field rations had become a trifle nauseating and there had been little else to do but get into sleeping bags before it got dark. The Mortain show had provided the Squadron with an excuse for a good piss-up but even that had fallen rather flat because pilots were tired and physically exhausted after the battle. It was going to take a little time for the Squadron to adjust itself and absorb the new blood. The CO, Jack Collins, had plenty on his mind knowing that it was impossible for him to find opportunities to give the sprog pilots a chance to get settled in from a flying point of view. He had never been one to send chaps up who weren't ready for ops but now he had no choice and they would just have to take their chance.

The first casualty happened shortly after their arrival. Stanford had returned after rocketing an SS headquarters, south of Caen, and noticing somebody's kit parked outside his tent had asked his chum Paddy Gray what it was all about. Paddy had no time to explain because he was called out on another show. When Paddy got back about an hour later he told Stanford that the chap who had left the gear outside wouldn't be needing it. 'He's just bought it', he said, 'I saw him go in'.

They both sat on the edge of their camp beds without saying anything. Paddy. as usual after a show, rolled back the cuffs of his battledress blouse, took his silver cigarette case out of his breast pocket and snapped it open. Carefully studying its contents he selected a fag and rolled the butt around in his mouth before lighting it. Inhaling tobacco smoke, he stared down at his flying boots with a fixed expression on his face. Meanwhile, Bob reflected that the poor sod who had bought it had only been on the strip for about an hour before he got his lot and that was tough. He had never set eyes on the man so there was no point in concerning himself about it. Yet, it gave him a strange pleasure to think that he had been able to survive for so long. He accepted that he had had more than his fair share of luck but there was more to it than that, he thought.

On the following morning the Squadron was briefed to give close support to our forward troops, who were having problems with Panzer tanks, south of Caen. There was a good deal of excitement in the Intelligence tent because of the successful advance of the 12th US Army Group which had taken Le Mans. The American line appeared to be bulging right across the southern sector making the British effort look very feeble by comparison.

Looking at the maps, however, gave everybody confidence that momentous things were about to happen and that the war was at last going our way. The stalemate had been a long drawn-out affair and it was a relief to see how much French ground was now in Allied hands. It wouldn't be long they thought, before they would be moving out of Le Fresne to a proper airfield and have a chance of seeing a bit of French life. The rate the Americans were going made Paris seem a distinct possibility!

After the show, Jimmy Wilson was told to pack up and go home. As usual, in these matters, the news came as a complete surprise especially as the Squadron was in a fairly fragile state after recent casualties. But there was nothing he could do about it and he was 'tour expired' and officially on rest. The tallish, slim, quietly spoken Edinburgh Scot who had been B Flight commander was replaced by Flight Lieutenant Archie Lamb who had just arrived on the strip having been with another Typhoon Squadron for some time.

245 Squadron lost one Scot but picked up another in Flight Sergeant Jock Darlington who had arrived with the first of the new mob. Jock came from Gartcosh, a small mining town on the outskirts of Glasgow and was obviously a tough little character. He told the boys bluntly, in his strong Glaswegian accent, that he was married with two 'bairns'. This rather shattered them and they couldn't understand why he should have volunteered for this kind of job or even gone into the Forces at all because mining was a reserved occupation. Jock said quite simply that he had always wanted to fly and this was his only chance. His parents had agreed to look after his family so he took the opportunity.

Benny Bennet was still shaking his head incredulously thinking over what Jock had said when he was called over to Flights together with Jock. Jack Collins told him that some replacement aircraft had arrived and needed air testing. 'You can take Flight Sergeant Darlington with you, Benny', he said, 'and give him some formation practice. Show him around the lines, will you? But no shoot ups, understand!'. This delighted Benny and when he got back to the tents he spread his map out over the log table and began explaining to Jock where they would go. Ches West ambled up behind them and stood there listening, chewing gum and grinning. He tapped Darlington on the shoulder, 'Jesus, man', he said, 'you going with him?', Jock nodded, 'Aw shit', Ches drawled, 'you're mad, Benny can't even find his way across Toronto, can you Benny?'.

In the event, Jock was given an extensive tour of the lines and his first introduction to flak when Benny got himself a little confused in the area of Vire just north of Mortain. Later in the afternoon of 11 August, the Squadron took off on an armed recce led by the CO. The day was sunny and warm and Bob Stanford sat outside his tent writing a letter home. These letters were getting a little difficult because he hadn't been anywhere recently and he obviously couldn't say much about the flying. He heard the Squadron coming back into the circuit and thought no more about it until Dud Nott came running in through the gap in the hedge. 'Jack's had it', Dud yelled, before disappearing out again.

At first, Stanford couldn't believe it feeling sure that he must have misunderstood Dud but when he hurried over to Flights he found that it was true. Jack Collins was dead. The Squadron had been crossing out over the lines when Jack's aircraft caught fire and he immediately baled out. His parachute hit the tailplane and became entangled around it and down he went. The irony of it all became clear afterwards. Jack had been 'screened', or taken off ops, before the show but had insisted on leading the Squadron for the last time. Those who went with him couldn't understand why his engine should have caught fire and exploded into flames or why his parachute should have caught the tailplane—it just seemed that his luck had run out.

Jack's death, particularly in view of the circumstances, came as a shock to all those on the strip who had known him well. He should have been on his way back to Blighty and this made it even more difficult to swallow. It marked the end of an era for 245 Squadron. The 'old hands' had known that Jack would be shortly departing the scene because he was overdue for a rest but to go out in that way was surely bloody hard lines.

The Squadron, for the time being, was rudderless and the question in most peoples' minds was who would be coming in to replace Jack. Some of them, like Stanford, couldn't imagine how anybody could possibly take over from Jack Collins. They talked about it amongst themselves knowing that it was naive to even discuss such matters but they couldn't help themselves. They had to get it out of their systems and when they finally realized that Jack would have left anyway they tried to forget it.

But it wasn't so easy because the continuity of Squadron leadership had disappeared almost overnight. 245 was now in the hands of Ace Miron, who had only recently been leading a Flight, and the unknown Archie Lamb, until a new boss arrived. Gray and Stanford talked about it later that evening in the tent before starting a game of crib. Gray's view was that Jack had been a nice chap and a good leader but life had to go on. As far as Miron and Lamb were concerned, he said that they would have to take their fingers out and do their job in much the same way as he had to do his. And that was all there was to it.

Chapter 8

Holocaust in the Falaise Gap

The influx of fresh blood began to pump new life into the Squadron although some of the 'old hands' adopted a wait-and-see attitude keeping themselves to themselves. Replacement pilots had never been spontaneously accepted until they had proved themselves and it was natural for the fraternity to stand back and watch points. The vitality and exuberance displayed by sprog pilots on the ground counted for nothing until they had made the grade in the air.

The new chaps didn't have to wait long before they were airborne on armed recces covering the Falaise, Argentan and Alencon area where the military situation was exploding. The 15th US Corps were driving north towards Argentan and the First Canadian Army was about to put in a major attack down the road towards Falaise. Simultaneously the British Second Army was advancing across a broad front south of a line between Bayeux and Caen.

The military plan, which could be seen clearly on maps in Intelligence, was to bottle up the German 7th Army and the 5th Panzer Army and use air power to destroy them before they could withdraw across the River Seine. This meant closing the gap between Falaise and Argentan thereby encircling the Germans on all fronts. If the brown jobs were successful then there would be plenty of business around for rocket Typhoon squadrons.

The Intelligence officer had explained that Typhoon rocket attacks on German armour at Mortain had not only prevented Panzer divisions breaking through towards Avranches but had helped the Americans to contain Panzer armies in the Mortain area.

Holding German armour at Mortain, he said, had been a key factor in the plan to trap German forces in the Falaise pocket. In the five days since they had attacked Panzer tanks at Mortain, the Intelligence officer and his aides had been frantically busy amending battle lines, moving them forward at an astonishing rate. It became obvious from the maps that the war in Normandy, which had been festering for over eight weeks, had suddenly erupted on the most gigantic scale. When the Canadians and Poles met up with the Americans and sealed the Falaise gap the stage was set for the biggest aerial massacre of German armies in the war to date.

The Squadron was suddenly called over to Intelligence and word got around that it was going to be a Wing show. Flight Lieutenant Ace Miron, acting as Squadron commander, drove the boys across in the jeep feeling rather chuffed with himself in his new role. Ace was a short, stubby French Canadian with a round face, sparse hair and little slitty eyes and had a reputation of being rather a madcap. He had taken over A Flight some weeks previously after Sam Slaney had gone down.

The Intelligence tent was humming with excitement, as it had been before the Mortain show, and when 245 entered many pilots cast an enquiring eye to see who was in command of the Squadron. There was always a natural curiosity amongst pilots to find out what was going on and today was no exception, but they didn't learn anything because Ace was only standing in.

They could see by the expression on the Wing leader's face that something big was afoot and they waited impatiently for him to get going. But first, the Intelligence officer filled in the background to the military situation in the Falaise-Argentan area where, he said, some six Panzer and SS divisions, and over 100,000 Germans were caught in the trap. Slowly and methodically he pointed to the details on the map and showed his audience the location of the pocket and the forward positions of Allied troops.

Wing Commander Charles Green made no bones about the fact that this was going to be the biggest show of their lives. He emphasized that the job for the Typhoons was to annihilate the German armies which were totally surrounded and there for the picking. He told pilots that squadrons would operate independently and maintain a cycle of attacks until the job was done. Once again, he warned them to keep a good look out to avoid mid-air collisions. 'Everybody is going to have a go at this lot', he said.

Wing Commander Tim Morice, the airfield commander, had already driven around the strip talking to his men in groups and giving them the news of the big break-through and the job that lay ahead for the Wings' Typhoons. He told them that this was their big chance to help in the destruction of whole German armies and so shorten the duration of the war. The Wing Commander always kept his men in touch with events and he did so in his own inimitable way by giving them the serious stuff and then spicing it with quips and gestures which they loved.

245 Pilots were in top form as they left the Intelligence tent and drove over to dispersals. The thought of attacking such a massive target for the first time excited them and they joked about it, saying that even Benny Bennet couldn't miss the whole bloody German Army! When they got out of the jeep they could see ground crews working furiously on all the Squadron's aircraft and it reminded them of Mortain. This time, however, they would have a rest between attacks while pilots from other squadrons took over. There was no need to consult maps because the area was a familiar Squadron battleground over which they had flown many armed recces looking for something to shoot up. But today they wouldn't have that problem!

Stanford had his usual pee against the tailplane and gave Spike Hughes, who was flying his number two, a thumbs up sign. He couldn't help looking across at the empty space where Jack Collins aircraft would have been and feeling a stab of sadness thinking how much Jack would have enjoyed leading this show. Glancing up at the weather and seeing a blue sky broken only here and there by a few chunky cumulus clouds he wondered how the Germans must be feeling knowing what was about to happen.

About fifteen minutes after take-off the Squadron was circling the Falaise area looking down on an incredible scene. The whole countryside was littered with tanks, vehicles and trucks jamming roads and country lanes. On some long sections of roads vehicles appeared to be head-to-tail and there was no doubt in anybody's minds that masses of armour and infantry were hiding under cover of trees and foliage. Typhoons from other wings were fast arriving on the scene and as the first waves started their attacks the Germans opened fire.

Then began the biggest shoot-up ever experienced by a rocket Typhoon pilot. The Germans who had desperately tried to escape across the Seine had taken over any transport that they could lay their hands on including horse-drawn wagons and carts. Targets were lined up in all directions as the Typhoons commenced their carnage. There was no escape for the Germans because Allied forces were massed around them on all sides and neither was there any respite from continuous air attacks. All they could do was to keep firing or take cover.

Hundreds of tanks and trucks were burning furiously as the Typhoons maintained their strikes and a great blanket of smoke hung over the pocket. Some pilots returning to base reported that they had encountered little flak, usually a sign that the Germans were either conserving ammunition or running short of it, but others said that the flak had been intense and so it went on. At the end of the day the countryside from Flers to Falaise and Domfront across to Argentan was riddled with bonfires and burned out hulks of vehicles but the battle was far from over and the Germans knew that the Typhoons would be back early in the morning.

It had been a highly productive day for rocket Typhoon Squadrons and 245 was no exception. All pilots, including the new chaps, had recorded 'good bags' and there was a bubbly atmosphere around the log table that evening. For those who had experienced their first real crunch of air-to-ground warfare it had been a splendid day and they were cock-a-hoop. Nobody had gone down and they were all conscious that the Squadron had performed well and had done a good job. Captain Cook was now 'Cookie', Lieutenant Cluelow, 'Clueless', and that long runner bean Gale was naturally 'Shorty'. They had done their stuff and so had little Jock Darlington and others. The Squadron was now back in business as a team and had recovered from its hang-over after the Mortain battle and the loss of Jack Collins.

But Bob Stanford wasn't feeling entirely chipper when he set up the cribbage board later that evening for the usual nightly session. His chum Paddy Gray was still outside the tent and he could hear him laughing and joking with Benny Bennet about Spike Hughes. Spike didn't drink and Dud Nott, Maxie Maxwell and a few others had held him down and stuffed a few tots of whisky down his throat for a prank. Bob thought it was a daft thing to do and told Paddy so when he came in but Paddy ignored him. He couldn't let the matter rest, saying that Spike was a damned nice chap and Dud and Co were nothing but a bunch of hooligans. When Paddy laughed at him he got up and walked out of the tent and marched down the cornfield in an attempt to cool off. It was getting dark and the air was soft and fragrant but he was too steamed-up inside to relax. He had to admit to himself, as he made his way through the long corn, that he wasn't mad with his chum or really about the Spike Hughes episode for that matter, but something had got into him to make him feel tense.

Then he remembered his last trip over Falaise. He had fired all his rockets and was using up his cannon shells flying quite low and pumping them into a line of vehicles on a country road and as he pulled back on the stick, looking behind him, he caught a glimpse of those poor bloody horses. It had sickened him at the time and made him feel that he never ever wanted to do that again. He couldn't care less about killing Germans but horses were different somehow. He knew that he was being a fool and a clot but it really had upset him.

The Squadron was taken aback when pilots were told that there would be a memorial service for Squadron Leader Jack Collins. It seemed a bit odd that anybody should have gone along with the idea but nevertheless it was to be held in the early evening on the strip. Pilots passed on the information that there was to be some kind of service for Jack but that was all. Personal views on the matter were not discussed openly and although there was no compunction to attend, the vast majority made their way across the strip at the appointed hour. The general feeling was to go and get it over with and not talk about it.

Any feelings concerning Jack were kept tightly under control during the service. Somehow, Doc Saunders who was also a Welsh organist, had managed to get hold of an ancient harmonium which he played with great skill. Hymns were sung and the Padre said some nice things about Jack while Squadron pilots avoided looking at one another and maintained blank expressions as if trying to insulate themselves from their emotions. It was a sad occasion and one which they had tried to put out of their minds.

It was more difficult for Tommy Thomson, the Squadron adjutant, who had worked so closely with Jack for a long period, and also for Doc Saunders. The Doc, being Welsh, was a bit emotional and a very kind man. He had set up a children's clinic in Le Fresne Camilly which had become a focal point for parents throughout the area. This act had not only helped the sick kids but was a marvellous piece of public relations for the Allies until the medical establishment stepped in to curtail the use of drugs for these purposes.

Pilots returned to their tents after the service talking about other things. They had heard that Flight Lieutenant Paddy Moore, from one of the sister squadrons, had been told over the RT while he was on a show that he was to be promoted Squadron Leader and would take over 245. Shortly after he landed, Paddy had collapsed and had to be wheeled off by the medics so the Squadron was still without a CO.

After the service some of the chaps were in the mood for a piss-up but there wasn't enough booze on the premises so they decided to go off on a recce after dinner. Gray and Stanford cooked up an egg-and-potato mixture which they spooned out of billy-cans. A bar of chocolate made an excellent sweet washed down with mugs of compo tea. As it was a fine evening they meandered down to the village and called in at the farmhouse to collect their washing and pick up any eggs that were going.

The farmer, whom they hadn't met before, was in the kitchen and he stood up when they came in and solemnly shook hands before disappearing outside. His wife, Louise, was obviously in a very cheerful mood and talked excitedly about the war at last moving away from them. She told them that she had walked all the way up to Brettville to meet a friend of hers, who lived in a little cottage opposite the church, and her friend had given her the good news.

She had just handed over their washing, all beautifully pressed, when her husband returned, carefully carrying a dusty old bottle. Reverently, he placed it on the kitchen table and gently extracted the cork, rubbing it in his huge hairy hands and sniffing it. He told them in a most serious voice that this would be the finest Calvados that they would ever drink in their lives.

Stanford hated the stuff and only drank it because he didn't want other chaps to think that he couldn't take his booze. When they had gone into the cafe at St Aubin after the swimming fiasco he had managed to secretly get rid of some of his into a flower pot and he looked around the farm kitchen to find a suitable receptable but there was nothing. Much to his horror, the farmer began to pour liberal quantities of the stuff into mugs, taking extreme care not to spill the minutest drop.

They could both see that this was obviously going to be a special occasion because grandfather staggered out of his rocking chair from a shadowy kitchen corner and came up to the table rubbing his hands. The farmer raised his mug and they all drank to Normandy and 'down with the Boche'. Stanford sipped his at first and found it smoother and less fiery than previous Calvados although it had a big message when it reached the lower echelons of his stomach. After a second refill he was able to take small swallows and found that he had little difficulty in speaking fluent French. It seemed to bubble out of him as he put his arms around Louise and her husband cuddling them. 'Nos amis', he said to Paddy, 'Vive La Normandie, Vive La France. Up les Boches—right up!'.

Both of them felt terrific when they left the farm with Bob Stanford still singing snatches of the song '*J'attendrai*' and weaving about a little in the process. 'It's OK for you, Paddy', he said, 'you're only carrying the bloody washing. But I've got the eggs!'. The rich smell of farmyard manure was overpowering as they entered the lane leading up to the strip and Bob stopped to light his pipe. He managed to place the eggs on the ground quite safely and sat down among the brambles. 'You know something, Paddy', he muttered as he lit up, 'it's been a bloody marvellous evening, after all'.

When they got back to the tent it was getting dark and the air was cold and clammy. There was only one thing to do and that was to pull on extra socks and a jersey and wriggle into sleeping bags using flying jackets as eiderdowns. Neither of them was in the mental condition or the mood to play the customary game of cribbage so they lay there talking.

Bob had been upset by Jack's memorial service and had found it difficult to 'put a face on it' with pictures of Jack floating across his mind. He thought that some of the other chaps might have felt as he did but nobody gave any indication. He wasn't going to admit any sign of weakness on his part to Paddy but he said quite nonchalantly that he didn't think that the memorial service should have taken place at all and it was a mistake. Paddy hadn't replied and obviously didn't want to talk about it. Bob knew him too well not to recognize the symptoms and had long since realized that he was an old softy under that rugged and assured exterior. Paddy put on an act just like the others and although they had been chums since well before D-Day neither of them had ever had really serious discussions about anything.

Lying there, half awake, listening to the distant rumble of gunfire, Bob thought it was probably better that way because there was no future in becoming interested in anything. Even the serious business of flying Typhoons on ops rarely came up in conversation because 'talking shop', as it was called, was generally frowned upon. Only the funny or stupid things that happened during flying were bandied about because anything was good for a laugh.

It was rare for Bob Stanford to turn things over in his mind before going to sleep. Normally, he sank straight into oblivion but that evening he was restless and couldn't switch off. The waxy smell from the candle stub, which Paddy had blown out, still lingered in the tent and its walls were wet with dew. The air was cold and he pulled his flying jacket over his head and tried to doze off but couldn't.

When he burped, his breath smelt of stale Calvados, which was quite revolting under the cover of his jacket and forced him to stick his head out in the open. His mouth was dry and he was thirsty but he

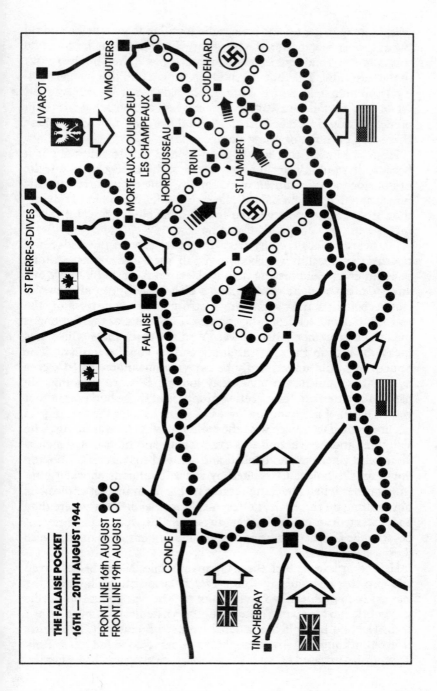

THE FALAISE POCKET
16TH — 20TH AUGUST 1944

FRONT LINE 16th AUGUST ●●●
FRONT LINE 19th AUGUST ○○○

LIVAROT

VIMOUTIERS

COUDEHARD

ST PIERRE-S-DIVES

MORTEAUX-COULIBOEUF

LES CHAMPEAUX

HORDOUSSEAU

TRUN

ST LAMBERT

FALAISE

CONDE

TINCHEBRAY

wasn't going to get up and unlace the tent flap to go outside and fill his mug with water from the jerry-can. The only thing he could do was to lie there and wait for sleep to catch up with him but he wasn't in the least tired. The thought suddenly struck him that he had absolutely nothing to look forward to. In the old days at West Hampnett when they got ten days leave every six weeks he knew that with a bit of luck he would soon be back in his local haunts. But stuck out here there was no hope of going home.

He told himself that it was plain bloody daft to think about it because it wouldn't get him anywhere so he tried to look on the bright side to make himself more cheerful; the chaps were a terrific bunch and that was no bullshit; he enjoyed the excitement of flying, the thing that he most wanted to do, so he couldn't really expect much more out of life if he was honest.

He heard voices coming from the other side of the hedge and realized that the shift was about to run up the Sabre engines. After a series of cracks and hissing noises, the aircraft blasted into life one after another and he could picture bleary-eyed ground crews in closed cockpits staring at glowing instruments and appreciating the warmth blown back from the engines. The sound of the Typhoons made him remember that he wasn't on the early show which was lucky for him in the circumstances and he could sleep late. The Squadron would undoubtedly be carrying out more armed recces over Falaise and he wasn't exactly looking forward to going. He hadn't forgotten catching fleeting glimpses of those horses, but that was only part of it. Flying low over Falaise he had, for the first time in his life, come fact to face with the reality of what he was doing. The slaughter and destruction was everywhere and he had had a clear view of it whenever he banked and weaved his aircraft. Looking down on the holocaust created by other Typhoons shocked him. Many times when attacking targets he had seen instant explosions but nothing on this scale, not even at Saint-Barthélemy where they had rocketed an entire Panzer division. That had been different because the Germans were advancing and full of fight but at Falaise they were helpless.

He knew perfectly well those German Armies had to be destroyed and also that he would be flying over Falaise again. Therefore, he was crazy to even think about it. Not that he was going soft but he was entitled to his own private thoughts particularly at what he had seen. He told himself that a sensitive person couldn't help being affected in some way by these things. He had been sad when Roly Temple disappeared because Roly was a nice chap and had a family.

He felt more so about Jack Collins and was glad that he hadn't been up there and seen him go down.

Jack had always looked after his NCO pilots and made them an integral part of the team and Bob wondered whether the new CO would do the same. It mattered a great deal to him because he had been on the Squadron for just over a year and was one of the 'old hands'. Only he, Terry Gray and Tubby Sago were left now from the NCOs who were on the Squadron when he joined. Dud Nott, who would have made it four, had been commissioned and the rest had either 'bought it' or been posted.

He pondered over the question of survival and wondered why the remnants of the old brigade had come through. His chum Paddy thought that experience had much to do with it. Being able to keep one's eye on the target in the dive and, at the same time seeing where the flak was coming from, was important, Paddy had said, and also watching points when breaking away from the target. Paddy was right, of course, but he thought there was much more to it than that, including having more than one's fair share of luck.

He had never had any doubt that he would come through. The fact that, so far, he had been a survivor gave him confidence and convinced him that he was a bloody good pilot and a lucky one. If he hadn't thought that way he couldn't possibly have stayed the course. He had learned over the past year to take each day as it came and tried hard not to look forward to anything, which sometimes had been difficult because of his natural enthusiasm for life and living.

On some occasions when he had had a particularly narrow squeak and nearly 'bought it' he was forced to control himself. During those terrifying seconds his heart raced madly and his body was rigid until he was able to breathe out and feel the tension flowing out of his system. Fortunately, it didn't often happen and he was able to absorb this kind of punishment without worrying about it too much. But there were odd times when his mind and body staged a minor revolt before he was about to take-off on an especially sticky show. It seemed as if his brain and working parts demanded an explanation of why they were about to be subjected to another boiling-up session.

This took the form of a nagging desire to pull out prior to a sticky op and he knew immediately that he was at the crossroads. Any attempt on his part to find an excuse would be regarded by the others as 'chickening out' and he was well aware that if he did it once then he would undoubtedly do it again and that would be the finish of him. It was possible to 'bale out' of an op without too much trouble by either overpriming the engine so that it failed to start or finding some electrical or mechanical fault with the aircraft—trouble with the RT was an obvious excuse and was difficult to pin down. He knew that he could get away with it once but if he continued to try it on he would become a marked man.

Luckily for him, he had never given way to the temptation. At briefings, sometimes, he had had a touch of the nadgers when he saw bloody great red blobs on the target map denoting areas of heavy flak but he got over it on the way to dispersals. In the jeep or truck he was in the close company of the lads and became infused with their spirit of companionship. They were all going together and that was all that mattered.

Fronting up to the challenge of continuous ops and having the moral fibre to press home rocket attacks was beginning to take more out of him than he realized. When diving down on targets they could see how each other performed. The Squadron operated as a team in accordance with a set pattern and everybody had to conform. Any departure from this discipline was usually a sign of nerves on some-body's part. He had, on one or two occasions, seen rockets flying over his head in a dive and had known that somebody behind him had either got wind up or fired by mistake. He wasn't going to make an exhibition of himself like that if he could possibly help it but some-times he found it hard going to hang on and press home his attack with all the shit being chucked up at him.

If a pilot regularly made a clot of himself on ops he knew that it wouldn't be long before he was quietly posted off. Nobody said anything because it was only too bloody obvious that the poor chap couldn't take it. There might be an odd joke perhaps about 'old so and so' who couldn't keep in the same sky as the Squadron but it was soon forgotten. Stanford had always felt damned sorry for such a man because he knew that it could happen to any of them. Many pilots had an inherent fear that one day they would wake up and be unable to make the grade.

Whenever his nerves became a little frayed he had only to think about being labelled as LMF to pull himself together. On those occasions he used to look around at the others to see if they displayed any signs of tension but they never seemed to. He knew that he couldn't be the only one to feel the strain from time to time but he daren't mention anything, not even to his chum Paddy. He had long since joined the fraternity but found it hard sometimes to maintain its carefree attitude.

After the battle of Mortain when 245 had lost so many pilots the new chaps fully expected that the Squadron would be 'stood down'

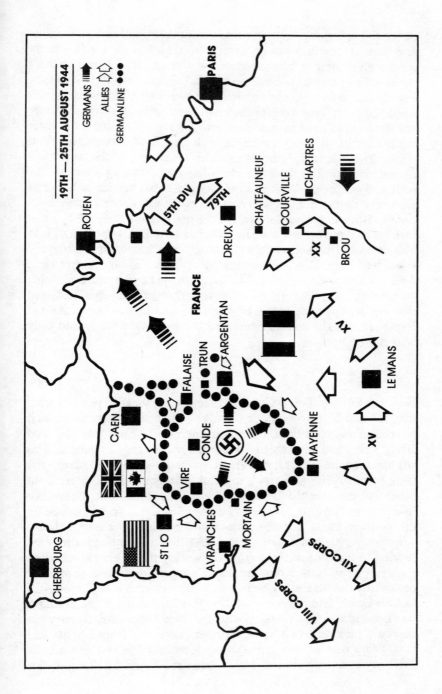

on the following day. That evening one of them said that he felt they had been bloody lucky to get away with it and surely the hierarchy would give them a break tomorrow but the 'old hands' hadn't thought like that and a 'stand down' had never crossed their minds. For them, tomorrow was another day and their chances tomorrow would be exactly the same as they had been today. His friend Paddy had listened to the conversation without saying a word but a little while later he suddenly came out with a profound statement. 'You know, Bob', he said, 'when a gambler has a run of luck he usually carries on gambling because he thinks that winning shortens the odds and vice versa. We're gamblers in our own particular way and we know that it doesn't work as far as we are concerned'.

After fidgeting about for most of the night in his sleeping bag and turning things over and over in his mind Bob finally drifted off into oblivion until he was rudely awakened by Ches West shaking his shoulder. 'Hey, Bob', Ches snorted, 'get your ass outta that sack. Archie wants you over at Flights. You betta get a move on man!'. He groaned and was shovelling his feet into flying boots when he heard the jeep's horn and looked through the gap in the hedge. Archie Lamb, his Flight commander, and the lads were ready and only waiting for him.

*   *   *

Warrant Officer Terry Gray was feeling reasonably pleased with life. He and Tubby Sago, or Glen as Terry called him, were well organized and comfortable living in their home-built 'château' and lately Terry had been able to procure a wider range of delicacies to supplement the field rations that they had been drawing from the cook house. News of Terry's ingenuity had spread and pilots from other Squadrons called in to take a look at his handiwork. They were told that the 'mansion' was a 245 design, inspected and approved by the establishment, but the plans could be had for a nominal fee!

Although he was repaying the RAF for his past indiscretions, leaving him only a pittance from his weekly pay, Terry always had plenty of spare cash. Knowing that the Squadron would be moving out shortly he had already done a deal with his American jeep but still had his Italian Guzzi motor cycle. He had been thinking that it might be a good idea to take a look around the Caen-Falaise area to see what he could pick up when Spike Hughes came over from Flights and told Terry that he had been 'stood down' for the rest of the day.

Now was a good time to have a bash at Falaise, he thought, but

Previous page Smoke trails from a rocket attack over the target area *(USIS)*.

Above A rocket Typhoon attacking out of the sun at Mortain *(Minin Verlag GMBH)*.

Below A German tank blown into the ditch at St Barthélemy, near the Haize-Almin farm *(Infantry Journal Press)*.

Top right This Panzer V didn't get very far *(Imperial War Museum)*.

Right Tanks destroyed at St Barthélemy *(R. Vitard)*.

Below right A German tank destroyed amidst the ruins of St Barthélemy *(M et Mme Maloizel)*.

Previous pages 'The Office'—from here pilots could command the firepower of a small warship, although in this particular example the weapon selector switches, normally near the fuel control (lower right) are missing.

Above *L'Angevine*, Dr Buisson's house, which had been transformed into a blockhouse by the GIs during the battle on the nights of the 6th and 7th August 1944 *(Dr Gilles Buisson)*.

Below left Major General Leland S. Hobbs, Commanding General 30th US Infantry Division who held the line at St Barthélemy *(Infantry Journal Press)*.

Below right Private First Class Wendell Westall who said that 'the Typhoons saved our butts on the day of August 8th when we were holed up at Mortain'.

Opposite Mortain today, and as it was in August '44 when the Typhoons attacked the German armour *(Dr Gilles Buisson)*.

Above Typical of the sort of damage a Typhoon could sustain and survive, this flak-hit example crossed the Channel and landed safely at Lydd *(Douglas Maxwell)*.

Below 7 June 1948—the Mayor of Mortain, M Hordin, receives the *Croix de Guerre avec Palme* awarded to the town of Mortain by the President of the *République*, Vincent Auriol *(Dr Gilles Buisson)*.

Glen Sago who normally went with him was on call and couldn't make it so he looked around for someone else who might like a spin out on the Guzzi. Spike was going down to Le Fresne for 'erfs', but Stanford said he could come along as he had just finished a show. He told Terry that they had pranged 'flak happy wood' once again. Terry grinned, 'You mean Le foret de Bretonne, or something like that', he said.

They took the road through Le Fresne which was quiet and deserted. The farmyard stench was even more overpowering than usual as Terry opened the throttle and they shot up the hill passing the old church. The place looked war-torn and derelict with windows boarded up and its grey stone walls pitted by shrapnel and bullets. Bob Stanford glanced across at an old château standing back off the road on their left as they turned the corner and accelerated away up the straight tree-lined road towards Brettville. 'I bet the Krauts took that place over', he yelled to Terry.

At the crossroads Terry turned right and, jumping a high curb, pulled up outside a small café opposite a church, the spire of which seemed to have been sliced in half. Bob had never been in the café before but thought that some of the boys must have used it because a wink from Terry produced two glasses of Calvados. He could see that the chap behind the bar had a monumental twitch and Terry explained that the poor sod had been an engine driver and knew all about Typhoon attacks.

A small deal was concluded in the kitchen behind the bar and Terry emerged with a bottle which he carefully wrapped up in a sock before placing it in a canvas bag on the side of the Guzzi. Then they roared off along the main road from Bayeux to Caen sending up clouds of dust and small stones as Terry really let the Guzzi go. Bob held on to his handlebars tightly, crouched behind Terry, thoroughly enjoying himself and leaning over as Terry negotiated a line of tanks and trucks like a trout swimming upstream.

The road was familiar to Bob because he had seen it many times from the air. He shouted to Terry that Carpiquet airfield would be coming up and he would like to take a look at it at ground level when they reached it. Terry pulled off the road and zigzagged along the cratered surface of the perimeter track. The whole area had been pattern-bombed and was littered with burnt out vehicles. Only the remains of runways and wrecked hangars gave it the appearance of once having been a major Luftwaffe base. Even the wine cellar of the demolished German officers' mess yielded nothing but an odd bottle of Vichy water which Terry reckoned that one of our brown jobs must have left behind because he couldn't stand the stuff.

Bob was keen to wander around Caen and Terry took him to the outskirts where the land sloped down towards the centre and the port. The landscape was a mass of rubble and ruins with church spires pointing up like pine needles and a few large edifices seemingly untouched. The castle with its battlements perched on a hill, overlooking the Caen Canal and the River Orne, dominated the desolate scene. A few small groups of people were chatting to one another amongst the surrounding debris and Bob walked over to have a word with one of them.

The man, smallish, slightly built and wearing a beret was sitting on a wall with his feet dangling down. He spoke reasonable English and when Bob told him that he was a Typhoon pilot, the little Norman became quite excited and shook hands, politely handing Bob his card which read, 'Monsieur Robert Lequesne, 124 Rue Saint Pierre, Caen'. He said that unfortunately this house no longer existed and Bob asked him whether it had been destroyed by shellfire during the battles but the man shook his head and told Bob that it had been bombed by Lancasters.

Finally, Bob managed to extricate himself and get back to Terry, who had been remarkably patient, and he gave him the gen. This place, he said pointing to Caen, went up in smoke shortly after two o'clock on the morning of D-Day just like Coventry. Once fires got going in the narow streets and timber buildings the wind blew up and that was it. The chap told me that the fires burned for a week or more and nobody has any idea how many people got the chop. The Norman said that on D-Day afternoon, the 21st Panzer tried to get through Caen and move up to the invasion beaches but couldn't negotiate the debris. He saw some of their infantry trying to march through and said they had a lot of casualties. 'So', Bob thought 'at least the bombing did some good!'

Terry then made his way around Caen heading south in the direction of Falaise where they saw three great pyramids of clothing and boots piled up twenty or thirty feet high in a compound just off the road. Canadian soldiers told them quite bluntly that the stuff had been taken off the corpses of their chums when they had advanced down the road towards Falaise. Some reckoned that as many as 18,000 were killed during that push but that wasn't the worst part of it, they said, the RAF had bombed their chaps by mistake, just after midday on 14 August, shortly after the advance had begun.

Terry and Bob looked at one another. There was nothing much they could say in the circumstances except to mumble about it being tough luck and how sorry they were. Terry took Bob aside and told him he knew that the Yanks had done the same thing over in their sector so this was the second time it had happened. Bob felt pretty sick at seeing all that gear piled up and couldn't help thinking of those poor bastards who had been blasted by our own bombs.

The Canadians warned them that they wouldn't get far if they went on towards Falaise because everything was chaotic down there and the place literally stank for miles around. Terry just grinned and got their OK to rummage around the piles for a pair of despatch rider's boots or anything else which might come in handy. Bob knew that Terry wouldn't take any notice of what the Canadians had said if he had set his mind on going to Falaise. But he wasn't going to join Terry and prod about in that heap.

The soldiers he had been talking to were French Canadians and he remembered that those boys had been a pretty wild mob and spoiling for any fight when they had been based in Southern England training for the Invasion. They all seemed to be a trifle wild and enjoyed close combat. He had no doubts about the way they and the Poles would tear into the Krauts and it was a bloody shame that they should have been on the receiving end of Bomber Command.

When they left the compound Terry confided in Bob that he had really been looking for motor cycles and that he had got a deal laid on. He also told Bob that they were now going to have a run round the battle area because he wanted to get his hands on some 9-mm Lugers amongst other things. Bob was in no position to argue but he had a funny feeling that he wasn't going to like wandering around the killing area.

Terry had an uncanny instinct in being able to find his way through a labyrinth of country roads and lanes and they got into the Falaise pocket without any trouble. Bob was aware of a sickly aroma long before they got there and Terry told him quite cheerfully that it was the sweet smell of death and not to worry about it because corpses couldn't do anybody any harm.

Shortly afterwards Terry explained that he was making for slit trenches and dug-outs. His Warrant Officer friend from 7th Armoured Division Workshops had told him where to find them and what to do. 'You won't find anything on the bodies lying in the top of the trenches', he said, 'because they've been gone over for Lugers and watches. You've got to dig a little deeper if you know what I mean!' Bob wasn't going to have anything to do with it and said so. He was already horrified at what he had seen in burned out vehicles and tanks and he nearly vomited when they came across remnants of horse-drawn transport.

While Terry went off to do his dirty work Bob lit his pipe wondering whether they would both be shot for looting. He had thought, at first, that Terry was talking a load of bullshit about taking Lugers and watches from corpses but now he knew better. He looked around him thinking that this was an awful place and he wouldn't spend a night here for a fortune amongst the wreckage and the dead and he was relieved when Terry suddenly appeared through the foliage looking very chuffed with himself having procured a couple of Lugers and several watches.

Terry was completely oblivious to all the ghastly scene around them and told Bob that he had rocketed horse-drawn artillery on one of his recces over the Falaise Gap. And what's more he said, it's all written in my log book as claimed and confirmed. Bob didn't exactly feel like arguing with him and was only too anxious to get back on the saddle and out of the area.

It came as a relief when they left that terrible smell behind and approached the environs of Caen. The fresh air was invigorating and Terry suddenly stopped outside a ruined building pointing at the roof. The fins and back end of a Typhoon rocket were sticking up out of the slates. They both laughed when Terry said that it must be one of Benny Bennet's.

The news that the Squadron was going to pull out of the strip and move up the line came suddenly on the morning of 28 August. The new airfield was an established ex-Luftwaffe base called St André de L'Eure a few miles south of Evreux and only a few minutes away in a Typhoon. There was no time for pilots to do anything but pack up and prepare for take-off. This was a little unfortunate for Stanford and Gray who had a load of washing being done by the farmer's wife down in the village. Other pilots had also been caught on the hop because the Squadron was only given about one hour's notice to be ready to move out.

Everybody had been looking forward to a change of scenery and moving into more established quarters, preferably within reach of a decent-sized town. They had been camping out for over sixty days at Le Fresne and apart from the flying they had had little to occupy them there. Now they thought that the brown jobs had at last 'taken their fingers out' and got a move on, everything was possible. News that the French Armoured Division had already entered Paris was received with particular interest!

For most of the period that they had spent on the strip the war had been a ding-dong affair with battle lines remaining static and the

Allies pouring in an endless stream of men, equipment and supplies. It was only during the previous two weeks, however, that the tide had turned dramatically with the advent of the Falaise Gap which finally achieved victory in Normandy.

While pilots had been concerned about the progress of the war during the stalemate situation, morale had always been very high and nobody had ever expressed any doubts about the eventual outcome. Such morale applied to everybody working on the strip from ack-ack gunners and cooks to clerks and ground crews. Working under field conditions had brought everybody together and 121 Wing operated as a large family with Wing Commander Tim Morice as its father figure. When Warrant Officer Terry Gray, for example, had procured extra goodies from NAAFI stores and paid for out of pilots' funds there was a party in the Flights tent for ground crews and they all received an extra week's ration including booze and fags 'on the house'. This spirit had been fostered right from the early days when the strip had been shelled and people were all in the front line together and was to remain with the Wing throughout. Tim Morice, of course, played the leading role in making his Wing the best in the business and later he was to be promoted to Group Captain and awarded the Distinguished Service Order to add to his Military Cross, but he always maintained that his DSO had been given to the Wing as a whole.

During those hectic days on the strip the Typhoon had indelibly imprinted its name on the pages of aviation history as being the most lethal air-to-ground attack fighter to emerge from the Second World War. The battle of Mortain, for example, was the first time in history that a great weight of attacking armour had been halted and destroyed by air power alone. The Allied Supreme Commander, General Dwight D. Eisenhower, issued a communique to the effect that the Typhoons of the 2nd Tactical Air Force had played a large part in crushing German forward positions by rocketing armoured columns and damaging and destroying numerous tanks and a considerable number of more vulnerable vehicles: 'This vigorous action of our land and air forces resulted in the halting of the attack and a threat was reversed into a great victory. For once the weather was in our favour and was ideal for aerial operations. If our machines had been grounded the enemy would have succeeeded in reaching Avranches and this would have compelled us to drop supplies to our troops by air to the north and east of the corridor thus restricting their manoeuvreability'.

The battle of the Falaise Gap had been on an even more gigantic scale than that at Mortain. Six Panzer Armies and over 100,000 men had been trapped in that pocket and they represented an enormous stationary and virtually helpless target for rampaging rocket Typhoons. Most Typhoon pilots who flew in both battles would probably agree that Mortain was a battle but Falaise was a massacre.

Both actions had called for maximum performance from the aircraft over sustained periods of attacks and the Typhoon met and overcame that challenge. In the first place, the aircraft had been operating from make-shift wire mesh runways, laid on rough undulating farmland, which constantly put pressure on under-carriages and airframe construction especially as the aircraft carried heavy armament. Sir Sidney Camm, Chief Designer of Hawker Aircraft had had this in mind in 1937 when he and his design team first worked on a high altitude chaser able to operate out of tempo-rary airstrips or even fields. Hence the wide undercarriage and sturdy frame. However, as a top echelon fighter the Typhoon had performed like an overfed duck and was outclassed by the Spitfire in rarer atmospheres. Camm, ironically, had the Germans to thank for the continuation and ultimate success of his Typhoon project. Low flying Focke-Wulf 190s carrying out hit-and-run bombing raids along the South Coast had enticed the Typhoon down to lower levels where it was the only aircraft capable of catching them. Its ability to carry heavy armament combined with a terrific performance under about 12,000 feet finally put it in a class of its own as an air-to-ground attack fighter. In November 1942 Beamont of 609 Squadron was authorized by Air-Vice-Marshal 'Dingbat' Saunders to carry out a wide range of low level attacks during which he pioneered the techniques of Typhoon ground strikes.

Any aircraft attacking Panzer armour had not only to be able to pack a punch capable of knocking out a tank but also be rugged enough to withstand flak damage and keep on flying. But the battles of Mortain and Falaise demanded even more from the aircraft in that it had to maintain a continuous cycle of attacks over a long period going virtually flat out. Its ability to build up speed in seconds during the dive and to turn tightly when pulling out were key factors in rocket attacks. Pilots were able to maintain visual contact with their targets because of this radius of manoeuvre and keep attacks going which eventually wore down Panzer gunners. Although heavily laden with armament and under considerable pressure from high 'G' forces for long periods, the aircraft had behaved admirably.

Leaving the strip at Le Fresne Camilly for the last time was the end of an era for the pilots—a period when their flying time on ops averaged only about twenty or thirty minutes and targets came into view before they had time to get settled in their cockpits. It had been a strange contrast from the days when they had flown from bases in Southern England and had spent half-an-hour each way crossing the Channel. At least, when they got back to base then, they had had plenty of opportunity to 'live it up'.

At Le Fresne Camilly, a pilot had more ops experience in a day than he might have gained during several weeks on a home station. Even the 'old hands' had found it a little difficult at first to adjust themselves to the pace of the game. Everything seemed to happen so quickly and no sooner were they airborne than the German guns opened up and didn't stop until they came back into the circuit for an approach and landing.

The Squadron had changed considerably with the influx of new pilots and it had been good to see two of the old stalwarts back in business. Bill Waudby, now commissioned, had rejoined after walking out of occupied France and also Bob Monk, who had recovered from the flak wounds he had received while wearing his famous American flak suit. The news had also come through that Flying Officer Ken Dickie and Flight Sergeant Tubby Noakes, who had both gone down in Normandy around D-Day time, had managed to get back to England so there was a chance that they might both turn up sometime.

Now events were moving fast and they were going to have to change their base in order to catch up with the front line but nobody had any idea what was going to happen next or what life would be like when they got to St André in about thirty minutes time!

St André de L'Eure was some eighty miles to the south east of Le Fresne and sixty miles west of Paris almost directly due south of Rouen. It felt good to land on a proper runway again and put up one's camp bed in permanent quarters but the Squadron was only there for a day or two and was just getting settled in when it had to move up the line once more and do another short hop across country to an airfield at Beauvais.

Chapter 9

The 'lost' Squadron

The brown jobs were advancing rapidly through the Low Countries in the direction of Antwerp and the Squadron had barely 48 hours to settle down on the airfield outside Beauvais before the news came through that it was going to move up the line to a base called Vitry just outside the town of Douai. Much to everyone's surprise 245 was briefed to carry out an armed recce in the Charleville-Mézières area on its way to the new airfield at Vitry.

The Germans were retreating eastwards and the plan was to shoot up their road transport. Pilots' tubular frame camp beds were dismantled and stacked into the gun bays of their Typhoons together with personal kit. The quick advance through Northern France towards Brussels had generated an air of excitement and pilots could see from their maps that the airfield was close to Douai, which looked to be a sizeable town, and also had Arras on its doorstep. After their monastic and rather grim life on the strip they thought that at last there would be opportunities for Squadron piss-ups and having a bit of fun.

There were a few jokes during the briefing session about taking their camp beds with them and plastering the enemy with shaving soap when they fired their cannons. Everybody was in good form and not particularly concerned when the Met officer warned them to look out for thunderstorms in the general target area. Archie Lamb was going to lead the show as the Squadron was still without a CO. Flight Lieutenant Paddy Moore had been taken ill immediately after being promoted to command 245 and then Flight Lieutenant Granny Grantham, from a sister Squadron, had been clobbered and had to bale out after hearing the news over the RT that he would be taking over 245. In effect, the Squadron had lost threee commanding officers within a few days and word was beginning to get around that there was some kind of jinx on it.

There were signs of heavy cumulus cloud building up when they took off from Beauvais. Great towering masses of swirling vapour with dazzling anvil tops and dirty dark grey skirts edged their way across a pale blue sky. The RT crackled with electrical interference as they flew east towards Charleville-Mézières combing the countryside for anything on the roads. The Squadron avoided the hills between Soissons and Laun and flew low across the plains banking and weaving in open formation but finding nothing.

Archie Lamb led them in a seemingly endless roundabout until suddenly they flew straight into an electrical storm in the Reims area; compasses were spinning and they could get nothing on the RT except crackling noises. Keeping tight formation was difficult in thick cloud because of heavy turbulence which bounced aircraft up and down and pilots were continually using throttles to keep station. Nobody had the faintest clue where they were and relied on Archie Lamb to get them out of it.

Lightning occasionally tore through the murk and Lamb was getting worried. His compass was useless and the only thing he could do was to turn the Squadron through 180 degrees by guesswork to get back on his tracks and out of the storm. Finally, they broke cloud into blue sky and sunlight and Archie looked around to try and pin-point his position. The Squadron had been airborne for about one hour and forty minutes and was fast running out of fuel. Pilots could faintly hear Jock Darlington's voice, amidst the crackling on the RT, saying that he was almost out of juice and would have to force-land in a few minutes.

Jock had been on the arse-end of the formation and had used more petrol than most when pumping his throttle to maintain station but the others were dangerously low. They were all aware that the show had been a fiasco and nobody had even fired a shot but now it looked as if the entire Squadron would have to force-land, probably on the wrong side of the lines.

Pilots had previously adjusted controls to give them maximum economical cruising but now it was a question of cutting right back in a desperate attempt to remain airborne until they reached their own lines. As Jock Darlington's engine began to cough they saw a large airfield with long runways pockmarked with craters and with German aircraft lined up on the tarmac outside the HQ area. There was no sign of life but it was obviously impossible to land on the runways. Jock's engine finally stopped and somebody who had spotted a grass area seemingly untouched alongside the main hangars called him up and told him to try to get down on it. It was about 600 yards long but nobody had any idea whether it was mined or indeed if Germans still occupied the buildings.

People in the surrounding area looked up in astonishment to see Typhoons circling the airfield. When Jock Darlington put his wheels down they went wild with delight, embracing and kissing one another. The moment they had been waiting for during four long years of German occupation had at last arrived and they thought they were about to be liberated.

Only about half-an-hour previously the last members of the Luftwaffe had left Amy airfield in vans and trucks and local people had been in a state of suspense wondering how long it would be before the Allies broke through. They had expected to see British tanks and infantry which they believed to be about twenty miles away and were amazed when they saw the Typhoons suddenly appear out of the blue.

The little town of Roye was a mile-and-a-half from Amy airfield which had been a major Luftwaffe base. Pattern-bombing since the Invasion had put it completely out of action and recently the Germans had been busy laying mines and booby trapping the aircraft which they had been forced to leave behind. About seventy miles north-east of Paris, the town was only forty miles from Beauvais from where the Typhoons had taken off. It was a small place and, except for the airfield, of little consequence. There was no hotel but there were a few cafés and a couple of restaurants in the tiny market square. The local mayor, however, was Colonel of the Resistance for the region and was out seeing his men when the Typhoons dropped in. As soon as the aircraft had landed the inhabitants of the town made for the airfield of Amy en bloc.

The pilots watched anxiously as Jock Darlington glided down towards the grass strip and saw him make a perfect approach and landing on a dead engine. As he rolled forward they all held their breath hoping that the patch wasn't mined. He got out of his aircraft and waved, beckoning them in, as one after the other they descended over electric pylons along the perimeter and made precautionary landings, parking on the edge of the grass opposite the main hangar.

Their immediate reaction was one of intense relief at getting down on the ground. The previous fifteen minutes or so had been a nightmarish experience, flying with an eye on the fuel gauges and expecting the engine to die on them at any second. Any dead-stick landing in a Typhoon was well known to be a very hairy business and they thought that Jock had done bloody well to get his wheels down instead of being content to do a belly flop. They were glad that he hadn't because there wasn't much width to that stretch of grass which was the only place where they could have possibly got down.

Dud Nott counted only seven Typhoons and could see no sign of Archie's aircraft; he had apparently vanished. He saw the tall angular figure of Bob Monk jump off the wing of his aircraft brandishing his .38 Smith and Wesson revolver. The crowd of them stood in a group for a minute or so not knowing what to do and looking anxiously around half expecting Germans to come running in and firing at them at any second.

Monk was the first one to take any positive action and told everybody to keep their revolvers handy and put a bullet through their petrol tanks if there was any trouble. 'We don't know where we are or what is going on around here', he said. 'So I suggest that we stay with our aircraft for the time being and if any French arrive on the scene don't say anything until we know what the score is'. They stood out in the sun waving at odd aircraft flying high overhead and joking about what was going to happen at Group when it was learned that an entire rocket Typhoon squadron, except for Archie, had disappeared into thin air. Nobody knew when Archie had vanished and the theory was that as the leader he would have had more petrol than anybody else and had gone for help.

Monk let out a yell and ran towards a Heinkel III where Spike Hughes was standing on its wing and about to open the cabin door. He roared at him to get away from there. 'It's booby trapped, you silly bastard', he said, and Spike, rather shamefacedly climbed down. 'Yesh', Spike muttered, 'shorry Bob', as he walked down the line of German aircraft with his mouth wide open. Dud Nott was just suggesting that it might be a good idea if a couple of them were to do a small recce when a crowd of French people, mostly women, came running towards them waving their arms. The pilots were embraced, kissed, hugged and fussed over, feeling a bit like lemons, but there was no escape from the mercurial emotion and explosion of feeling pouring out of the local people. Some women had brought babies, which had to be kissed and patted, others adorned the cockpits with flowers and a group of women were busy setting up wooden trestle tables which they had dragged out of the hangar.

Black bread, cheese and jugs of wine were produced and the first of the liberation parties to be held that day got under way. It was a crazy, almost unbelievable atmosphere for the pilots who knew damned well that they hadn't really liberated the place at all. One of the French Resistance chaps, wearing an armband, with an automatic slung over his shoulder, asked Bob Monk what time the British tanks would be arriving. Bob put on a serious face, looked at his watch and waved his hands in the air saying that the tanks were on their way and that was all he knew. The Frenchman beamed and said that he was surprised that the RAF had got here first and Bob said, 'So are we!' and left rather smartly.

Bob Monk told the lads that the only thing they could do was to keep up the old party spirit and not mention anything. 'We shall just have to take a chance that an aircraft will spot us', he said. 'And that the pilot will have the sense to get hold of the brown jobs to come and bale us out. There are Germans still retreating all over the place here, so let's hope the Krauts won't have time to bother with us'.

After the celebration outside the hangar they were taken into Roye in some strange-looking transport including a battered old taxi and a horse-and-cart. Nobody was in any state to worry whether they might bump into any Germans and they arrived in the market square feeling happy and ready for anything.

Bob Stanford had been taken over by a tall and buxom French girl who introduced him to a rather serious and tubby Frenchman sucking a squelchy pipe and taking off his glasses every few seconds to wipe them with a filthy rag. The man told him that he was one of the Captains of the local Resistance and dragged him off to meet the mayor who was his Colonel. It was a lovely old house with a walled garden and Monk was already there putting the mayor in the picture. The upshot of their discussions was that a despatch rider would be sent off to try to get through the lines and deliver a message. Meanwhile, the mayor in his capacity as Colonel of the Resistance would do his best to keep his chaps happy until the tanks arrived.

Monk knew that it wasn't going to be easy, especially when the Resistance men realized that the RAF were bluffing and had no back-up in the form of tanks and infantry. This was bound to cause resentment amongst the Maquis who appeared to be a rather headstrong and undisciplined crowd. Apart from that, there was a very real danger that retreating Germans might band together and attack the airfield to destroy the Typhoons. Monk doubted whether the Maquis would be able to stop them but he was in no position to voice an opinion.

The mayor, M. André Coël, and his wife were very charming people and to mark the occasion they dug up some bottles of champagne which they had buried in their garden when France was occupied by the Germans. It was decided that the pilots would sleep in the hangar that night and the mayor was rather astonished to learn that they had brought their beds and kit along with them in the gun bays of their Typhoons.

They were still excited but rather tired when they finally got back to the hangar and started to kip down for the night with the aid of torches. Still having a laugh about the events of the day as they got into sleeping bags, they heard voices and shots rang out with bullets ricocheting around the metal walls of the building. The Resistance fighters had arrived!

They looked a particularly scruffy and dangerous bunch armed with automatics, rifles, pistols and hand grenades and were obviously in a mood to create trouble. A line of them swaggered into the hangar watched anxiously by the pilots, who had rapidly got out of their sleeping bags and were sitting on the edges of their camp beds wondering what was going to happen next. There was a complete silence until the Frenchmen passed the odd bottle of wine around and set up a couple of wooden trestle tables. They had brought black bread and an assortment of cheese which they laid on the table and invited the pilots to join them for supper. The pilots had little choice but to accept the offer cheerfully. The Resistance were making a lot of noise and jabbering away in French which made it difficult for the pilots to understand what was going on.

It was pretty clear, however, that the Maquis felt that they had been badly let down by the RAF because there had been no actual breakthrough by the British Army and the sight of the Typhoons on the airfield might well result in a German counter-attack. The pilots had been bluffing of course, and the Resistance fighters knew it. Bob Monk, being a Flight Lieutenant and the senior officer, had taken command and he was suddenly confronted by the Resistance leader who said that his men had rounded up some Germans at the edge of a wood about a mile or so outside the airfield. Monk gathered that the Frenchman wanted to take some of the pilots with him to shoot some Germans which his mob had captured. As far as he could make out they were now being made to dig their own graves.

He took the Resistance leader on one side and apparently sorted matters out because the Maquis calmed down and no more was said about going out on a night recce to shoot Germans. The pilots were not going to do that anyway, not in cold blood, but Monk had been very skilful in his handling of the situation. As far as the boys could gather, he had firmly told the Frenchman that he was the senior, serving British officer present and that the allies would shortly be arriving. He would report any attempt to shoot Germans in cold blood to the appropriate authorities and anyone concerned in such an action would be tracked down and made to answer for it. It sounded melodramatic at the time but the pilots were under no illusions that this ill-disciplined mob were capable of anything in their boozy state. They could easily have knocked off the Germans, or the pilots for that matter, and vanished into the surrounding countryside without trace. It was rumoured that their leader had told Monk that either the pilots came out with them to shoot the Germans or they would shoot the pilots and he could take it or leave it!

Nobody got much rest that night and they were awakened early by the Resistance returning and firing bullets around the hangar again. They felt more confident in daylight, however, as other people from Roye and the surrounding area began to turn up. Once again they were stared at, touched, embraced and kissed as if they had been long-lost sons returning from the grave. Life over the past 24 hours since they force-landed had been an incredible experience, almost like Alice in Wonderland, and they were only just beginning to realize what had actually happened to them.

The night had been very frightening because they would have had no chance of defending themselves with .38 Smith and Wesson revolvers against men with automatics if it had come to the point. Those maniacs could have shot them, blown up their aircraft and disappeared, making it look as if the Germans had counter-attacked. The problem was that they didn't know whether the Resistance chaps had been bluffing or not, especially about shooting the Germans in cold blood, but there was no doubt that it had been an ugly situation in which anything could have happened.

The thought hadn't really struck them that if the Germans had attacked the airfield, the Maquis would have been shot out of hand. The pilots couldn't understand why the Maquis were so put out because they had refused to go along with them to knock off some Boche. They considered that even the Maquis should have known that the British would never shoot prisoners in cold blood. If the worst happened and the Germans retook the airfield they would be lucky enough to have the protection of the Geneva Convention and could be expected to be taken prisoner but the Maquis could only expect a bullet.

It seemed incredible to the pilots out there in the morning sun that nobody should have spotted the seven rocket Typhoons sitting on an airfield situated well on the wrong side of the lines. Odd aircraft which had flown over obviously hadn't seen them because not one had dived down to take a closer look. Surely, by now, they thought, Group must have heard that an entire Typhoon squadron had disappeared and should have sent out reconnaissance aircraft.

They had tried several times to make radio contact but could get nothing but crackling noises. It was frustrating because their position was only about thirty miles from Beauvais from where they had taken off and fifty miles from Douai which was to be their new base. It had looked on their maps as if they were in some kind of pocket about fifteen or twenty miles in front of their own lines with remnants of German units possibly retreating on either side of Amy airfield.

There was absolutely nothing they could do except to hang on and hope that the mayor's despatch rider had got through the lines and raised the alarm. Most of them were aware that when they got back, the RAF wasn't going to be particularly pleased that they hd managed to lose themselves and run out of juice but Archie would have to take the can for that. He had pissed off and was probably sweating over the whole thing.

Later that morning, much to their atonishment and relief, a group of British tanks escorting a petrol bowzer suddenly appeared over the horizon slowly grinding its way across country towards the parked Typhoons. The head and shoulders of a Major stuck out of the leading tank and as he got closer they could see he had a superior grin on his face and they knew what he was thinking!

Bob Monk, who had led the Squadron since they landed on the airfield, had the bright idea of giving the citizens of Roye and especially the Maquis a fair old beat-up before setting course for Vitry airfield just outside Douai. The idea appealed to everyone and after take-off they climbed into the distance and disappeared from view. Then, right out of the sun, they dived down on the deck and streaked across the airfield in open formation breaking into a steep climbing turn before coming round again to repeat the performance.

Bob Stanford could see the town square packed with citizens looking up and waving as he shot across the roofs following Dud Nott who had nearly clipped the flag pole outside the town hall. He had felt damned helpless in that hangar last night and was glad that it was all over. There were bound to be a few questions asked when they got back but he didn't care because he had nothing to worry about. He hadn't been leading the show so they could all take a running jump as far as he was concerned. All he wanted to do when they landed at Vitry was to nip into Douai or Arras and see a bit of life.

Apart from a few jokes about the Squadron actually liberating a town, little was said about the Roye episode and it was soon forgotten. There was really nothing for the powers that be to enquire into because no pilot had gone down and no aircraft had been damaged or lost. As usual, nobody mentioned anything or even admitted to one another that they had been a little 'twitched up' when the Maquis played fun and games.

Chapter 10

Breakthrough

The style of operations changed considerably when the Squadron started flying from Vitry, or to give it its full title Vitry-en-Artois. Longer armed recces, lasting an hour or more, were carried out north of Ghent and over the Dutch Islands where a large ship of some 1,500 tons was attacked and severely damaged. During this attack Jeff Jeffreys spotted a U-boat in the harbour and went down on it firing his rockets. The submarine exploded and sank and Jeff reckoned that one of his rockets must have either gone down its conning tower or pierced the hull. Very heavy flak was encountered on these trips leaving the pilots in no doubt that Jerry still had a lot of fight left in him.

Pilots could see from Intelligence maps that the British Second Army was moving fast up the coast towards Antwerp and the Americans were also advancing over on the right flank. This lightning thrust into the Low Countries generated a wave of optimism making people feel that the war might well be over before Christmas. News came through that Squadron Leader Jack Collins had been awarded a bar to his DFC posthumously and that Maxie Maxwell and Dud Nott had won the DFC. Warrant Officer Paddy Gray had been awarded the American DFC for his part in the battle of Mortain and Bob Lee a DFC for his courage in staying alive when trapped under his aircraft for several days. These were the first decorations that the Squadron had received for at least two years so there was much to celebrate!

Squadron piss-ups had suddenly returned to a degree of normality after the long stint on the strip. There were plenty of local bistros around and Douai and Arras were on the doorstep. One night in Douai they discovered a building with a high wall surrounding it and heard music and laughter coming from within. It was obvious that something interesting was happening in there and it sounded like a party so they banged the knocker on a solid-looking door inset deep into the brickwork. After a few hammerings, the door was opened slightly and an American voice told them to 'get lost'; the door was slammed shut and they heard it being bolted.

This was a challenge so Spike Hughes was lifted up and sent over the wall to investigate. It was very funny to bunk up old Spike, they thought, because he was a bit religious and the place might well turn out to be a brothel. Presently, he came creeping back in the dark. 'Yesh', he whispered, 'I looked through the French windows and shaw ladiesh and gentlemen all danshing round. There'sh a band in the corner and a gallery upshtairsh with little cubiclesh and curtainsh. It sheemsh a nice placesh. I think I shaw the Shenior Medical Offisher in there'.

Shortly after Brussels was liberated, Bill Smith, Dud Nott, Maxie Maxwell and Paddy Gray borrowed the Squadron jeep and drove some seventy miles into the city. The whole place was a mass of flags and the streets were crowded with people still 'whooping it up'. The Belgians must have hidden the flags during the Occupation because there were Union Jacks everywhere in addition to their own national flags. They discovered that they were the first pilots to enter the city and as they wandered around the streets feeling glad to be back in civilisation, people around wanted to take them into cafés and restaurants and buy them lunch. The entire population seemed to have blown a safety valve and was letting off steam after the Occupation.

The pilots were carried along in a wave of euphoria which swept through the city. During the afternoon they called into a café and, much to their astonishment, the proprietress offered them a selection of fancy pastries and iced cakes on a tray—delicacies which they hadn't seen since pre-war days. Paddy Gray had a particularly sweet tooth and was studying the assortment when Dud Nott, airing his knowledge of French, pointed to the tray and announced to madame that he would have a piece of that 'château' over there.

On Sunday 17 September, thirteen days after landing at Vitry, the Squadron took off for Deurne which was an airfield on the environs of Antwerp. At this time the Germans were firing off V2 rockets aimed at the Greater London area and one of these misfired and came straight down on a NAAFI wagon parked on the perimeter of the airfield. There was an enormous explosion followed by bits of cakes and biscuits dropping out of the sky. Sadly there were many casualties but the chaps made jokes about being sprayed with 'char and wads' and it came as a sharp reminder that life at home in London and the Home Countries wasn't all that comfortable.

The Squadron had leap-frogged its way from Le Fresne Camilly in Normandy through Belgium and finally into Holland in four short hops over a period of nineteen days. It had followed on the heels of the brown jobs whose spearheads of the 21st Army Group had pressed on from Brussels and covered a distance of 95 miles in four days just as the Germans had done in 1939. On the day that the Squadron landed at Deurne, thousands of Airborne troops were being dropped in the Arnhem area as 'Operation Market Garden' got under way. Everyone soon got to hear of the tragedy which took place there.

Unfortunately, the weather immediately clamped down with low cloud and rain and remained that way for several days so that rocket Typhoon squadrons were unable to provide back-up for the Paras. This was a disaster because a Panzer division, which had been concealed under cover of woods outside Arnhem, was able to make mincemeat of the more lightly armed Paras. As soon as the weather cleared, the Squadron took off on armed recces covering the Arnhem area but it was too late to help the British and American Paras.

The plan to establish bridgeheads over the rivers Rhine, Waal and Mass, and thereby make a lightning thrust into Germany itself had failed. Most people were disappointed after the excitement following the rapid advance through France and Belgium which had given rise to the feeling that the German Army was crumbling. All sorts of stories had been going the rounds at this time including a strong belief that civilian morale in Germany had collapsed and the Germans were about to throw in the towel.

Nobody on the Squadron took much notice of rumours but it was the major talking point that the Allies had suffered a severe setback at Arnhem. But pilots had their own job to do and felt that it wasn't their affair. There was no point in them looking forward to a quick end to the war because the next op would be coming up at any time and then the one after that 'ad infinitum', if they were lucky enough to survive. The great thing was to have fun, and in Antwerp they were to find plenty of that.

Sitting in Flights one afternoon on standby, Warrant Officer Paddy Gray was passing the time carving a chunk of perspex with his penknife, trying to make it into the shape of a Typhoon fuselage, when the knife slipped, severely gashing his thumb and he had to go over to see the MO who stitched it up. He came back with it covered in an enormous bandage and held it aloft, announcing to his Flight commander that he was bloody sorry but he was off flying for a day or two.

His namesake Terry Gray who was also on standby looked down his nose. 'I don't want to say anything, Paddy, but . . . this is obviously a self-inflicted wound and you have a touch of the old LMF'. Instead of taking the remark as a joke and saying, 'Up yours Terry!', Paddy stalked off in a rage. The mere suggestion that he had done it deliberately had sent him berserk. But Terry Gray never gave a damn what he said. He had often asked new pilots when they arrived on the Squadron what size collars they wore because he could do a good trade in shirts if they didn't make it. He couldn't have cared less if they took umbrage, saying that if they were that bloody sensitive then they shouldn't be there.

Recce parties had managed to find a suitable night club in Antwerp and had organized a Squadron table. The place was full of Yanks who had the money to pay for the booze and the Squadron had to rely on smuggling in a bottle of Scotch and decanting it into teapots in the privacy of the 'loo'. They sat round listening to Paula singing while pouring out cups of neat whisky and adding milk and sugar to keep up appearances. Paula was a terrific looking girl of Rita Hayworth proportions and she wore a tight-fitting bottle green dress which shimmered in the soft lights and clung to her supple body. Her favourite number was *My Heart Belongs To Daddy* and when the band started this tune she would come over to the Squadron table, sit on big Bill Waudby's knee stroking his blond hair and gazing into his pale blue eyes.

When Tubby Sago, the Australian Warrant Officer, joined the gathering for the first time and his eyes got accustomed to the dim lights he looked about him and came out with a classic remark, 'Cor', he said, 'my mum wouldn't 'alf give me a leatherin' if she knew I was in a place like this'.

Squadron piss-ups in the night club were becoming regular functions and as it was a long drive from the airfield into the city centre, a recce party was organized to find hotel beds. The chaps discovered a place called 'The Florian' which was up a convenient side street and looked to be pretty useful. The foyer was attractive with nice carpets, plants and reception desk and it all looked clean and comfortable. Dud Nott, who was doing the bookings, asked for five rooms which, he said, the chaps would share. Madame, shortish, broad-bosomed and wearing a black dress looked him up and down and asked what time the gentlemen would be arriving. When Dud told her that it would be some time after six o'clock, she smiled and said that would be perfectly all right. Dud, who had rapidly worked out the terms, translating Dutch guilders into sterling, reckoned that seven-shillings-and-sixpence per head was pretty damned reasonable although he had stayed at the Park Lane Hotel in London several times when on leave for a pound, including bed and breakfast.

The following evening Terry Gray, Tubby Sago, Bob Stanford and Paddy Gray arrived a little early and booked into the Florian. Madame looked at her watch and said that Mr. Terry Gray's room was ready but Mr Bob Stanford would have to wait for a few minutes. Terry disappeared with Sago while Stanford and Gray sat in the foyer noting points. Several young girls in black dresses tip-toed past them looking over their shoulders and giggling. Paddy remarked, 'I know what, Bob. They must think we're a couple of pansies, sharing a room!'

Their room was quite large and comfortable with a big double bed and lots of buttons on either side which Stanford started to push. 'That's funny', he said to Paddy, 'I can see your arse on the ceiling'. There were mirrors all over the room and every imaginable form of lighting so that they could see themselves in different colours from all angles.

Bob pushed a button marked 'Chambermaid' and in a minute or two there was a tap on the door. The sight of a pretty girl standing there in her black dress must have unnerved Paddy because the only thing he could think of saying was 'Bath towel' and Bob called, 'Make it two and deux bierres, s'il vous plait'. Large, rough hot towels and two cold beers on a tray with glasses and opener were delivered pronto and the girl gave them a little wave as she went out. Bob immediately opened his bottle, 'Enormous cheers', he said to Paddy, 'now this really is the life'.

The Squadron soon discovered that the hotel was not a brothel as they had at first suspected but a place where the locals took their girlfriends for the afternoon. The pilots made jokes about it especially when they arrived before time and had to hang about. It was difficult to keep a straight face when a couple stepped out of the lift and madame, behind her reception desk would give them a wink!

During his past five ops Bob Stanford had been flying a new Typhoon with a question mark painted on the side. At first, it had given him a strange feeling because 'MR-?' had been Jack Collins' markings. His own aircraft 'MR-U' had been badly damaged by flak when a shell went clean through the starboard mainplane, fortunately without exploding. The shell had caused rather a nasty hole and some of the metal skin had been rolled back which had disturbed the airflow over the wing and made it difficult for him to control the aircraft. He had been forced to undo his straps to enable him to put enough weight on the spade grip of the control column to keep the aircraft stable but he had managed to get it down all right.

His first op in his new 'MR-U' was on 26 September when the Squadron carried out an armed recce in the Arnhem area. The weather was still fairly 'clampers' with a lot of low cloud and the Dutch countryside below was wooded, flat and very watery. Three rivers, the lower Rhine, Waal and Maas carved up the landscape and these waterways were confusing at first, making it difficult to locate exact pin-points. The prime target was a certain wooded area concealing Panzer armour in the environs of Arnhem and the Squadron was also to look for barge transport on the rivers.

Flying north-east over new territory, which they were going to know intimately before long, they were close to the German border with the Ruhr and the Reichswald forest on their starboard side as they crossed over the labyrinth of rivers. The low cloud base forced them to make a shallower dive than usual when attacking the wood and accurate light flak came up from different quarters leaving no doubt in anyone's mind that there was a lot of stuff hidden under those trees. Shooting up forests had become standard practice for most of them and the lead Typhoons made straight for the sources of flak, firing their cannons in the dive to keep the gunners' heads down. On the way back they spotted some barges on the River Maas and strafed them with cannon fire finally landing back at Deurne having been airborne for an hour and ten minutes.

Shortly after landing, Stanford learned that Dud Nott, Maxie Maxwell and Paddy Gray were packing up to go home. He had been expecting that they would be 'tour-expired' soon knowing that they had been on ops for eighteen months or more but it came so suddenly that he felt a trifle stunned. He was going to miss them, especially dear old Paddy, and the inevitable games of cribbage. Paddy was all smiles as he carefully folded his gear and stuffed it into his kit bag and Bob suddenly realized that only he, Tubby Sago and Terry Gray were left out of the old brigade.

He felt resentful watching Paddy getting ready to leave and could see the change in him by the look on his face. Paddy was already a new man, talking about the things he was going to do and the people he would contact when he got back. It irritated Bob that his friend could now look forward to living and picking up the old threads back in Blighty. The RAF was right, he thought, any chap coming off ops should disappear at once and the sooner the better!

245 was still without a CO. Ace Miron and Archie Lamb had taken turns to lead the Squadron but Ace had gone down and there were other gaps to fill. On 30 September, the Squadron in its depleted state was ordered to pack and fly to a place called Volkel some twenty miles north-east of Eindhoven. The airfield was a very large one situated just outside a small village where the Squadron was billeted in a children's school run by nuns.

Pilots set up their camp beds in the upstairs rooms but the wing at the far end of the building contained the nuns and was completely shut off. The children had obviously left and the place was littered with tiny tables and chairs and the 'loos' were of similar proportions, which caused a great deal of amusement and leg-pulling. There was no heating of any kind or sign of the nuns, except for the twitch of a curtain when the Squadron passed by.

The road leading to Grave ran straight through the village and was choked with tanks and vehicles moving towards the front line in a continuous stream. Volkel was only a tiny little country place and its only buildings on either side of the road had been taken over as billets and messes for the Wing. The airfield, however, with its long runways and strategic position, provided a forward base for Typhoons and later Tempests to attack targets in Germany itself and was to accommodate several Wings.

The pressure was on for the military at this time to consolidate their positions after their rapid advance. Failure at Arnhem had precluded any possibility of a breakthrough into Germany before winter set in and there were still many tough cleaning-up operations to be done against German forces holding out on islands and in the Dutch countryside. Meanwhile, Germans were retreating east to take up new defensive positions in front of the Rhine and were vulnerable to rocket Typhoon attacks whenever they moved in daylight either on roads, by rail, or in barges.

River and canal traffic was obviously going to provide good business for the Typhoons because the fleeing Germans would have to cross major waterways to get to their natural defensive position on the only range of hills in Holland. These hills were in the neighbourhood of the Reichswald forest where the northern end of the old Siegfried line petered out.

The Squadron had no sooner got bedded down in Volkel than it began to receive another blood transfusion of pilots and most important, a Commanding Officer by the name of Tony Zweig-

bergk. Tony, who was always known as Skip, had previously commanded Number One Squadron and he brought Moose Mossip and
Bob Hornell along with him. 245 already had a reputation as a jinx
squadron as far as COs were concerned but Skip, who was a placid
and easy-going chap, didn't seem to worry.

There followed a period of intensive operations during early
October when the Squadron carried out a series of armed recces
whenever weather permitted. It was a mixed bag of strikes against
ferries and barges, trains and trucks, Panzer headquarters and the
Reichswald Forest. During this period other replacements arrived
including Jock Campbell, 'Nuts' Nutter, Al Brown, Harry
Bathurst, Arthur Leighton-Porter, Sully Sullivan and Mick Young
to bring the Squadron up to its full complement of pilots.

Terry Gray, who had been with the Squadron for well over eighteen months, found it rather odd that he hadn't been tour-expired
like the others but cheerfully accepted his situation. He had procured two motor cars, one of which was a large Dutch saloon called
an Imperia and the other an eight-cylinder Delage with an electric
gear box. In addition (as 'Wing Commander Gray'), he had acquired
various radio sets when he visited a Philips Electrical factory outside
Eindhoven so he was making life as comfortable as possible for
himself.

He hadn't had the Delage for very long before the airfield commander, Tim Morice, took a fancy to it and Terry obliged. This was
at a time when all transport had to have numbers and Terry's
Imperia was registered as *121W-001* and, under Tim's patronage,
Terry was allowed the facilities of the car maintenance unit.

The Squadron was now starting to attack targets in Germany and
attracted a great deal of heavy flak from the Ruhr. The usual method
adopted to get through this flak belt was to employ the 'Russian
roulette' technique of climbing high over our own lines and then
diving through it. Flight Lieutenant Harry Bathurst who had taken
over A Flight, had a curious attitude towards the dangers of flak and
used to tell pilots not to worry about it. Whenever he led the Squadron he would climb steadily towards Germany right through the flak
belt without attempting any evasive action whatsoever.

This was a rather nerve-racking and needless exercise and earned
him the nickname of 'flak happy Harry'. Nobody knew whether he
did this out of personal bravado or if he was trying to see if anybody
would 'chicken-out' and break formation but flying through those
dirty great boxes of heavy flak was a bastard! However, Harry was to
learn something about flak when one afternoon a German jet

whistled across the airfield dropping 'butterfly' or anti-personnel bombs. Harry immediately dived for cover, but he was too late and collected a large number of metal splinters in his arse. He was taken off to Eindhoven hospital and given a massive dose of penicillin before the medics got busy digging out the bits—which must have been a very painful process. Later, the boys went to visit him and found him kneeling in a wheel chair, for obvious reasons, but they cheered him up by saying, 'You don't want to worry about flak, Harry boy. It won't hurt you!'

Bob Stanford had been in his cockpit when the attack took place and hearing the airfield's ack-ack guns opening up he swiftly lowered his seat and ducked down behind the armour-plating while shell splinters rattled on the sides of his cockpit. His aircraft settled down on one side when a tyre burst and he jumped and ran, expecting it to go up in flames at any second.

After the Me 262 had vanished the adjutant, Flying Officer Tommy Thomson, who had been in the Flights tent was seen running around in sheer delight holding up his thumb. He was as happy as a clam because he had been wounded in action—a shell splinter had sliced off the top of his thumb. All the pilots liked Tommy because he looked after them and they kidded him about filling in an application form for a wound stripe.

Shortly after the incident Skip Zweigbergk told Bob Stanford that he was to go to Eindhoven the following morning for a commission interview with the Air Officer Commanding, Air-Vice-Marshal Harry Broadhurst, and wished him good luck. This news had come right out of the blue and Bob was taken aback. The thought had crossed his mind several times lately that he must have been passed over because he had been on the Squadron for well over a year and was now a very experienced pilot.

Ross Brown, Ches West, Spike Hughes and Jock Darlington had all flown as his number two and he had become an established section leader. Only the week previously he had flown as number two to Pitt Brown who had taken over from Charles Green as Wing Commander Flying and Pitt, who had a slight stutter, had told him that, 'he had p-put up a g-good sh-show'. So there was nothing wrong with his flying and his mother had ensured that he wouldn't need a knife and fork course and could speak properly so there was no reason why he shouldn't be an officer. Terry Gray had often told him that being a Warrant Officer was the best rank in the Air Force. 'You've got seniority in the mess', he said, 'no bloody officers' mess bills and nobody can kick you around. What more do you effing well want?' This had been the NCO attitude and they had all agreed with Terry at the time but when it came to the point nobody as yet had turned down a commission.

Bob really wanted his commission because he felt that he had earned it the hard way and it would please his family. Preparing for his interview he did his best to look smart, polishing his buttons and shoes, pressing his trousers and tie under his sleeping bag and doing his best to get odd stains out of his number one shirt. Spike Hughes lent him a pair of gloves and told him, 'To shpeak up for himself', and Ches West drawled as he went out, 'You sure are a bullshitting bastard, Stanford. That's what you are man!'

As Bob marched into the AOC's large room in Eindhoven he saw Broadhurst sitting behind a vast desk looking down at some papers. His hat, covered in scrambled egg, was lying on the corner of his desk and he appeared to take no notice of Bob who had put up a terrific salute and stood rigidly to attention feeling somewhat nervous. Broadhurst was a stocky figure with a pug-like expression and piercing, powerful eyes. His chest was covered with combat ribbons and his sleeves displayed the thick and thin rings of an Air-Vice-Marshal. It was like standing before the Almighty, Bob thought, as Broadhurst looked him up and down asked how old he was and how many ops he had done. Bob said that he was twenty-one and had completed eighty-three and that concluded the interview. When he arrived back at Volkel they all wanted to know how he had got on and all he would say was that it had been 'a piece of cake'.

The sleeping quarters in the convent were primitive and apart from bare boards the only furniture consisted of little wooden chairs and tables which the children had used. The accommodation, however, was preferable to being under canvas especially as the weather was getting colder and very damp but there was no hot water for washing clothes. The nuns who might have been persuaded to lend a hand with the domestic chores had remained in seclusion.

Outside in the yard there was an ancient iron boiler which Flight Lieutenant Nuts Nutter managed to get going with odd bits of wood he had collected and this soon became the central laundry. The boiler was filled up with water, bits of soap, shirts, socks, and underwear as Nuts stoked it up and the nuns could be seen peeping out from behind a ground floor window. After a day or two during which Nuts had succeeded in producing different coloured smoke from chemicals he had nicked from stores, the Mother Superior came out of hiding and took over. The Squadron responded with bars of chocolate and other goodies while the nuns did the washing and ironing, leaving Nuts to carry on in charge of the boiler.

The weather was becoming uncertain and whenever it cleared the Squadron piled in the ops. These were mainly armed recces known as the milk run, covering the area of Arnhem, Apeldoorn, Emerich, Zutphen, Hengelo and Wesel, searching for hidden armour, road, rail and river transport. Occasionally, close support targets would turn up where the brown jobs had problems and it was obvious that the momentum of the war was getting bogged down again.

Stanford's commission came through and Skip Zweigbergk asked him to join him in a trip up the line to liaise with the Army chaps. They set off in the Squadron jeep with Skip driving and Bob doing the map reading as they headed towards the River Maas. Bob, like everyone else, had found Skip easy to get on with and accepted him as a father figure who knew more about aeroplanes than any of them, having been a civvy pilot before he joined the RAF.

There was a raw, damp cold in the air as they drove along winding roads towards the front. Bob couldn't help noticing the blasted trees and animal carcasses as the countryside assumed a weary war-torn look with the earth churned up into a quagmire. He recalled the time when he and Roly Temple had suddenly looked down into the filthy abyss which had once been St Lo and hoped that it wouldn't be like that when they met with the brown jobs.

Skip didn't say much but Bob could see that he was taking an odd glance now and again at the scene and putting a glove against an ear when the guns opened up. Suddenly he had to brake hard when a Corporal appeared out of nowhere and waved them down. The road ahead was muddy, bumpy and devoid of trees or any cover whatsoever and the Corporal shouted that this stretch was being shelled every now and again and he would give them the signal to go like hell and make for the wood at the far end.

Skip reached inside his leather flying jacket bringing out a bottle of whisky and took a couple of rapid swigs before offering it to Bob who shook his head. Then the Corporal dropped his arm and Skip revved up and let the jeep go, bumping and sliding along the muddy track until they reached the cover of the trees. The ground then sloped away down into a clearing where the brown jobs were dug in and they were stopped by a Sergeant who threw up a salute and directed them to what appeared to be some kind of dug-out, timbered up and with steps leading down to it.

Stanford was astonished to find down there a group of Army officers being served drinks by an orderly carrying a silver tray. The Regimental Colonel greeted them and offered them sherry in the most beautiful crystal glasses. In a far corner he caught a glimpse of the mess silver all highly polished and noticed that the Army chaps were all neatly dressed in collars and ties and he felt scruffy by comparison. Both he and Skip were in flying boots and battledress with grimy silk scarves around their necks.

They had had no idea that they were going to be received by the Colonel and his officers in such a formal manner especially as they were supposed to be in the front line. The brown jobs, however, appeared very friendly and said some nice things about rocket Typhoons and the splendid job that they were doing. A Major remarked that Bob looked very young and seeing his thin blue Pilot Officer's stripe asked him if he had just joined his Squadron. When Bob explained, the chap shook his head, 'Do you mean to say', he remarked, 'that you have done all those ops and you are only a Pilot Officer'.

The Colonel asked Skip, who had got down to some serious drinking, whether he would like to fire a mortar. Jerry, he said, on the other side of the river was bound to fire one back and that would give him the feel of things around here. Stanford looked across at his CO standing with his feet well apart, which was his usual drinking stance being a beer man by nature, and wondered what he was going to say. He was obviously enjoying knocking back monumental sherries and without batting an eyelid he played the Colonel's ball right off his toes. 'I've fired them before', he said, 'but Stanford would like to have a go. Wouldn't you, Bob?'

The Major alongside Stanford said that he would come along too and as they stepped out of the dug-out a Sergeant saluted Bob crisply. Bob looked at him in astonishment, suddenly realizing that he was now an officer, and he gave him a sheepish kind of wave. The ground sloped down to the River Maas with fields of vegetables on either bank and this area, the Major explained, was the front line. Bob, who couldn't see any sign of life and thought it looked all very nice and countrified, nodded. He was then handed field-glasses and told to focus them on a church tower on the opposite bank. 'There's a Jerry artillery spotter up there', the Major said, 'and our chap is in a steeple around the corner just behind you. We'll go and see him later'.

The wretched mortar was in a sandbagged position just outside the dug-out and the Sergeant had got everything prepared for firing. Bob was allowed to stuff the bomb down the tube and then he had to duck and put his hands over his ears when the gun went off with a terrific bang making his ears ring. The Major told him to stay down whispering confidentially, 'They'll fire one back in a minute, you see'. Jerry returned the visiting card a minute later and Bob hoped that honour was satisfied and they could go back into the dug-out, but there was more to come.

He was taken to a church about a hundred yards up the road to be introduced to their artillery spotter who happened to be high up in the spire above the belfry with only a rope ladder for access. Stanford already had the uncomfortable feeling that he would be required to climb up that bloody ladder and he was up tight about it because heights made him feel giddy. He had never been able to lean over the parapet of a tall building, for example, or look down from the top of a cliff without a sense of nausea but, oddly enough, he could be upside down in his aircraft without giving it a thought.

Now he was really caught out but dared not funk it because the Major was gallantly holding the bottom of the rope ladder for him and telling him to get up there and have a word with the chaps. It was one hell of a climb so Bob shut his eyes and kept going until his head hit a trapdoor and he was hauled in. An Army Captain looked at him in amazement 'I know you', he said. 'You're Bob Stanford, aren't you?'. They discovered that they had been at school together in Bath and laughed about meeting again in the top of a church steeple overlooking the front line.

By the time Stanford and the Major got back, lunch was about to be served and Bob could see that Skip was doing nicely. His ruddy complexion and weatherbeaten face was all smiles and he winked at Bob asking him how he had got on with his mortars, receiving in reply a discreet two-fingered salute.

They were mellow and in good form as they were waved off. This had been the first time that either of them had had any real liaison with the brown jobs and it had been a splendid party. Both agreed that they would have been complete misfits in the Army but it was all right for those chaps. Skip was trying to work out how much booze he had consumed when once again, the Corporal waved them down as they approached the road which was under shellfire. This time when the Corporal dropped his arm and yelled, 'Go—now!', Skip let in the clutch rather more gently and they coasted along quite happily without worrying about getting blown up.

When they arrived back at Volkel Bob was very sorry indeed to hear that Jock Darlington had gone down at Wesel. The little Scot had had tremendous courage, he thought, to get out of a mining community to do this kind of job and more especially because he had a wife and kids. Ironically, Jock had recently written his home address down on a scrap of paper and asked Bob to look up his family if anything should happen to him. Bob had joked about it but kept the address.

There were flurries of snow next morning and the weather was bitterly cold. The Sabre engines of their Typhoons had long since been covered over at night with padded quilts but ground crews still had to run them up at regular intervals—which was now becoming a most uncomfortable chore. After lunch the weather cleared sufficiently to allow them to rocket a village inside the German border which the Krauts had made into a strongpoint.

The cloud was nine-tenths when they took off and the weather quite murky but they had no trouble in locating the village which was spread along both sides of a main road. This was the first occasion when the Squadron had been told to demolish a complete village and it had seemed a little odd at the time until the Intelligence officer explained what the Germans had done. Dug-in tanks were under cover of ruins, he said, and they had made the place into a fortress to stop the Allied advance up the main road into Germany.

The village showed up just as it had appeared on the map and as the Squadron circled the target the Germans opened fire, sending up a variety of concentrated flak. It looked as if the Krauts were determined to remind the pilots that this was part of Germany and they would fight for every square inch of it. There were too many sources of tracer to make selective attacks so pilots dived on the village firing cannons and rippling rockets down the length of it on either side of the road.

They dived through an inferno of bursting shells and criss-cross tracer with seemingly little chance of coming through but surprisingly nobody went down. Buildings had been shattered and fires started but it was impossible to see in all the smoke and débris what damage had been done to the strongpoints beneath the rubble.

After the Squadron landed back, Bob Stanford was given seven days leave plus a voucher for fifty pounds to return home and get himself kitted out. Skip told him that a truck would take him to Eindhoven in the morning and he would be flown home from there, probably landing at Northolt.

Bob couldn't quite believe that he would actually be home tomorrow. He had been able to put all those thoughts out of his mind for a long time but now he could think about all the things he wanted to do and he was determined to pack a lot into seven days. Leaving Flights in a rosy glow he walked back to the convent to clean up. Nuts was producing blue smoke from the boiler and a nun was

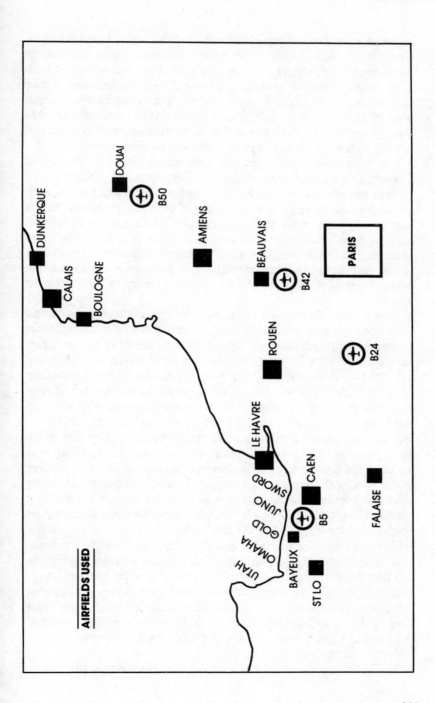

AIRFIELDS USED

UTAH OMAHA GOLD JUNO SWORD

ST LO
BAYEUX
CAEN
B5
FALAISE
LE HAVRE
ROUEN
B24
BEAUVAIS
B42
AMIENS
DOUAI
B50
DUNKERQUE
CALAIS
BOULOGNE
PARIS

199

carrying a load of washing back into her quarters. Spike Hughes, Ches West and Terry Gray were standing around warming themselves by the boiler and he told them his good news but only Terry spoke saying 'It's all right for some'. He realized then that he was no longer one of them and for a fleeting moment he was sad and wanted to join their circle but they had turned away from him. He was too uplifted to think about it as he dashed upstairs to wash and get a few things packed up ready for the journey home.

His camp bed was in the far right-hand corner with Moose Mossip's on one side and Arthur Leighton-Porter's on the other. Both chaps were very experienced pilots and had joined the Squadron at Volkel doing their second tour of operations. He had often wondered what it must be like to come back for a second tour and have to chance one's luck all over again, thinking that they must either be lacking in imagination or 'bonkers'. It had never occurred to him that chaps like them might have no alternative and after a rest period were simply posted to another Squadron to do it all over again.

Moose Mossip was man of iron, both mentally and physically, and thoroughly enjoyed his ops. The big Canadian had been a foreman in a lumber camp and had built up a great reputation as a crack train-buster and a devastatingly efficient low-level attack specialist. He had married an English girl and his one '*bête noire*' was to be taken for a Yank. A strong-willed, impulsive and tough character, Moose had already influenced the Squadron with his personal leadership and buccaneering spirit. Moose had arrived on the scene, Bob Stanford thought, just when the Squadron needed a man like him to fill the gap left by Jack Collins; not as a commanding officer, Moose was too wild and headstrong for that, but to sharpen up the cutting edge of the Squadron by personal example. Stanford had missed Collins who had been the linchpin, and was enjoying Moose's friendship which did a great deal to bolster his confidence and on odd occasions keep black dog depression off his back.

Sitting on the edge of his camp-bed, sorting out his laundry, Stanford thought about the changes that had taken place since the Squadron had been brought up to its full strength at Holmesley South shortly before D-Day. Many new faces had arrived then and a number of those had since gone down. Then another great batch came after the Battle of Mortain and again at Volkel. It seemed incredible to him that the Squadron had undergone three major blood transfusions in seven months.

But he had had no sense of time and it seemed like years since he had first joined the Squadron at West Hampnett although it was only a little over sixteen months ago. He imagined it was because he couldn't look forward to anything that time didn't pass quickly. Each day was incredibly long and they had to pack as much fun as possible into every minute of it. He came to the conclusion that he had only been able to think backwards because there might be no tomorrow.

Now, for the first time in months he could restart his time machine and plug in the forward gear for seven days at least. Thinking about it opened the sluice gates of his mind allowing him to conjure up images of girlfriends, draught beer, parties, dances and generally living it up, packing everything into his leave. Life was going to be terrific and he would be able to get his new uniform and stooge around his old haunts playing it by ear!

He had remembered the look on Paddy's face when Paddy was told that he had finished his tour. It was as if somebody had suddenly taken the bung out of his system and got rid of all the pressure making him into a changed man. He supposed that being given a passport to living would make anyone be like that. It was the only occasion when he had felt resentful towards Paddy, who had been pre-occupied with packing up and getting the hell out of it, and afterwards he felt sorry, but even so, dear old Paddy had given the impression of being 'I'm all right, Jack!'.

It was a bright crisp morning when the Dakota took off for Northolt with everybody sitting on its metal seats facing one another and looking very chipper. Stanford first called at Moss Bros in Covent Garden to buy all his gear and was told by an assistant that he could kit him out completely for a little under his £50 allowance from stock which had been traded in. The man said that everything was as good as new but Bob realized where it had come from. He didn't like the idea of wearing dead men's clothes but couldn't afford to be squeamish about it. When he walked out in all his splendour he was glad that he hadn't!

*   *   *

After a terrific leave which seemed to pass in a flash he returned to Volkel to find that Terry Gray and Tubby Sago had both left, being tour-expired, and that De Kerdril, the French pilot, had gone down. He was sorry to hear about DK, who had nearly got the chop on so many occasions, but hardly surprised. Now he was the only one of the old gang left on the Squadron and knew that he would soon be packing his bags if he managed to survive.

The great thing about coming back after leave was to see the chums again who wanted to know all about the piss-ups and parties. He felt immediately at home rejoining the fraternity and was able to shrug off that empty feeling in the pit of his stomach, knowing that he would probably be back on ops tomorrow. It had nagged him in the plane on the way over and several times while on leave he had become introspective, arguing with himself whether or not he would be able to face up to reality when he got back.

The commission business had brought matters to a head because people at home had gone out of their way to buy him drinks and pat him on the back. His own family had taken him around as if he was some kind of prize exhibit when all he wanted to do was to go his own way and meet strangers whom he could really talk to. There was nobody in whom he could confide his fears and he was never going to do that with people who might pass the word around.

Now he was back in the fraternity and they would never mention anything. He had a quiet laugh to himself when Arthur Leighton-Porter drifted back from the mess. It was snowing outside, bloody cold and miserable and he was putting on extra socks and jerseys before wriggling into his sleeping bag. Arthur sidled up with a grin on his face, 'Nice to see you back, Bob', he said. 'Hope you had a good time. By the way, you do know don't you, that you're on the morning show tomorrow, chum. It's Rheine airfield. Bloody good luck, mate!'. Stanford was in a state where he couldn't bloody care less so he pulled his leather flying jacket over his face and flaked out.

Rheine airfield was a forward base for German jets and very heavily defended, with flak lanes guarding every approach. Stanford cursed his luck when he arrived for the briefing session knowing that they would be diving through heavy flak coming up from the Ruhr before getting to the target and Rheine airfield was a mass of guns looking after the Me 262s which used it.

This show was to be a co-ordinated effort preceeded by attacks from heavy and medium bombers then followed up with four Wings of Typhoons whose job it was to rocket and shoot up the airfield. The first two Wings were to act in an anti-flak role, firing cannons to keep the gunners quiet and the remainder would make rocket attacks.

Stanford learned that 245 would be the final Squadron to go in on the attack and he would be last-but-one to fire his rockets by which time, he thought, German gun barrels would be red hot. It wasn't exactly the sort of show he was looking forward to when he came back from leave but there was no point in worrying about it. He had got past the stage of hoping that his engine wouldn't start when off on a sticky show but at least he had Spike Hughes flying his number two which was a comfort.

He had the usual pee against the tailplane of his favourite machine and checked all the adjustments carefully, especially the tension of the throttle nut and the length of the rudder pedals in case some long-legged bastard had been flying it while he was away. When starting up he must have accidentally overprimed the engine because it coughed, spluttered and blew back a shower of oil and wouldn't pick up. He fired a second cartridge with the same result. By now he was in a cold sweat as the engines of the other Typhoons around him were roaring away. On the third cartridge he just caught her and coaxed her gently into a broken rhythm until she let go an enormous belch and at last broke into a steady thunder.

They had to wait for take-off because there were so many Squadrons going and he gave his engine a good belt to clear it thoroughly but still didn't quite like the sound of it. She was running hot but that was to be expected: the oil pressure was all right, but she was definitely a bit rough when he opened the throttle against the brakes. He sensed that she was off-key on take-off but was giving plenty of power so he tried to forget it. Moose was leading the Squadron as they climbed hard over our own lines preparing to dive through the Ruhr flak. It felt great to be airborne again and back in Squadron formation with the lads. Looking around he could see heads turning as pilots scanned horizons for any sign of the Luftwaffe and being the last Squadron they would probably be the first to get bounced.

Down below the air seemed to be full of Typhoons, some silhouetted against cloud, as the whole giant formation commenced a shallow dive building up speed to get through the flak belt. The usual heavy stuff burst around them as pilots concentrated on keeping station and preparing for the attack. Stanford was thinking that being top echelon had its points because no buggers would be diving down behind him. Suddenly his engine gave an almighty bang and stopped for a second. Immediately he throttled back, checking his instruments, his heart pounding, and prayed that the bastard would keep going. She picked up again as if nothing had happened and Spike, who must have noticed something, came up alongside but Bob gave him a thumbs-up sign. He decided to carry on as he could see fires and smoke coming up from the target dead ahead and he could make his dive and nurse the bloody thing back if necessary. Worrying about his machine, he was hardly conscious of the flak, being only too anxious to fire his salvo of rockets and get it over.

He fired his rockets in the general direction of a hangar and could see that the place was a shambles as he pulled out of the dive, determined to make as much height as possible without pushing his engine. The cylinder-head temperature had crept up a little but the oil pressure was holding as he flew back through the Ruhr flak, trailing well behind the Squadron. Spike, as usual, had kept station and he called him over the RT to tell him what had happened.

It was a nail-biting business creeping home, coaxing the engine with eyes glued on the instruments and hoping like hell temperatures wouldn't suddenly go up and she would catch fire. The Sabre was really popping and banging as he called for immediate clearance. He made a steep approach and landed, switching off as soon as he was clear of the runway, jumped out and ran like hell!

*   *   *

Towards mid-December the weather became unbearably cold with fog, ice, sleet and snow. The Dutch winter had clamped down on the airfield as ground crews worked in shifts by day and night to keep Sabre engines warm and aircraft defrosted in the most appalling conditions. But the main road through Volkel was still jammed with tanks and vehicles moving slowly towards the front line. There was nothing the pilots could do except to keep warm and try to amuse themselves.

On 16 December, much to everybody's astonishment, came the news that von Rundstedt's Panzer divisions had unexpectedly broken through the Allied lines. Nobody paid much attention to it at first, thinking that it was simply a flash-in-the-pan. But when they heard that over twenty German armoured divisions had carved their way through the American lines it suddenly became a very serious situation. The German offensive had come at a time when Allied Tactical Air Forces were grounded because of fog and within a few days von Rundstedt's armour had penetrated some forty miles into the Ardennes. As soon as the fog lifted, the Typhoons were unleashed to provide back-up for the Americans and were able to catch a weight of German armour out in the open silhouetted against the snow. This battle, code named 'Herbstenebel' or 'Autumn Fog', cost the Germans over 100,000 casualties and was Hitler's last throw of the dice as far as a major military action was concerned.

The Battle of the Bulge, as it was later called, was the second time that rocket Typhoons came to the aid of American forces and Squadrons received generous credit from the Yanks for 'doing their stuff'. Both at Mortain and in the Ardennes the Typhoons were rocketing advancing German armour in highly dangerous situations. These battles were the direct result of personal gambles by Hitler himself when he threw in his Panzer divisions in a desperate attempt to drive a wedge between the British and American Armies and reach the coast.

On Christmas Eve, after the Battle of the Bulge, 245 Squadron was pulled out of the line and flew to an Armament Practice Camp at Warmwell Airfield in Southern England to do a rocket and cannon firing course. The posting couldn't have come at a better time and it was probably a tribute to the Squadron's performance throughout the Invasion that they made it home for Christmas!

On 1 January 1945, while the Squadron was completing its course at Warmwell, several hundred German fighters attacked Allied air-fields in Belgium and Holland achieving complete surprise. Over 300 Allied aircraft were destroyed but German losses were also very heavy at a time when the Luftwaffe needed every aircraft it could lay its hands on for the defence of the Reich.

The Squadron flew back to Volkel on 6 January to pick up the threads of war, once again having been well fed and watered! It had been a fantastic two weeks break and everybody was raring to go. A few days later Bob Stanford was walking towards the mess having landed from a close support show in which the Squadron had pranged gun positions. Moose Mossip and Bob Monk caught him up and Moose put an arm around his shoulder asking him in an off-hand manner how long he had been with the Squadron. Bob Stanford gave him the gen and wondered what it was all about. 'Well', said Moose, 'that's long enough for anybody, Bob. Now's the time to have a break, old son'.

Stanford was only given time to collect his papers, pack up and have a hurried lunch before the truck would arrive to take him to Eindhoven. He took his log book along to be signed and was given a 'Tour Expired' certificate to take back with him. This certificate was a flimsy piece of paper headed, 'ROYAL AIR FORCE—SUB FORM 780', and somebody had written in ink at the top the words 'TOUR EXPIRED'. It was in fact a fourteen-day leave pass and the sentence 'Completion of Op. Tour' had been typed alongside the words 'Type of leave'. He smiled when he saw the word 'Flying' which denoted the duties that he had performed!

This fragile piece of paper meant more to him than anything that he had ever received in his life and he couldn't help staring at it almost in disbelief. It suddenly dawned on him that he had finally made it and he gave a great whoop of sheer joy.

Retrospect

Any Typhoon squadron was a changing entity. It had a number, a crest and a motto which were its only permanent fixtures. In the case of 245 Squadron, its crest depicted an albatross flying over the sea and its motto was '*Fugo Non Fugio*' which translated means 'I fight not run away'. The fact that 245 was formed during the First World War as an anti-submarine patrol squadron probably accounts for the albatross but the motto could be applied to any fighter squadron. Few pilots either knew or considered such matters—only regarding themselves as being 245.

In writing this book, the author has used the name Bob Stanford to get away from the first person and to be able to stand back and give an objective view of events. The only other pseudonym is that of 'Cartwright' because the pilot concerned killed himself. Everything else is real and all the ops are taken from my log book in which I wrote notes regarding each show. All the personalities involved are as I saw them during that period. The slice of 245 Squadron life which I have described is naturally focused on those who were my immediate associates during my tour of operations which lasted from September '43 until January '45. The major part of the book is devoted to Squadron life on the strip at Le Fresne Camilly where the log table became the focal point for post-flying chit-chat. During this period of some two-and-a-half months the most traumatic events took place and the Invasion of Europe hung in the balance.

Recreating the characters and Squadron atmosphere, after forty years, was not too difficult because those were the most formative and vivid times of my life and were imprinted on my memory. I am not alone in this because when making tapes with other survivors I found it uncanny how easily they slipped back into the old jargon as if they had just put on their uniforms once again and I am particularly grateful to Paddy Gray, Dud Nott, Terry Gray, Robin McNair, Geoff Murphy, Doug Martin and Arthur Leighton-Porter for helping me to bring the Squadron back to life.

The basic ingredient, however, and the springboard for everything was the Typhoon itself. The aircraft embodied a spirit of aggression with its mighty Sabre engine, cannons and rockets, enormous nose, powerful airframe and vast three-bladed propeller. It was hardly surprising therefore that some of this should have rubbed off on the pilot. If a chap steps out of a Mini into a Ferrari, for example, he will undoubtedly change his personality and driving habits!

When firing his cannons and rockets a pilot could feel the enormous power and strength in his aircraft and it gave him confidence. Also, it was reassuring to know that he was encased in a rugged machine with armour-plating protection when the flak was coming up at him fast and he had to hold his bead on the target. But the Typhoon, as far as the pilots were concerned, was not simply a mobile firing platform but a character, each one being different and having its own idiosyncrasies.

The aircraft also had a big psychological influence on the enemy in different ways. The rocket projectile, or RP as it was called, was an accelerating missile and apart from the damage it caused it made a dreadful noise on its way down. The morale effect against those on the receiving end, especially tank crews, was very great. The Germans knew that its 60-lb head could penetrate steel and nobody wanted to be burned alive or compressed into a jelly inside a tank. The awesome reputation of the rocket Typhoon had been building up steadily since before D-Day and compelled the Germans to move their Panzer divisions by night thereby limiting their powers of manoeuvre—a significant factor on the military chessboard!

There are always the experts who, after battles have been fought and won, delve into the statistics and come up with their own views and philosophies. Usually, they run true to form and attempt to decry and deride those very actions which played a vital part in altering the course of the war. Rocket Typhoons, according to them, were inaccurate and didn't knock out nearly as many Panzer tanks as claimed by the 2nd Tactical Air Force during the major 'aircraft versus tank' battles. The inference was that rocket Typhoon operations were somewhat costly and inefficient!

If the people who made those assumptions had been with me on 10 September 1984 when I visited Mortain to meet survivors of the 30th US Infantry Division they would have revised their opinion. The Americans had their backs to the wall as a complete Panzer division came rolling towards them and there wasn't much they could do about it except pray until the Typhoons arrived on the scene and annihilated the German armour.

I was the first rocket Typhoon pilot that they had met and the survivors of the 'Old Hickory' Division, as they called themselves, left me in no doubt that 'the Typhoons had saved their butts'. Yet, our own military history books give only a passing mention to the part played by rocket Typhoon Wings in battles such as Mortain and perhaps this book will go some way to redress the balance.

The French, however, do rather more and the cover of Doctor Gilles Buisson's book *Mortain 44—Objectif Avranches* depicts rocket Typhoon attacks on German armour at St Barthélemy and highlights the battle giving full credit to the part played by Typhoon squadrons. Apart from attacking German tanks and vehicles along that road through St Barthélemy leading to Juvigny we had no idea what was going on down below and I asked Dr. Buisson to tell me what happened at that time. He said that the inhabitants of Mortain had thought themselves liberated by the 1st US Infantry Division three days previously. But the Luftwaffe severely bombed the town and then the Germans counter-attacked on the night of 7 August. The town was in flames and covered with a thick cloud of smoke and everybody evacuated it.

Nearly 700 took refuge in the galleries of a mine at Neufbourg which were crowded with people from surrounding areas who had fled to escape the fighting. They hid there for a week in the most deplorable hygienic conditions and without sufficient food but escaped with their lives. One little baby girl delivered there received the Christian name of Barbé in memory of the patron saint of miners.

A number of others fled to the east to the area of Rancoudray and the valley of the Selune where American troops were situated. Dr. Buisson escorted his parents to a friend's farm some twenty kilometres away before returning to Notre-Dame-de-Touchet where he spent several days caring for a large number of refugees who had had to evacuate the regions of Coutances and St Lo. Tiredness, fear and overwhelming emotions were the basic maladies but he also attended to two births. The women were installed on makeshift beds in the granary of a farm, situated near a battery of the American DCA which German aircraft were trying to spot. Another patient was sheltering at the Presbytery of Villechien between Mortain and St.-Hilaire-du-Harcourt and was attended by one of his colleagues whom the Americans had to find and bring in by jeep. No French doctors were allowed cars and they had to get around by bicycle. The telephone was not working. Some women had to care for themselves and their babies during these events alone in fields or ditches.

Buisson's house had been severely damaged and transformed into a blockhouse by American GIs. Trees had been torn up and the whole surrounds were full of debris, abandoned weapons and anti-tank guns. Three SS men were buried in a flower bed at a depth of only a few centimetres. At St Barthélemy, where the Typhoons had stopped the advance of the Panzers towards Avranches, the inhabitants had fled into the fields and taken refuge in farms which were burned one after the other. Gravely wounded civilians stayed without medical attention and slept in the open between the lines for several days. On all sides the civilians offered themselves as scouts to the Americans and guided their patrols.

During my visit to St Barthélemy I met the schoolmistress, Mme Lerendu, who had taken refuge in a farm just off the main road where she saw the leading Panzer tanks rocketed and blown sideways into the ditch. I also talked with Doctor Lemonnier who was the head of the Resistance at Juvigny-Le-Tertre and he told me that he had been hidden in a wood about three kilometres away and watched the rocket Typhoons scream overhead as they pulled out of dives.

The photographs of Mortain and the battle of St Barthélemy reproduced in this book were kindly loaned to me by Dr Buisson who also gave me a detailed account of what happened on the ground during that time. Typhoon pilots will be interested to learn that the story of their attack on 8 August is kept alive in Remembrance services and exhibitions in the town hall at Mortain. Any pilot having the opportunity of covering 'old ground' would be assured of a warm welcome at Mortain.

While in the town I saw film of the liberation of Rennes and photographs of little towns and villages covering a wide area from St Lo to Avranches. The vast majority had been bombed and shelled into heaps of ruins and were evidence of the hard slog the Americans had in fighting for every inch of ground as they broke south out of the beaches of Utah and Omaha. These pictures also demonstrated in brutal fashion the terrible price that the French in those parts had to pay for their liberation. This was clearly portrayed in the old film of Rennes taken just as the city was liberated. One can only describe it as a fountain of human joy against a background of ruins and desolation.

The only Typhoon pilot I encountered during visits to Normandy for the D-Day celebrations was the distinguished Belgian pilot, Lieutenant Colonel Raymond 'Horse' Lallemant and we fought the war over again, amidst much noise and celebration, in a small restaurant beside the port at Le Havre. I shall not forget the enthusiastic welcome I received from the brown jobs outside Madame Gondré's café at Pegasus Bridge when they heard that a Typhoon pilot was around. This was of course for rocket Typhoon pilots in general and I should like to pass it on.

Typhoon squadrons, unlike regiments, were comprised of only a small group of pilots, some of whom came from various parts of the British Empire. After the war it became virtually impossible and certainly impractical to hold squadron reunions because a number of the chaps had disappeared to all corners of the globe. Quite apart from that difficulty, Typhoon squadrons were continually changing over a period of eighteen months to two years because pilots were either tour expired, gone down, wounded or posted off. 245 was no exception, so the Squadron as I knew it when I left Volkel on 22 January 1945 would have had many new faces by the end of the war in Europe some four months later.

The 'Old Reaper' took his toll and over 25 pilots were killed or wounded during my tour which meant that the entire Squadron complement of pilots had been turned over in eighteen months. This kind of arithmetic was rather alarming for anybody considering his chances of survival but nobody worried about it, or even if they did they never mentioned anything. There was only one thing to do, as far as a pilot was concerned, and that was to press on regardless.

The day of the Typhoon has become part of the aviation history relegated to history books and museums. The only complete surviving Typhoon in the United Kingdom rests in the RAF museum at Hendon but it seems that there is life in the old dog yet because some enterprising chaps have recently established a first-class Typhoon museum on the perimeter of Tangmere airfield on the outskirts of Chichester. The public relations officer, Ken Rimell, and his associates, have been busy locating and digging out some of the crashed relics and building up the story. Ken's photographic genius is responsible for sharpening up and restoring many of the photographs in my book and he has been enormously helpful in wiping away the wrinkles of faded prints.

Finally, I would remind the reader that the Typhoon project was very nearly scrapped in late '42 because as a high-altitude chaser, for which it was originally designed, it performed less than adequately. The Spitfire camp was obviously anti-Typhoon because their older generation of machines could outfly it at altitudes in excess of 20,000 feet. Politically they had an axe to grind and they almost got their way. No man did more to keep the project alive and ensure its ultimate success than Wing Commander Roland Beamont, CBE, DSO and bar, DFC and bar, FRAeS. 'Bee'. as he is universally known throughout the world aviation industry, was seconded to Hawker Aircraft in 1942 from the RAF to help sort out the teething problems of this *enfant terrible*. Joining the Hawker team, he played a vital role as a test pilot and politician. Testing the Typhoon to destruction when Sabre engines were seizing up and tails falling off for no apparent reason required enormous personal courage but that wasn't all. 'Bee' returned to the RAF, resuming his command of 609 Squadron, and with ruthless determination proved the potential of the machine as the most lethal air-to-ground attack fighter of its time.

Appendix 1

245 Squadron pilots known to the author

These names were jotted down in the author's log book at the time and he apologizes for any mis-spelling!

Austin, 'Chris'
Bassett, Peter
Bater
Bathurst, Harry
Bennet, 'Benny' (Canadian)
Brown, 'Al' (Canadian)
Brown, Ross (Canadian)
Campbell, Jock
Clark, 'Nobby'
Cluelow, 'Clueless' (South African)
Collins, Jack
Cook, 'Cookie' (South African)
Crabtree, Neil
Crosswell
Dakin, George (Canadian)
Darlington, 'Jock'
Dellar, 'Al'
Dickie, 'Ken'
Flynn, 'Johnny'
Gale, 'Shorty' (South African)
Golley, 'Johnny' (author)
Gordon, 'Scotty'
Greenhaugh, 'Greeners'

Gray, 'Paddy'
Gray, 'Terry'
Hawkins
Hornell, 'Bob'
Hughes, 'Spike'
James, 'Jimmy'
Jeffries, 'Jeff'
De Kerdril, 'DK' (French)
Lamb, 'Archie'
Lee, 'Bob'
Leighton-Porter, Arthur
Lush, Dennis, 'Lusho'
Martin, 'Doug'
Maxwell, 'Maxie'
Milne, 'Sheep' (Canadian)
Minet
Miron, 'Ace' (Canadian)
Monk, 'Bob'
Mossip, 'Moose' (Canadian)
Murphy, 'Spud'
McKillop, 'Mac' (Canadian)
McNair, Robin
Noakes, 'Tubby'
Nott, Dudley

Nutter, 'Nuts'
Reynolds, 'Bill'
Ryan, 'Buck'
Sago, Glen 'Tubby' (Australian)
Simm, 'Ken'
Slaney, 'Sam'
Smith, 'Bill'
Sullivan, 'Sully' (Canadian)

Temple, 'Roly'
Waudby, 'Bill'
Wharry, George (Canadian)
Webb (Australian)
West, 'Ches' (Canadian)
Wilson, 'Jimmy'
Zweibergk, 'Skip'

Appendix 2

245 Squadron bases, 10 October 1942 - 22 January 1945

West Hampnett	*10 October 1942-30 April 1943*
Holmsley South	*30 April 1943-12 May 1944*
Eastchurch	*12-22 May 1944*
Holmsley South (rocket course)	*22 May-27 June 1944*
B5 Le Fresne Camilly, Normandy	*27 June-28 August 1944*
B24 St Andre de l'Eure, France	*28 August-2 September 1944*
B24 Beauvais-Tille, France	*2-4 September 1944*
B50 Vitry-en-Artois, France	*4-17 September 1944*
B70 Deurne, Belgium	*17 September-1 October 1944*
B80 Volkel, Holland	*1 October-24 December 1944*
Warmwell, Southern England	*24 December 1944-6 January 1945*
Volkel, Holland	*6 January 1945*

Author left the Squadron 22 January 1945.

Bibliography

Monty, Master of the Battlefield 1942-44, Nigel Hamilton (Hamish Hamilton, 1983).

Rommel in Normandy, Vice-Admiral Friedrich Ruge (Macdonald & Jane, 1979).

Stalingrad en Normandie: La Bataille de Normandie, Eddy Florentin (Presses de la Cité, 1981).

Mortain 44 Objectif Avranches, Dr Gilles Buisson (Editions OECP, 1984).

The Typhoon File, compiled by C.H. Thomas (Air-Britain and the British Aviation Archaeological Council).

Typhoon and Tempest at War, Arthur Reed and Roland Beamont (Ian Allan Ltd, 1974).

Other PSL books for your enjoyment

The Flying Dutchman

An exciting true story of war in the air
Hans Van der Kop
Foreword by Prince Bernhard of the Netherlands

Nearly killed on his first operational mission over enemy-occupied Europe, Hans
Van der Kop went on to survive 78 sorties in B-25 Mitchells of No 320 Squadron
during and after D-Day. The authentic story of this expatriate Dutchman who
volunteered for the RAF makes engrossing and exciting reading and clearly shows
the strong camaraderie which grew up between English, Dutch and
Commonwealth aircrew.
248 pages, illustrated, hardback.

Castles in the Air

The story of the B-17 Flying Fortress crews of the US 8th Air Force
Martin W. Bowman

Based on interviews and letters from surviving Flying Fortress officers and men,
this is an absorbing personal account of 'Mighty Eighth' operations from 1942 to
1945 which really puts the reader into the cockpit while flak explodes all around and
German fighters race into the attack.
208 pages, illustrated, paperback.

The Spitfire

Fifty Years On
Michael J. F. Bowyer

Fifty years after it first flew, the Spitfire is still the most glamorous, revered and
beautiful of all fighter aircraft. Michael Bowyer's book — which includes
unpublished wartime colour photos — examines this superb aircraft's place in
history, relates what it is like to fly and shows where you can still see surviving
Spitfires today.
136 pages, illustrated, paperback.

All these, and many other fine books on subjects ranging from astronomy to
railways, may be obtained through your local bookshop. Our complete catalogue is
available free of charge from: Patrick Stephens Limited, Denington Estate,
Wellingborough, Northants, NN8 2QD.

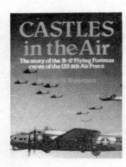